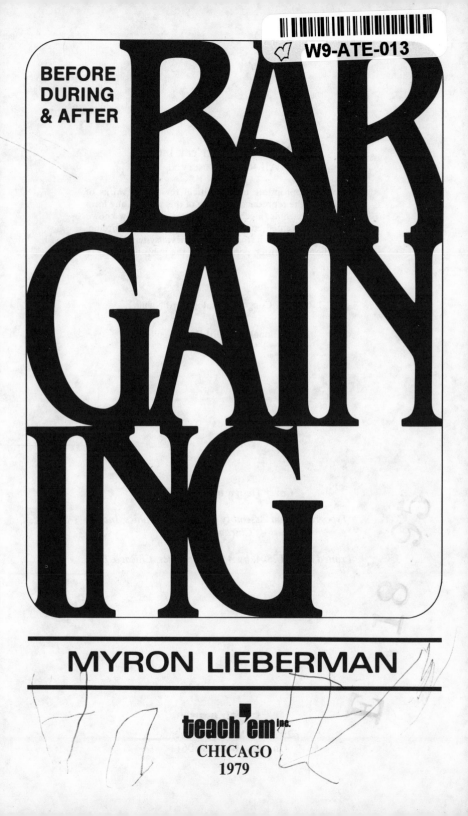

BEFORE
DURING
& AFTER

BAR GAIN ING

MYRON LIEBERMAN

teach'em inc.

CHICAGO
1979

Library of Congress Catalog Card Number:
79-66017

International Standard Book Number:
0-931028-09-4

Cover Design by Phillip Gill

*Typography and Assembly by Accent Graphics, Inc.,
Chicago, Ill.*

Printed in the U.S.A. by Active Graphics, Chicago, Ill.

teach em inc.
625 North Michigan Avenue
Chicago, Illinois 60611

*For
Rachel, Warren
Loren, Larry,
and Nancy*

PREFACE

This book is intended to help school boards, and those who must work with school boards, in the collective bargaining process. It deals with issues boards must face before bargaining begins, during the bargaining process itself, and after an agreement is negotiated. Although most attention is devoted to the practical issues boards face in bargaining, certain public policy issues related to bargaining also are discussed.

Obviously, what board members and boards do affects the roles and responsibilities of others in the negotiations process. For example, the superintendent will be affected by whether the board employs an outside negotiator, and by whether the outside negotiator reports to the board or to the superintendent. How much authority should be delegated to the board negotiating team is another example, and dozens of others could easily be cited. The point is that an analysis of the role of school boards inevitably deals also, by implication if nothing else, with the roles of other parties involved in negotiations. For this reason, it is intended and hoped that the book will be helpful to superintendents, central office staff, principals, outside negotiators, media representatives, impartial third parties, and other parties involved in school district negotiations. In fact, the treatment of some issues is not specifically related to the board of education because its importance to all parties is so evident.

The issues discussed here have seldom been fully explored. The objective was to bring together material that would be immediately helpful; the omissions are regrettable, but any attempt to be exhaustive would have been unrealistic.

Some of the material has been published previously in article form. In those cases, the original article has been reviewed for current relevance and applicability, and changes have usually resulted from such review. In addition, the material has been grouped to provide in-depth treatment of various problems or problem areas.

The author wishes to express his appreciation to the editors of *The American School Board Journal*, where much of this material appeared, and to the other contributors to this book. Needless to say, I am responsible for any shortcomings in my own material and for the choice of material by others.   M.L.

POLICY ISSUES IN BARGAINING

1. Must Boards Bargain?

The first policy issue some boards face in bargaining is whether they have to bargain collectively at all. Although this option no longer exists for many boards, it is a useful point of departure, since it helps to clarify several policy issues related to bargaining.

Many observers have noted the tremendous public employee unionism in the past decade. Public employee unions have increased enormously in membership and resources; private sector unionization has hardly maintained previous growth levels.

The decline or stagnation in private sector unionization has many causes, including technological change and shifts in the economy. Nevertheless, there are also some unique reasons for the rapid growth of public sector unions.

Fully half of all public employees are unionized. In the private sector, where unionism began, no more than one worker in three carries a union card. One reason for this disparity: Private employers oppose the unionization of their employees more vigorously and effectively than public employers, such as school boards, do. Indeed, it's not unusual for management in the private sector to launch a strong no-representation campaign the moment a union organizer is seen on the premises. The idea of these campaigns is to convince employees that they're better off if they do not unionize and bargain. In fact, many companies don't wait for union organizers to appear before conducting campaigns intended to discourage unionization.

Do these no-representation campaigns work? Sometimes they do. Sometimes they are so successful that unions can't muster even the employee support necessary to call a representation election, let alone win one.

Why can't school boards and superintendents do the same thing? Probably they can in some districts. Whether they should is a much different issue. Granted, school boards and teacher unions are natural adversaries, and, for the same reasons they are elsewhere; unionization increases costs and decreases managerial control over district operations.

The actual expense in dollars and cents may not be evident even to the parties. Quite often, the extra district expenditures required by unionization do not necessarily add to the well-being of teachers. For example, instead of providing increased employee benefits, the additional spending often is devoted to bargaining personnel and legal fees. Furthermore, bargaining often leads to grievance arbitration, the cost of which can be substantial. Not only must a board pay for the preparation of its case, but it also must pay its share for the arbitrator's services.

Many other indirect but substantial costs of collective bargaining have nothing to do with teacher salaries. A district may agree to an upper limit on class size in the contract. Then enrollment increases, perhaps because of consolidation of schools or the opening of a new, parent-pulling business in the community. Thus, the district is required to hire more teachers. The upshot is substantially higher operating costs, which may be unjustified in relation to other important district needs and priorities.

In many school districts, unions frequently try to embarrass board members and administrators to achieve bargaining concessions. More often than not, these efforts are not justified. In fact, board members and administrators who do their jobs well are usually subject to more abuse from unions than those who do not. In other words, unionization is likely to restrict management options, and may result in only marginal economic advantages for employees. At the same time, it escalates and institutionalizes conflict generally. From management's point of view, there's nothing a union can do for employees that can't be done voluntarily and at less cost in the absence of unionization. Conversely, many disadvantages can be avoided when unions are not present.

Why, then, do school boards usually accept unionization without a struggle? One reason is that the idea of launching a no-representation campaign simply has never occurred to some school officials. Another is that resistance seems hopeless, like raising a seawall against the wave of the future. Of course, the first reason may be an outcome of the second, so let us consider the latter briefly.

The tide of unionism in school districts is indisputably high, but ripples are running the opposite way. Colleges and universities, for example, are increasingly active in efforts to turn back union drives. On four-year campuses, collective bargaining was rejected by the faculties of 59 of the 239 institutions where the issue prior to 1979 was put to a vote. Among institutions with faculties who rejected unionization are the University of Massachusetts, New York University, University of Pittsburgh, and Syracuse University.

In private industry, management's no-representation campaigns have met with still greater success. Fewer than a third of the private sector employees who are legally authorized to bargain collectively has elected to do so. In recent years, employers who have conducted aggressive campaigns against unionization frequently have been successful in this objective. It would appear, therefore, that school districts that merely assume nothing can be done are ill-informed.

On the other hand, a school board and administration must take the long view. It is hardly worthwhile to oppose unionization if such opposition will be successful for only a year or two. Such short-lived opposition may serve only to antagonize a successful union, inflame its militancy, and intensify its anti-management attitude. Furthermore, unionization differs in the public and private sectors: The differences make it more difficult to oppose successfully the unionization of public employees. For instance, local teacher organizations are typically established in school districts long before efforts to bargain collectively. Similarly, so are the civil service type of organization representing non-certified personnel. In contrast, when organizers from a private sector union first solicit support among workers at a factory, they rarely are greeted at the gate by dues-paying union members. If an organizing drive fails in the private sector, there is usually no ongoing dues-paying membership until the union achieves majority status.

Recent developments in California illustrate the differences. The California School Employees Association enrolled 70,000 dues-paying members before the passage of the Rodda Act, the 1975 legislation affording bargaining rights to school district employees.

Furthermore California employee organizations have the right to represent their members, even if the organizations fail to achieve collective bargaining rights. This puts California school boards at a distinct disadvantage, since they have to deal with an employee organization regardless of whether or not it represents a majority of employees in an appropriate bargaining unit. Fortunately, for school officials elsewhere, this type of legislation appears to be unique. Nevertheless, union influence is pervasive throughout education, whether or not employees bargain collectively. The National Education Association and the American Federation of Teachers, for example, have been a presence in school districts for decades. In fact, until a few years ago, many school administrators were members — indeed, leaders — of NEA locals. In some districts, they still are. Consequently, teacher organizations may be perceived by school administrators as familiar, if not friendly, forces. In any case, NEA and AFT organizers typically encounter a warmer welcome from school administrators than union organizers get from managers in private industry.

Another difference relates to the time that must elapse between union organizing drives. Several states set one year as the minimum time span between one union organizing drive and the next. Clearly, it would be unfair to the employer were state law to allow unions to try again for recognition immediately after employees have voted to reject unionization. Likewise, it would be unfair if a no-representation vote were to bind employees forever. From management's point of view, the longer the time span between votes, the better. School boards would be well advised to seek at least a two-year limitation when agreeing to consent elections, when drafting new legislative proposals, or when seeking to amend existing statutes.

The degree of financial and management support the union receives from teachers, the depth of the union's traditional involvement in district affairs, and the time limit imposed on organizing efforts are some of the crucial elements for board members and superintendents to consider before launching a no-representation campaign. Another factor is whether supervisors or principals or both have the right to bargain collectively. In districts where they

5

do, the likelihood that top management will receive their support in a no-representation campaign is reduced greatly.

On the other hand, many district employees aren't eager to unionize. One frequent problem is that what employees read and hear on the subject tends to come from the union. As a matter of fact, some school administrators believe that it is illegal to urge school employees to stay out of a union or to vote against union representation. This belief, of course, is not true; freedom of speech still lives and still applies to management as much as to organized labor. School officials do have the right to urge their employees to reject unionization, i.e. collective bargaining. How that right is exercised, however, is another matter.

Management can't tell teachers they'll be fired, transferred or deprived of any benefits because of their support for the union. In addition, it cannot interrogate employees about their views on unionization. Although school management can express its opposition to collective bargaining, such expression must not be coercive or promise a benefit in exchange for an employee vote against unionization. Management must be careful to observe these limits on its rights to oppose unionization. There's no point in having employees vote to reject the union only to have that vote set aside because of illegal employer conduct.

Precisely what management can say and do to discourage unionization varies somewhat from state to state. Usually, a board can urge its employees to reject a union's attempt to call a representation election. In its rationale, a board can point to the costs of union dues and assessments and to the possibility that these will increase. School officials are free to quote NEA or AFT contracts that require union membership or the payment of service fees as conditions of employment. They can make it clear that if the union wins recognition, employees then may be required to bring their problems to the union instead of to their supervisors. It is also appropriate to tell employees that neither the board nor the administration wants or needs the union and that employee benefits in the district compare favorably with salary and other benefits in unionized districts.

Finally — and this can be highly effective — a school board and superintendent may stress that, while the union can always out-promise management, it cannot deliver a single benefit that is not agreed to by the administration and the board. This point can be persuasive because most bargaining laws stipulate specifically that neither party is required to agree on any proposal or make any concession during bargaining.

Of course, every school district is different, and the variables make it impossible to prescribe a detailed no-representation strategy suitable for everyone. In general, however, boards should avoid extreme positions of any kind that are not based on objective assessments of district strengths and weaknesses. Whether anything can be done to oppose union efforts to win bargaining rights is a practical more than a legal question. As a practical matter, opposition may not be worthwhile; nonetheless, boards should not assume automatically that opposition is prohibited as a matter of law. If a no-representation campaign is appropriate, it is essential to avoid actions that will violate the state bargaining law and jeopardize a favorable election result. Practically, this means that boards should employ experienced labor counsel before embarking upon a no-representation campaign. Otherwise, they probably will have to employ one anyway to get out of the troubles they have created in their districts.

Boards should be aware that they typically underestimate employee support for collective bargaining, and that relatively few board campaigns against it have been successful. Indeed, such campaigns seem to be successful only in rural or high salary districts; rarely, if ever, are they successful in urban or larger districts.

2. Teacher Bargaining Reconsidered

In 1962, the first significant collective bargaining contract covering teachers was negotiated in New York City. Since then, collective bargaining in education has developed nationally at an impressive pace. At present, approximately 35 states provide teachers with bargaining rights, and a growing majority of teachers (perhaps 60 percent or more) works pursuant to collective bargaining contracts. Membership in teacher unions has increased enormously; simultaneously, union dues have increased, so that the resources available to teacher unions may exceed $500 million annually. Since 60 to 80 percent of school budgets is spent for personnel, virtually every aspect of education has been affected by this dramatic shift to collectively bargained terms and conditions of employment.

Since 1962, collective bargaining has been sold to some legislatures and school boards on a "try-it, you'll-like-it" basis. It has been inherited by others as a fixture on the educational scene, just as its absence was taken for granted in an earlier era. Regardless of how it is presented or experienced, however, there is one crucial difference between the present situation and the 1960's: We now have a wealth of experience in teacher bargaining to guide us. What was advocated or opposed in the Sixties on the basis of logic or intuition or speculation or analogy can be tested now against a body of experience. Today, there is no excuse for debating whether or how collective bargaining in education differs from collective bargaining in the private sector. The differences are real and important, and they justify this conclusion: Providing public employees collective bargaining rights similar to those provided private sector employees is undesirable public policy.

In the 1960's, the appeal to "equity" was the major public policy justification for teacher bargaining. Without bargaining rights, teachers, like other public employees, are allegedly second-class citizens. Privately employed guards can unionize and strike; publicly employed ones cannot. Bus drivers for a privately owned company can strike; if the same routes were taken over and operated as a public utility, the drivers could not bargain or strike.

Similarly, teachers in private schools can organize and bargain; those in public schools cannot.

For the sake of argument, let us agree that teachers ought to have "equity" with private sector employees. To assess the equity argument objectively, however, we must consider all of the crucial differences between public and private sectors of employment, not just the absence of bargaining rights in public education. Among these, perhaps the most important difference is that teachers often play an important role in determining who is management. For example, teacher organizations frequently are active in school board elections. In some situations, they have a decisive influence upon who is elected to the board. In contrast, private sector employees have no legal or practical role in selecting management, and ordinarily it would be futile for them to try to do so.

In some jurisdictions at least, the political influence of teachers upon public management has been extremely advantageous to teachers. This influence affects not only what is proposed, accepted, rejected and modified, but the timing of concessions, the management posture toward grievances, and the extent of management support services for bargaining. Sometimes even the choice of management negotiator is subject to an unofficial but effective teacher veto.

It is easy to underestimate the impact of teacher political influence on teacher employment relations because typically it has to be shared. Often, the influence is more veto power than "do" power. One should not be misled, however, by the fact that teacher-backed candidates do not always support the teachers, or may even oppose them on occasion. Such situations notwithstanding, the political dimension constitutes significant teacher advantages over private sector employment.

In this connection, teacher opportunities to influence the choice of state officials also must be considered. True enough, private sector employees have equal opportunities to influence or to elect such officials. The point is, however, that state officials seldom affect the context or substance of private sector bargaining. Typically, the governor of a state has no role in collective bargaining for private sector employees. Such bargaining is regulated by the National Labor Relations Board, a federal agency. On the other hand, the governor frequently plays a decisive role in whether there is to be public sector bargaining at all, and, if there is, in such matters as the scope of bargaining, the nature of unfair labor practices, the relationship of bargaining to budgetary schedules, the impasse procedures, and the balance of bargaining power between the parties. In addition, governors often play a crucial role in substantive matters subject to bargaining. For example, the governor typically is the most important single individual in the annual aid to education controversy. Since states provide almost half of public school revenues, the gubernatorial role is much more important to teachers than it is to most private sector unions. For teachers, as for other local public employees, the implications are obvious. Political activity at the state level pays the teacher a larger dividend than it does the factory worker or the farmer.

The fact that NEA and AFT are once again seeking to enact federal legislation providing bargaining rights for state and local public employees in no way negates the foregoing analysis. Obviously, if public employee unions can achieve their goals by one legislative enactment instead of fifty, they will do so. As a matter of fact, while they are striving for federal and state bargaining laws, they also are seeking state legislative benefits on matters normally considered subject to bargaining. Every group has the right to use the ballot box to advance its interests; my point is that the opportunity to do so is more advantageous to teachers than to private sector employees.

The political dimension to public sector employment works to the advantage of teachers in several different ways. For example, the turnover is greater in public than in private sector management. More importantly, private sector management tends to have a greater direct and personal stake in resisting unreasonable union demands. This is particularly apparent with pension and retirement benefits. Public management frequently achieves bargaining agreements by excessively generous pension and retirement benefits. Such concessions may not require any immediate tax increase. Thus the management officials responsible for the agreement can be heroes to the public employees for being generous, and to the public for not raising taxes. Unfortunately, the practice saddles taxpayers with enormously expensive long-range commitments. Significantly, the tendency to "end load" agreements this way has become evident in local, state, and federal agreements. It is difficult to see the equity in requiring taxpayers to provide public employee retirement benefits that greatly exceed their own, but that is the present situation.

Another crucial point is that public management has less incentive than private management to resist union demands. If private sector management makes a concession that impairs the long-range profitability of the enterprise, that fact is reflected *immediately* in the value of the company. Thus, unlike public sector management, management in the private sector cannot avoid *immediate* accountability by agreement to excessive deferred benefits. Although these observations are subject to exceptions and qualifications, they reflect a significant teacher advantage over private sector employees.

The major disadvantage of public employees relates to revenue raising and ratification procedures. Normally, the private sector employer can negotiate an agreement without public or political opposition. When the employer representative signs off, the employer is bound. Raising revenue and ratification by a public agency can be more difficult, and the difficulties may serve as a brake on what management is willing to do. For example, a school board may be unwilling to face the opposition to higher taxes needed for justified increases in teacher compensation.

Teachers do have some advantages in revenue raising and ratification. The school board's financial situation is known to the union, as is the board's room to maneuver. Indeed, teacher union representatives are sometimes more knowledgeable than school administrators about the district budget. My observation is made not to advocate secrecy in government; it is to point out that teachers have an inherent information advantage over private sector employees.

Another tactical advantage of teachers is that they have very little, if any, obligation of loyalty to their employer. On the other hand, private sector employees are under some obligation not to damage the employer. In the context of a labor dispute, private sector employees can urge the public not to purchase the employer's product or service, but otherwise their rights to criticize the employer's product or service are limited in ways that do not apply to teachers. Again, I am not advocating restrictions on teacher rights to criticize school boards and administrators. The fact is, however, that teachers enjoy legal rights to criticize their employers that exceed such rights in the private sector; this is an advantage over private sector employment, especially in view of the political dimension to teacher bargaining.

The fact that public enterprise cannot move constitutes still another advantage of public sector employment. Although the employer's ability to move varies from industry to industry and within industries, the inability of school boards to relocate as a response to employee pressure is obviously advantageous to teachers. Multi-national corporations have moved operations from one country to another to resist unionization; sometimes even the threat of relocation has helped to moderate union demands. But you cannot move the schools of Tucson to Mexico, or even to the Tucson suburbs, to avoid excessive demands by Tucson teachers.

Another major advantage of public over private employment is that teachers are entitled to certain rights of due process even in the absence of a collective agreement or statutory protection. For example, teachers who have acquired an expectancy of re-employment may not be fired without due process. Note that this protection is grounded in the federal constitution, not state statutory enactments. *Thus teachers without bargaining rights frequently have more protection against arbitrary and unjust employer action than do private sector employees with bargaining rights.* In fact, teachers sometimes have the benefit of an extensive system of statutory benefits that exceed the benefits negotiated in the private sector. In California, by statute, teachers and teacher unions have the following benefits, among others:

    1. Strong protection against dismissal or suspension;

2. Ten sick-leave days cumulative without limit;
3. Right to due process even as probationary employees;
4. Substantial notice before termination;
5. Layoff rights;
6. Military, bereavement, personal necessity, legislative, industrial accident and illness leave;
7. Sweeping protections in evaluation;
8. Limits on district authority to reduce benefits;
9. Protection against non-certified employees doing teacher work;
10. Duty-free lunch period;
11. Right to dues deduction;
12. Right to prompt payment of salary;
13. Right to notice of school closing;
14. Protection from legal actions for action in the course of employment;
15. Protection from being upbraided, insulted or abused in the presence of pupils; and
16. Limits on the work day and work year.

In the private sector, collective bargaining is the means of self-help to these benefits; bargaining rights were not superimposed on them. Providing bargaining rights in addition to this vast complex of statutory benefits is not equity for teachers; it is more than equity by a wide margin. In the private sector, employees presumably would have had to make various concessions to get these benefits, if they got them at all. In California, as in many other states, the benefits existed prior to bargaining, and no employee concession was or is required to achieve them. This is an enormous advantage to the teachers.

Theoretically, California could repeal all of the statutory benefits mentioned in the foregoing and the teachers could bargain from ground zero. For this reason, it may be argued, the existence of statutory benefits for teachers does not constitute an inherent advantage to public employees. In fact, the legal possibilities are not so clear. In some states, such as New York, public employee pension benefits may not be reduced constitutionally by the state. Unfortunately, this fact did not seem to lessen the generosity of the legislatures, which now must grapple with the problem of funding public employee pension and retirement benefits that require alarming proportions of state revenues.

According to teacher unions, the most glaring inequity between public and private employment is the fact that, in most states, teacher strikes are prohibited. If we limit our analysis to the legal right to strike and ignore the practical difficulties of enforcing penalties for illegal teacher strikes, there appears to be an inequity. This inequity is more technical than practical, and the typical legislative remedy for it has added to the advantages teachers have over private sector employees.

We must recognize that teacher strikes are not an economic weapon. If they are an economic weapon at all, they are a management one. The "loss of production" resulting from a teacher strike is hardly noticeable. Who can say years or even months after the fact what difference was made by a few lost days or weeks of schooling? From the standpoint of putting economic pressure on the employer, the loss of the right to strike in education is no loss at all. On the other hand, because teacher strikes are political, not economic, weapons, not having the right to strike strengthens the political effectiveness of teachers. The public is not aware of the economic ineffectiveness of teacher strikes, while it tends to be sympathetic to the argument that something should be done to help employees who cannot strike.

Because teachers generally don't have the right to strike, state legislation usually prescribes considerable time for bargaining and for impasse procedures. As a result, school management often concedes more than it would in a strike settlement. After all, the longer management is at the table, the more it gives away. The concessions management makes to avoid protracted negotiations and impasse procedures often are much greater than the concessions it would make to avoid or settle a strike.

Legislatures ought to be concerned about the fact that too much, not too little, time is devoted to public employee bargaining. Instead of providing a minimum amount of time for bargaining, legislatures should consider a maximum. Teacher unions still could be amply protected against lack of time for management preparation through the mechanism of unfair labor practices.

The emphasis on mediation and fact-finding in public education has been very costly to the public for another reason which is widely ignored. This emphasis has been a significant casual factor in teacher persistence in unreasonable demands. A teacher union that had to settle or strike, and thereby expose its members to the loss of income, would be more reasonable than a union whose options were to settle or invoke the statutory impasse procedures.

As long as the alternative to settlement is an impasse procedure, teacher persistence in unreasonable demands is only to be expected. In fact, the very existence of impasse procedures often strengthens teacher determination to concede as little as possible, lest they weaken their position in the impasse procedure. Thus in remedying a legal inequity whose practical importance is vastly over-rated, the legislatures have enacted impasse procedures that are more damaging to effective management than the legalization of teacher strikes would be.

The weakness of the equity argument is dramatically illustrated in cases where a board of education tries to discharge striking teachers after the board has bargained in good faith to impasse. In the private sector, the employer has the right to replace strikers under these circumstances; "equity" would appear to justify a similar right for school boards. Nevertheless, striking teachers have argued successfully that they can be fired only pursuant to the causes and procedures set forth in the tenure laws. These procedures typically require a board hearing for each individual teacher; the practical implications are to make it impossible to fire striking teachers in many districts. We are thus treated to the hypocritical spectacle of teacher unions crying to the public about the inequitable absence of a teacher right to strike, while they urge their members to strike because it is practically impossible to discipline or fire striking teachers. This is a major inequity favoring teachers.

What is the impact of collective bargaining upon pupils? Four positions on this issue are:

1. Collective bargaining is good for pupils.
2. Collective bargaining is bad for pupils.
3. Collective bargaining has no visible impact on pupils one way or the other.
4. We don't really know what the impact of collective bargaining is, and it wouldn't matter much if we did.

Theoretically, each of the four positions might have been valid at one time. Certainly, in the 1960's we probably did not know enough to draw valid conclusions about the impact of collective bargaining upon pupils. Today, however, this agnosticism is not so defensible.

The proposition that collective bargaining is good for pupils has its origin in politics, not in education. Probably the most important single difference between public and private sector bargaining is the political dimension to public sector bargaining. Essentially, it is a contest for public opinion. Whoever can appear to be the defenders and supporters of children has an enormous advantage in the struggle for favorable public opinion. For this reason, teacher union propaganda is almost invariably couched in terms of the welfare of the pupils.

Such appeals have a certain plausibility, but only because at some points teacher interests appear to coincide with pupil interests. For example, teachers want small classes, and small classes appear to be beneficial to students. Teachers want more preparation time, and who can be opposed to adequately prepared teachers?

Even teacher proposals of demonstrable benefit to pupils (and most are not) do not support the conclusion that teacher bargaining is an over-all benefit to pupils. Look at teacher proposals on issues where teacher interests conflict with pupil interests. For example, about 10 times a year, I negotiate on teacher proposals that teachers be dismissed when pupils are. A common variation on this theme is that teachers be dismissed when pupils are dismissed on Fridays and days preceding a holiday or vacation. Such proposals are hardly in the best interests of pupils; on the contrary, they are obviously in the interest of teachers to the detriment of pupils, as are many other teacher proposals from New Jersey to California.

In short, teacher interests sometimes conflict with and sometimes support the interests of pupils. When teacher interests can be made to appear as pupil interests, the teacher union will do its utmost to persuade the community that teachers are primarily interested in pupil welfare. Nevertheless, if teacher bargaining is not harmful to pupils, it is only because school boards do not agree to most teacher proposals.

Actually, teacher proposals frequently generate more public support than they really deserve. To illustrate, consider most teacher proposals to limit class size. A wealth of research clearly invalidates the assumption that there is an invariable positive correlation between lower class size and student achievement, but let us assume the correlation exists. Assume also that teachers are successful in achieving limits on class size in negotiations. Nevertheless, it would be fallacious to conclude that bargaining had a beneficial effect upon students or student achievement. After all, the practical issue is not only whether lower class size improves student achievement; it is whether the use of district funds to reduce class size is the most optimum use of the funds. Pupils may need textbooks or physical security or a decent meal even more than lower class size. The fact that such alternatives are typically ignored in negotiations helps to explain why most teacher arguments on the subject are nothing more than rationalizations of positions taken solely because they are in the interests of teachers. In saying this, I do not denigrate teacher self-interest or challenge their right to pursue it. My point is that from the teacher point of view, pupil welfare is a secondary or even tertiary consideration in teacher bargaining.

Realistically and practically, why should it be otherwise? How can it be? The teacher union is legally and practically the representative of *teachers*. *Pupils* did not elect teacher unions to represent *pupils; teachers* elected them to advance the interests of *teachers*. In this connection, the advent of collective bargaining clearly should end the controversy over whether teaching is a "profession." This controversy has been around for a long time, and most educators are probably bored with it as a semantic morass not worth stepping into. The issue has been definitely resolved by teacher bargaining, by the way, in favor of the proposition that, under collective bargaining, teaching is not and cannot be a profession in the traditional sense. I say this even though I formerly advocated collective bargaining as a means of professionalization. What puzzles me now is not that I was mistaken, but that the mistake was so obvious. At any rate, let me describe briefly the intellectual process by which I came to the erroneous conclusion that collective bargaining would be supportive of, or at least consistent with, professionalism.

More than 20 years ago I wrote a book entitled *Education as a Profession*. Writing it, I defined a profession as an occupational group that *inter alia* emphasized the service to be rendered, rather than the economic gain to the practitioners, as the basis for the organization and performance of the service performed.

I then asked this question: What was preventing teachers from professional status as defined? My answer was this: Teachers could not achieve professional status because their organizations were weak. Their organizations were weak because they were dominated by employers, *i.e.* by school management. This domination was used to frustrate association efforts to "professionalize" teaching. Example: Superintendents desperately needed teachers, hence their association influence was used to oppose efforts to raise certification standards.

My thought was that under a system of collective bargaining, management would be excluded from teacher organizations. Such exclusion would enable the organizations to become more vigorous and effective advocates of the higher standards administrators would not and could not support because of their position as management representatives.

In retrospect, part of the analysis was substantially correct. Collective bargaining brought about the exclusion of school administrators from teacher organizations, and these organizations became much stronger in the process. Unfortunately, another crucial consideration was overlooked. In representing teachers, a teacher union cannot be guided strictly or even primarily by public interest considerations. It must necessarily be guided by the interests of its members — an interest basically adverse to the public interest.

On this issue, the case is no different from the employment of an attorney. An attorney represents a client, not the public interest. This does not mean that there are no limits or constraints upon the representational function, but all of us expect our attorneys to act in our interests, whether we are suing the government, trying to stay out of jail, or seeking government approval to rezone a building.

Teachers frequently object to the proposition that their organizations are primarily oriented to teacher welfare. Nevertheless, this is not only the fact of the matter, but it probably would be dangerous if this were not the case. For example, suppose a district desires to dismiss a teacher for alleged incompetence. If the teacher union were to be the judge instead of the teacher advocate, the teacher would be without effective representation. This would be a most undesirable outcome, since effective representation is so important in our society.

Paradoxically, teacher organizations would lose rather than gain support among *teachers* if their organizations adopted a public interest posture in fact as well as in rhetoric; at a rhetorical level, there is no problem because most teachers believe that what's good for teachers is good for the country. At least, I have yet to hear a teacher union assert that more money for teachers, shorter hours, smaller class sizes, lighter loads, and more teacher benefits generally were not also in the best interests of the community — and I'm not holding my breath.

Assuming that the previous analysis is substantially correct, what of it? What policies or actions does it suggest; who should do what?

I am troubled by the foregoing analysis; I am troubled especially by the immense practical difficulties of doing anything constructive about it. Clearly, we cannot go back to the pre-bargaining days. For better or for worse, we have institutionalized collective bargaining or something like it in most states. The personnel and resources available to teacher and other public employee unions virtually ensure the continuation of collective bargaining in the public sector. Thus the political influence of public employee unions — the same factor that gives them an undue advantage in bargaining — is also a major deterrent to remedial action at the legislative level.

Furthermore, it is useless to look to higher education for any help in this matter. Many institutions of higher education have departments that are supposed to study and analyze labor legislation. At the same time, the professors in these departments often moonlight as mediators, arbitrators, conciliators, and fact-finders. To avoid jeopardizing their moonlighting roles, they avoid criticism of labor legislation generally, and especially of legislation that encourages and promotes the use of extended impasse procedures. They frequently even promote such legislation, having no problem whatever in finding it in the public interest. The relationship is not necessarily conscious and deliberate; my point is, however, that the philosophy for what's good for General Motors is good for the country lives in these departments, as indeed it does in education generally.

As previously noted, the differences between public and private sector bargaining are not all favorable to public employees. In my opinion, however, most of them are, even though their practical importance varies from state to state. Clearly, the justification for public employee collective bargaining is much stronger in states such as Mississippi, which has virtually no statutory benefits, than in states such as California, which has very substantial statutory benefits. Paradoxically, bargaining has emerged first and foremost in the states where it has the least justification and has yet to emerge in many states where its justification is comparatively greater. It must be emphasized, however, that most of the advantages of public employment are ineradicable, regardless of the political jurisdiction involved. Short of disenfranchising public employees, we cannot eliminate their additional leverage on their employers through the political process. Similarly, the rights of public employees to due process are grounded in the federal constitution, and it is not realistic to anticipate the elimination of these rights through the political process. If, therefore, equity is to be achieved, it must be achieved by adjusting the representational rather than the constitutional rights of public employees. To compensate for the inherent advantages of public employment, such adjustment should provide representational rights, which are different from, and significantly less than, private sector bargaining rights.

3.   Board Mistakes in Bargaining

Assuming that the board must bargain, what board actions are required? And what are some of the frequent or costly mistakes boards can avoid in these critical early decisions?

The role of school board members in teacher negotiations is of paramount importance. The philosophy of the board, its basic posture, and the nature and extent of its involvement in the bargaining process often spell the difference between a successful bargaining experience and a disaster.

On many crucial issues, school boards can look to their own experience or the experience of the administrative staff for guidance. This is not the case, however, with school boards negotiating one of their first written agreements. And, while the experience of negotiating a first agreement is valuable, it never encompasses all of the problems likely to arise in a subsequent agreement. In fact, the second time around is often as different from the first as the first was from the pre-negotiations era. The following suggestions should be considered, regardless of whether the board has previously negotiated with unions representing district employees.

1. If you don't know what you're doing, hire someone who does.

More costly mistakes are made by school boards in their initial reactions to negotiations than at any other time. It is not unusual for the entire course of negotiations to be dominated by board mistakes made at the very outset, when board members are not aware of the consequences of a seemingly sensible, innocent action.

Example: I was once employed as a negotiator by a board that had insisted upon *open* negotiationg sessions, *i.e.* sessions open to the general public, prior to my appointment. This insistence had led to procedural problems that made effective negotiations all but impossible. When I recommended discontinuation of open sessions, the board said, in effect: "We agree that open negotiating sessions have proved to be undesirable. However, we made such a public issue of having open sessions — over the objections of the teachers — that we'd look foolish, now, changing our position."

This reaction is a good example of why the board should not have advocated open negotiating sessions in the first place. It is always more difficult to change a position advocated publicly in newspapers than one advocated only around a negotiating table.

But the real point of this anecdote is that the board adopted its original position before seeking advice from someone with a practical background in negotiations. *Any* experienced negotiator would have saved this board considerable time and expense, if the board had only consulted him before, instead of after, getting into trouble.

Here's another example: I was employed as negotiator by a board that had previously and publicly agreed to negotiate with teacher organization "A," over the protests of teacher organization "B." Unfortunately, "B's" protests were justified, so I recommended that the board suspend negotiations until the issue was resolved by a representation election. The board felt that it could not retreat from its publicly advocated and reiterated recognition of "A." As a result, the board's negotiating team spent fruitless months negotiating with "A," only to have "B" upset the applecart by winning a representation election. Had the board been advised by any reasonably well-informed person *before* its unwarranted recognition of "A," it would have avoided months of expensive and time-consuming negotiations.

2. Board member should stay away from the actual negotiations!

One of the most common board blunders is for members—either the whole board or a sub-committee — to do the negotiating themselves. This blunder is often aided and abetted by superintendents who prefer to avoid assuming responsibility for the outcome of negotiations. Such avoidance may have a variety of motives. The most common is the attitude that negotiations are a "hot potato." If the board handles it effectively, there is no problem. And if the board botches it — which is more likely — the administration can always blame the board. This is all the more convenient if, as often happens, the administration is not experienced and knowledgeable about bargaining.

Look at it this way: Board members do not teach. They do not drive buses, cook in the school cafeteria, or coach the athletic teams. By the same token, they should not attempt to negotiate an agreement with their teachers. That task, like the others mentioned, should be delegated, through the superintendent, to competent personnel. If the superintendent can't recruit such personnel, the board should not attempt to perform these roles. It should, instead, recruit a new superintendent.

Board members should stay out of negotiations for a number of reasons.

Their most crucial task is policy-making. Anything else that takes up a lot of time weakens their ability to do their most important task. Negotiations are *extremely* time-consuming, to say the least.

Negotiations require a certain degree of skill and knowledge. Certainly, these qualities can by acquired, to some extent, by many board members. However, treating negotiations as an exercise in adult education for board members can be a very costly way to educate them — and the community — to the fact that the task is better left to more qualified personnel. Equally important, many board members do not have the personality traits required for effective negotiations. (This, incidentally, is as much a compliment as a criticism.)

Furthermore, having board members do the negotiating places the board at a crucial strategic disadvantage. Teacher representatives normally will insist that any agreement be ratified by the entire teacher organization. However, board members cannot ethically — and, in some states, legally — oppose ratification of an agreement they have personally negotiated. Many agreements are consummated in the early morning hours, as deadlines near, and the parties are fatigued. The board that negotiates virtually forfeits its right to consider ratification in a deliberate, non-crisis atmosphere, away from the pressure of a deadline and the frustration of a negotiating session.

Another reason board members should not negotiate: They lack detailed knowledge of the school system that is essential for effective negotiations with teachers.

Who *should* negotiate for the school board? A team of two or three administrators, headed by someone who reports directly to the superintendent of schools. A district administrator who has participated in past negotiating sessions — either in your district or in another district, either as a teacher representative or a board representative — might be suitable for the important position of team leader and chief negotiator.

If you do not have, on your district staff, anyone who has negotiating skills and experience, you should consider an outside consultant to head up your negotiating team.

3. Give your negotiating team authority to negotiate.

Some school boards recognize the need to stay out of the negotiating process. They establish a negotiating team — then fail to give it sufficient authority. Consequently, the negotiating team must refer every issue back to the board. It does not have the authority to agree to anything, except specifics previously approved by the board.

This is most unwise for several reasons. A board should retain the right to ratify an agreement, especially if the members of the teacher organization must also ratify the agreement. On the other hand, the board should not regard its negotiating team as mere messengers, relaying messages from the board to the teachers and back. Under such circumstances, the teacher negotiators will have a field day, ridiculing the board messenger service and criticizing the board for an unfair practice, *i.e.* being represented by someone without authority to negotiate. Just as board representatives would be wasting their time negotiating with messengers, instead of teacher-negotiators, so would the teacher-negotiators be wasting their time.

Many boards fear that delegation of authority to negotiate will mean abdication of their decision-making authority. This will not happen if the board knows *what* to delegate and to *whom*. If items involve *board policy,* then the board's negotiators should thoroughly explore these items with the board. If this is done, the board will not agree later to anything that will be rejected by the board, and the board will not by forced to reject an agreement that includes unpleasant surprises relating to "policy."

Many items involve *administrative matters,* rather than board policy. On these items, the board should normally accept the views of its administrative staff. If the administration says it can administer the schools effectively, pursuant to an administrative policy that is also acceptable to the teachers, the board should be extremely cautious in rejecting such a policy.

It is obviously important to avoid mix-ups over what is "administrative" policy and what is "board" policy. Ideally, the superintendent should make the decisions as to whether it is necessary to discuss an item with the board before the negotiating team discusses it with teachers. Hopefully, the superintendent knows the board and its policies well enough to make such decisions.

At the same time, the superintendent should give the board a complete list of the teachers' demands, making it clear that any board member should feel free to raise any question about any item.

From a practical point of view, the ultimate decision as to whether an item involves board policy or administrative policy *must* lie with the board. True, the board may unwisely decide many things that should be left to administrative discretion, but that is its prerogative.

4. Know how much money you're talking about.

It is essential that the board give its negotiating team a realistic idea of the total amount of money that will be available for the next school year. If negotiators do not know what this figure is, they will either be afraid to make any concessions (for fear the total package will exceed what the board is willing to pay) or they will find that they have agreed to items costing more than the board's "final" figure.

If you have complete confidence in your negotiating team and the negotiator who heads it, give the team the board's *actual* dollar limit. If you do not have complete confidence in the team, you can hedge a little. However, a board that cannot trust its chief negotiator with the board's bottom line positions should change either its attitude or its chief negotiator.

5. Don't agree to too much too soon — or too late.

Some boards come in with a firm offer very early, very hardnosed and very sure that they will make no further concessions. Meanwhile, neighboring school districts are settling for more than this "final" figure. By holding back too long and too much from the initial offer, a board infuriates its teachers and gets a strike. Then, after losing opportunities to recruit teachers all spring, the board finally ends up offering an amount which, earlier, would have produced a good agreement and avoided all the recruitment and personnel problems associated with a strike.

Delicate timing problems typically characterize negotiations. A board may decide upon the over-all limit of its settlement as early as November. In the ensuing months, inflation may increase significantly. Other districts may reach higher-than-anticipated settlements. Other public employee groups also may achieve unexpected benefits. State aid may be increased. In short, the amount that appears quite generous in November may be conservative in March.

And woe to the board that sets an early "final" figure, under no pressure, and then revises it upward as soon as the teachers strike or threaten to do so! The mistake here is not so often the upward adjustment as it is the earlier failure to take into account the effect of teacher pressure in estimating the cost of the package. The teachers rarely regard *any* offer made in the early stages of bargaining as "final." It is difficult for them to accept early offers. After all, a board can hardly lower an offer once made, so why not wait or put the pressure on to see if the offer won't be increased. In other words, don't assume that you will speed things up by offering all you can immediately. It rarely works out that way.

6. Don't require teacher concessions as a precondition to negotiations.

<u>Boards sometimes agree to negotiate only if the teachers meet some demands,</u> *e.g.* negotiations must be conducted at board meetings. In a growing number of states, such demands are illegal, since they force teachers to make concessions to be accorded their legal rights. Where boards are not legally obligated to negotiate, the temptation to require concessions as a precondition to negotiations is often irresistible. Of course, a board has the right — even the duty — to make sure that it negotiates only with an appropriate organization and under appropriate circumstances. Nevertheless, many boards not only want to designate their own representatives, they want to designate the teachers' representatives, too. <u>Boards should negotiate with whomever the teachers have duly chosen.</u> Perhaps the teachers have not chosen well. But board statements to this effect usually do more harm than good. (Boards don't always choose their representatives so well, either, but a board should not change its union representative simply because the teacher expressed dissatisfaction with him.) For better or for worse, both sides should choose their own representatives, and then go forward to do the best they can.

Frequently, the board's attitude is that it will meet with its teachers but not with "outsiders," such as field representatives of NEA or AFT. A growing number of states have made this an unfair practice, as it ought to be. <u>Boards should accept the right of teachers to choose their own representative.</u> No self-respecting teacher organization would, or should, accept the board's veto power over its right to designate its representative. Instead of making an issue over this, the board ought to concentrate on getting the strongest possible negotiating team for itself. (The negotiations statute enacted in Tennessee in 1978 requires that the negotiators for both parties be full-time employees of the school district. It will be interesting to see how this works out.)

7. Don't get bogged down over procedure.

<u>Avoid long hassles over procedure.</u> The teacher negotiators may want the board (or its team) to approve a negotiating schedule for

months in advance, including specific times, places, numbers, agendas and so on. Of course, a board may not be able to avoid a hassle, if the teachers are foolish enough to press for these blueprints. In fact, the vast majority of procedural arrangements are not worth the paper they are printed on. If you can set up a tentative working arrangement, so that participants can plan their schedules effectively, it's all right to do so. But don't expect a detailed, rigid, long-range procedural agreement to work.

The task of a board is not to negotiate, but to ensure that negotiations are conducted by competent personnel. *Such personnel may or may not be employed by the school system.* If they are competent, they will take steps to provide adequate communication between the board and its negotiating team. Such communication should preclude erosion of board authority on the one hand, and insufficient delegation of authority to negotiate on the other. Boards should respect expertise in this area, but such expertise should not make basic policy decisions for the board. Rather, it should be used to clarify important alternatives from which the board must choose. In negotiations, as in so many other areas, the effective board is the one that makes correct decisions on a relatively *small* number of fundamental issues.

4. Negotiating With Middle Management

A few years ago, most middle management school personnel were opposed to collective bargaining with teachers. Today, the issue is not whether middle management supports collective bargaining for teachers but whether middle management supports collective bargaining for itself. As a matter of fact, middle management is, with increasing frequency, opting for collective bargaining, and this is creating some extremely difficult problems for school boards.

"Middle management" refers to school-level personnel who exercise administrative-supervisory roles: principals, assistant principals, and supervisors; department chairmen with significant responsibilities for hiring, tenure, promotion, and discipline; and some central office personnel (depending upon the nature of their work, size of system, appropriate legislation, and other factors). Management is "middle" between top management and teachers, not between upper and lower echelons of management.

Bargaining with middle management presents a number of special problems.

The first problem is whether to negotiate at all with middle management. In some states, legislation requires the board to do so. In California, Connecticut, Massachusetts, Michigan, New Jersey, New York and other states, the school board is required to negotiate with organizations representing virtually all certified personnel, except the superintendent and assistant superintendents. In these states, school management is likely to find that most of the questions related to bargaining with middle management are also resolved by statutory decision or state regulation. Should middle management be included in the same negotiating unit as classroom teachers? Should middle management have the right to be represented by the same organization that represents teachers? What impasse procedures should be utilized in case of an impasse between middle management and the board negotiators? Who belongs in the middle management unit, if it is a separate negotiating unit (often referred to as an administrative-supervisory unit)?These are some of the special issues related to negotiations with middle management.

Administrators in states without such legislation should be aware of experience in the states that have mandated negotiations with middle management. By and large, this experience confirms the view that it is not desirable to legalize collective bargaining by middle management. Significantly, management in the private sector is not required to bargain with middle management. Thus, many school boards and superintendents who used to lament "the introduction of industrial practices into education" are now singing the praises of "the enlightened industrial negotiations model."

Where there is no statutory obligation or prohibition relating to negotiations with middle management, the decision on whether to negotiate with middle management will rest upon several factors. Ordinarily, a board is unlikely to be faced with such a request unless it is already negotiating with teachers. Other than that, size of system is probably the crucial factor. A large urban district cannot determine conditions of employment for several hundred principals, assistant principals, supervisors, and coordinators on an individual basis. Some type of collective bargaining may be desirable, especially if the personnel involved desire collective representation. (Of course, it is necessary to require evidence of majority status before entering into negotiations with any organization that claims to represent an appropriate unit.)

Regardless of whether a board negotiates with middle management by statute or because of the practical realities of the situation, there are some unique and thorny problems involved.

First, school management is likely to be shorthanded in negotiating with middle management, especially if it is simultaneously negotiating with a teacher union and one or more organizations of non-certified personnel. Regardless, it is almost always preferable to negotiate with middle management *after* negotiations with other groups have been concluded. As a practical matter, boards cannot make concessions to middle management which will undermine their bargaining position with teachers. For example, it is usually not feasible to negotiate a higher percentage raise for middle management than for teachers if the middle management package is negotiated first. The teachers are not likely to expect a smaller percentage raise, and they will be extremely resistant to any such final offer. If the order of negotiations is reversed, however, the board has more flexibility. It can correct administrative inequities without raising teacher expectations to unrealistic levels.

In all cases, the board should be careful about making any concession to middle management which it does not intend to make to teachers at the *next* teacher contract. Consider a school board where middle management has asked for sabbatical leaves at full pay. The administration has just completed an agreement with teachers providing sabbatical leaves at half pay. In this situation, the board could hardly concede full pay for middle management sabbaticals unless it was prepared to do so the next year for teachers. In fact, it probably would have been a serious mistake to make any such concession unless the board had *first* made it to teachers. It would be much better for morale to have the teachers feel they had gotten this benefit for middle management than to have the teachers feel they got it only because the board had first conceded it to their supervisors and principals.

Some agreements with organizations representing middle management expressly base a benefit upon the teacher contract. For example, the administrator-supervisor salary schedule may be geared to certain steps on the teacher salary schedule. Despite the frequency of such clauses, they can be extremely undesirable and should be avoided. To illustrate, consider a district in which both the school board and the employees want to avoid negotiating a contract every year. Assume that there is a mutual willingness to negotiate a two-year or three-year agreement but deep uncertainty over the appropriate salary terms for the second or third year. The middle management personnel want a schedule so high that there would be minimal risk to them in accepting a two-year or three-year contract. This requires a higher commitment than the board is willing to make. Under these circumstances, gearing the salaries for middle management to certain steps on the teacher schedule appears to be an attractive solution. Nevertheless, it should be avoided.

Suppose the salaries in the second or third year of the contract for middle management are geared to particular steps on the teacher schedule, *e.g.* the bargaining salary for a teacher with a B.A. degree. It would then be very tempting for the school board to minimize salary increases for teachers at that step, to hold down the entire middle management schedule. This temptation would exist regardless of the step used as the base for calculating the middle management schedule. Suppose, for example, the step on the teacher schedule used as the base for middle management was the maximum for teachers with an M.A. degree. The board might then be tempted to pump more money into the early or middle steps of the teacher schedule. In other words, the board can, if it wishes, minimize the increases at the step used as a basis for paying middle management. True, the school board may have no thought of doing so when it reaches agreement with middle management. A year or two in the future, however, the pressures on the board may be too great for it to resist such temptation.

It is even more important to emphasize that this type of clause is also undesirable from the *board's* standpoint. Suppose the board agrees to a three-year contract for middle management, with salaries the second and third years to be a certain ratio above the first step on the teacher schedule. In the second year, the board may find it necessary to raise this step substantially, but not so much as it needs to raise other steps on the schedule. Now the board has a problem. It can no longer consider the teacher salary at the first step on its merits alone. It also must weigh the impact of its decision, at that particular step, on the entire middle management salary schedule. In order not to give the middle management group an undeserved windfall, the board may have to set the beginning salary for teachers at less than it otherwise would or should.

As a rule, boards should avoid tying salaries for one group to salaries for another group. If it does, it won't be able to consider the salaries of either group on their merits. There should be a relationship between salaries for teachers and for middle management, but that relationship should not be one of automatic, predetermined contractual increases for middle management, based upon the teacher schedule. On some occasions, middle management should get either a higher or a lower percentage raise than teachers at a particular step.

Grievance procedures for middle management are another troublesome area. In general, school boards and superintendents should have wide latitude in selecting and directing middle management personnel. Nevertheless, unjust treatment of middle management is a possibility.

Again, size of system is crucial. Suppose the middle management unit includes only 12 or 15 persons. If the grievance procedure provides for impartial arbitration as the terminal point in the grievance procedure, it might cost each member of the unit $50 to $100 per grievance going to arbitration. This cost would be prohibitive, unless a basic employee interest were involved. Nevertheless, middle management groups with fewer than 15 members sometimes ask that grievance arbitration replace a board hearing, even though the middle management organization could not pay for grievance arbitration except in dire emergencies.

Many middle management personnel have come to support collective bargaining because of the feeling that they have been "bypassed" in teacher-board negotiations. While this may be true, the answer to the problem is not necessarily collective bargaining for middle management. Instead, it should be the incorporation of the needs of middle management personnel into the positions ultimately adopted by the school board's negotiating team. This usually — but not necessarily — requires the inclusion of capable middle management personnel on the board's negotiating team. (An effective administration team will learn how various proposals and counterproposals affect middle management, regardless of whether such personnel are on the team.)

Boards tend to get the kinds of employment relations they deserve. If a board refuses to provide fair settlements with middle management, it is in effect inviting middle management to take a hard line with the board. Budgeting commitments made prior to negotiating with middle management should leave adequate resources and flexibility for dealing with middle management. The school board and superintendent who recognize this will not ordinarily find negotiating with middle management to be a traumatic experience.

5. Negotiating With Pressure Groups

In many districts, school administration has become almost synonymous with "confrontation management" in recent years. First, there was an unsettling upsurge in teacher militancy, culminating in teacher-school board bargaining. Then, other employee groups began to press for collective bargaining. Administrators were literally forced into annual or biannual confrontations on terms and conditions of employment.

But civil rights groups also began to demand curriculum and personnel changes, and their successes have contributed to the formation of other community pressure groups, all concerned with issues that have little or nothing to do with the actual conditions of employment.

Today, the school administrator suddenly finds himself faced with a bewildering collection of demands — for more liberal rules of dress or conduct, for curriculum change, for (and against) integration, for just about anything that catches popular support at the moment. Such demands may be made by students, by parents, or by community groups. They are often accompanied by threats of demonstrations, boycotts, or other forms of protest and persuasion. Because these growing demands frequently lead to "negotiations," it may be helpful to clarify some of the similarities and differences between non-employee negotiations and those involving employees.

In negotiating with teachers, there is usually no problem determining who represents them. The procedures for designating teacher representatives are often regulated by statute. Where they are not, procedures for determining representation are well established.

It is relatively easy to determine who represents students, too — at least, on a given issue. But deciding who represents parents, or a neighborhood, or a black community, can be extremely difficult. Dealing with persons who do not really represent the group they claim to represent can escalate problems. At the same time, refusing to deal with persons who are the *de facto* leaders of parents or a community can be equally troublesome. The problem is exacerbated by the fact that most school controversies flush out a considerable number of self-styled community leaders or representatives.

I recently witnessed a dramatic illustration of this problem. A group of black students had damaged some school property after one of their "demands" was refused. Subsequently, a group of parents, alleging to represent all parents, presented several demands to the administration, including amnesty for the students. The basis for their claim to represent all parents was simply that the local paper had carried an advance announcement of the meeting at which their demands were formulated. However, the announcement did not state the purpose of the meeting or indicate that it was open to all parents. The local press subsequently gave wide publicity to their demands, but raised no critical questions concerning the representative status of the leaders. As a result, the administration felt forced to negotiate with a group that really did not represent more than a handful of parents. In fact, many parents who had never heard of the group resented its claim to represent them.

The absence of a feasible representational system for parents or community groups leads to another basic difficulty in "negotiating" with such groups, *i.e.* their inherent lack of accountability. It is easy for students, parents, or community groups to demand certain changes in the curriculum or in school operations. Unfortunately, these same groups are not really accountable for the consequences of their demands.

For example, suppose students demand certain courses or changes in grading policy. Suppose, further, that the changes are made and have undesirable consequences in practice. The students who originally demanded the changes are not likely to be around when the consequences can be adequately evaluated. Even if they are, it is extremely difficult, if not impossible, to hold them accountable for advocating policies that turn out to be undesirable. It's the school administrator who is likely to be held accountable for undesirable outcomes, regardless of who initially requested them.

This being the case, administrators must be cautious in sharing their decision-making power with individuals or groups who are practically immune from any responsibility for the consequences. In fact, such immunity is one reason that administrators are often confronted by unrealistic, even irresponsible demands. It is easy to make such demands when the other fellow has to suffer if they don't work out.

Note the difference, on this issue, between teacher-school board negotiations and negotiations with students, parents or community groups. The teacher negotiators are either teachers themselves or full-time representatives of teachers. Their own level of compensation, or even their jobs, are likely to depend upon the effectiveness of their negotiations. Furthermore, they must live with the administration after negotiations are concluded. As a result, there are some built-in restraints on their negotiating behavior — restraints that do not apply to non-employment negotiations. Teacher negotiations are increasingly regulated by statute and governmental agencies, which prohibit unfair practices. "Negotiations" with community groups are more prone to irrational or unethical behavior, which makes it difficult to reach agreement.

Some time ago, I attended a meeting where a group of black parents made six demands on a high school principal. The demands included: increased employment of black teachers, introduction of black history, amnesty for black students who had damaged school property, and no restitution for property damage resulting from a recent outbreak of vandalism. The demands were made with a newspaper reporter present, and the school administration was given until three o'clock the next day to accept the demands, which were labeled "non-negotiable." Obviously, such behavior at teacher-board negotiations would constitute an unfair labor practice.

The scope of non-employment negotiations is also much different from negotiations over terms and conditions of employment. In fact, non-job negotiations frequently deal with curriculum, admissions, and other matters of educational policy. Many school administrators — including some in higher education — are courting trouble on this point. In teacher negotiations, they typically assert that educational policies are not negotiable. Inconsistently, they then negotiate such policies with groups who carry no legal responsibility for the outcomes. In my opinion, this is an additional reason why administrators should avoid the term "negotiations" in referring to discussions of this nature.

In the 1960's, the City College of New York (CCNY) administration "negotiated" an admissions policy that would have permitted half the incoming freshmen to be admitted without meeting the normal admission requirements. The agreement was later rejected by the faculty, but that is not the crucial point. What is crucial is that the entire sequence of events tended to legitimatize the notion that the administration should negotiate on admissions policies with community groups.

Negotiations with community groups are essentially *political* accommodations. And as such, they do have important similarities with teacher board negotiations. For example, in both situations, the parties need to save face and avoid the appearance of capitulation. In one school system with which I am familiar, the superintendent agreed to certain proposals made by a community group. The newspaper story referred to the superintendent's "capitulation" to the pressure groups. The story was unfair, but it illustrates a point. The administration must appear flexible and responsive, but it seriously risks public support if it seems to give in too easily to pressure groups.

Here, as with teacher-board negotiations, it may be crucial to have the parties keep talking during a crisis. It is also desirable to observe certain amenities in dealing with community groups. Even when it is necessary to disagree with them vigorously, a special effort should be made to avoid personal affront. They will often seem acutely sensitive to one who is accustomed to the rough-and-tumble of negotiations over conditions of employment.

In general, most of the techniques of negotiating with teachers are to some degree applicable to negotiations, "confrontations," or "consultations" with other groups. It is significant that the American Arbitration Association (AAA), which plays such a prominent role in mediation in employment relations, has recently established a mediating service in the area of community relations. Some of the AAA's most experienced labor and commercial arbitrators are now active in community relations.

True, "negotiating" with a community group over a pupil transportation policy, or a policy on student dress, does call for knowledge about those specific subjects. In employment negotiations, what other districts are doing — especially nearby districts — is very important, and this is also true with respect to other types of controversies. If all other nearby school districts bus elementary pupils one mile or more from the nearest school, it will be easier for the administrator to carry out such a policy in his district. The herd instinct is not confined to employment relations, as any experienced administrator knows. Thus, the technique of citing what others do has broad application. Likewise, as in teacher negotiations, the experienced admininstrator will avoid citing practices in other districts that increase, rather than decrease, his vulnerability.

The major problem, again, is that negotiations outside the employment context are so unstructured. In employment negotiations, there are certain constraints on the parties. These constraints do not eliminate all inexperienced and unsophisticated negotiators, or all the crackpots and irresponsibles. But they do have a healthy tendency in this direction.

In teacher negotiations, for example, the administration spokesmen will recognize the political needs of their adversaries. Thus, they will usually try to help the teacher representatives look good — to the teachers. By the same token, the administration negotiators usually will expect certain kinds of help from teacher representatives. In negotiating with community groups, however, the administration is more likely to be confronted by spokesmen who are ignorant or heedless of the long-range consequences of a particular tactic.

The best way to avoid excessive and unproductive negotiations with community groups is to have a positive program for constantly informing and involving *responsible* groups in considering issues that concern them. By taking the initiative here, with both student and community groups, a board has a better chance to structure their involvement in a satisfactory way. A board also stands a better chance of avoiding the kind of emergency *ad hoc* negotiations that have been so disastrous to school boards that have been unprepared for negotiations with teachers.

6. Maintaining Managerial Prerogatives in Bargaining

Many school boards have got themselves into serious trouble by making concessions that render it impossible for the board to manage the district effectively. When the board tries to recover its lost authority, it finds it impossible or extremely expensive to force the union to return the captured board authority. For this reason, the most important rule in bargaining is: Don't give up your board authority in the first place. Second rule: When you do concede board authority, make sure you understand exactly what you're giving away. Don't bargain away what you can't live without.

What follows in this chapter are some specifics for retaining and increasing school board authority. The first line of defense is a management rights clause. If the contract doesn't have such a clause, get one. And don't settle for a clause that simply says the board retains all the management rights it has under state and federal laws. You have those anyway! Spell out your rights to hire, fire, demote, transfer, discipline, establish curriculum and select textbooks. The union will not readily admit that the board has such authority, but in the end, the teachers must recognize it. The union must also, if it wants to maintain its own credibility. I've been in tough arguments with some hard-headed union leaders over specific management rights clauses. I've asked: "Who's the boss, the board or the union?" And: "Since the board has the right to hire and fire teachers, what's wrong with putting that in the contract?" I've yet to find a union bargaining team that can win that argument.

The management rights clause is an obvious instrument to preserve board authority. It's direct and meets the problem head on. But there are other, more subtle ways to give the board more power. One of the best ways is to *decrease* union authority, and the griev-

---

This chapter has been prepared by Raymond G. Glime, a school board attorney and negotiator, Mt. Clemens, MI. (Portions were published previously in *The American School Board Journal*, March 1978.)

ance clause of the contract is the most fertile place to start. The grievance clause is the vehicle the union most commonly uses to enforce the contract, so start by defining "grievance" as narrowly as possible, preferably as a "violation of the express terms of the contract." Then impose as much responsibility on the union as you can. Insist, for example, that a statement of grievances must be in writing, must be filed no later than X days from occurrence of the grievance, must clearly set forth the facts, must cite the contract provisions violated, and must contain a clear statement of the appropriate relief sought.

A second way to increase board authority is to limit the authority of the arbitrator in contract disputes. Confine the arbitrator within the four corners of the contract; don't let him or her interpret questions of law. Let the union sue over violations of law if it wants to. The lawsuit remedy is considerably better for boards than the arbitration remedy. Courts are prepared to deal with questions of law, and if a board disagrees with the court, its rights of appeal are clear. If a board disagrees with the arbitrator, however, its rights of appeal are unclear. Since there is no defined appeal procedure, the board is likely to end up in court anyway. For this reason, it may as well exclude arbitrators from deciding questions of law — leave those to the judge.

Furthermore, courts are reluctant to interfere with an arbitrator's award unless the arbitrator clearly exceeds his authority or there is fraud or collusion (all of which are difficult to prove). Even if the arbitrator misinterprets the law, the court usually will not set aside his decision. In one 1975 case in Michigan (*Chippewa Valley Schools v. Hill;* 62 Mich. App. 116, 1975), the teacher association contended that a teacher on maternity leave was entitled to be paid her accumulated sick leave days for her disability. The arbitrator decided, erroneously, that federal law required that the teacher be paid for the sick days used for maternity purposes. The U.S. Supreme Court has since struck down that position. But the Michigan Court of Appeals said the arbitrator's view of the law was binding, since both parties had agreed in advance to accept his decision about benefits.

Another good way to increase board authority is through old-fashioned horse trading — getting something you want in exchange for something the teachers want. The trick, of course, is to be able to appraise accurately the value to each party of the items traded. That's what collective bargaining is all about, and that's where it's advisable to have professional skills. The idea is to make sure the board is getting something at least as valuable as the item it is giving away. One thing to trade for is money — increases in salaries and fringe benefits. The board will probably spend the money anyway, so it may as well get something for it. Too many school boards don't connect or relate salaries with management rights. They divide the issues into "economic" or "non-economic" items, bargain the non-economic items first, and then move on to salary concerns. There's a better way: Take the approach that you can buy anything and that everything is for sale. With that attitude, negotiators can do wonders to increase board authority.

The timing of contract proposals is important, too. If you want a strong layoff provision, one that allows you to lay off the least qualified employees first (and not be stuck with seniority, as the union wants), negotiate that provision before you really need to use it. In other words, don't wait until a year when you're faced with declining enrollments or a fiscal crisis that would mean reductions in force. Likewise, don't try to negotiate a "no strike" clause during a strike. It is far more difficult to get agreement on such controversial items when the union is under the gun than when it is not.

You also can regain school board authority by having reasonable expectations about collective bargaining. If you gave everything away last year, don't expect to get it all back this year. That goal is unrealistic. You can, of course, declare war on the union, demand the return of your management rights, and let the union strike or withhold services. Through injunctive relief, unfair labor practice hearings or binding arbitration, you may recapture, over a period of a few years, some previously lost board power. Of course, you can fire all the teachers, destroy the union, and start fresh with a clean slate, a new contract and a new union. But that approach is very costly, in terms of money, time and disruption to the educational process.

A better, and easier, way is to understand the union and deal with it intelligently. Don't treat the union as the enemy (even though it may be). Use a modern personnel manager's approach. Be informal, attempt to understand exactly what problems the union bargaining team is trying to solve, and look at the problems through the union's eyes. If the teachers have a legitimate complaint, or something that doesn't cost much to resolve, bow to it. Try to handle the matter administratively, without adding to the collective bargaining agreement. If the teachers sit on a problem all year, only to bring it up at bargaining time, chastise them. Remind them you have a grievance procedure to remedy problems during the school year. You don't have to change the contract to satisfy every whim. If the problem is a temporary one, or one you can resolve with a simple assurance, handle it with a letter of intent.

Remember, too, that the union is a political entity. Try to understand and tolerate its propaganda so that you can live, work and achieve together. If you can give union leaders something of little consequence to make them look good, give it. You don't have to fight every step of the way; save the fight for something that matters. When you have to add to your contract, look around for something to trade for the addition. If your contract lacks a strong management rights clause or a narrow grievance clause that limits the arbitrator's power, start there. If your contract is loosely written and deals in generalities, strengthen the language. Get rid of phrases like "no employee shall be treated unfairly" or "every child is entitled to a quality education." They're too vague.

To summarize, school boards can increase their authority through collective bargaining. The bargaining atmosphere for boards of education has clearly improved in recent years. Boards have muscle, and teachers are rightly concerned about being fired in a very tight market. So, if a board proceeds carefully, fairly and firmly, it may indeed be able to increase or recapture its authority.

7.   More Sources and Suggestions on Policy Issues

AASA Model Public Employee Collective Bargaining Law, American Association of School Administrators, Arlington, Va., 1976. State public bargaining laws are virtually always initiated by public employee unions. Typically, public school management is not aware of all the deficiencies in such union-drafted legislation until it is enacted. Partly to help solve this problem, AASA sponsored the development of model legislation that would avoid legislative mistakes and oversights in states that have enacted public employee bargaining laws. This model legislation would be useful in evaluating proposed changes, as well as initial legislation on the subject.

Jones, Ralph T.: *Public Sector Labor Relations: An Evaluation of Policy-Related Research,* Contract Research Corporation, Belmont, Mass., 1975. This publication attempts to provide a comprehensive survey of policy-oriented research bearing on public sector labor relations.

Labor-Management Services Administration, U.S. Department of Labor: *A Directory of Public Employee Organizations,* Superintendent of Documents, Washington, D.C., 1974.

Labor-Management Services Administration, U.S. Department of Labor: *A Directory of Public Employment Relations Boards and Agencies,* Superintendent of Documents, Washington, D.C., 1975.

Labor-Management Services Administration, U.S. Department of Labor: *A Directory of Public Management Organizations,* Superintendent of Documents, Washington, D.C., 1974.

Midwest Center for Public Sector Labor Relations: *Sources of Information in Public Sector Labor Relations,* Indiana University, Bloomington, 1977. This is a useful directory for districts or agencies that desire to establish an information system on school district labor relations.

Myers, Donald A.: *A Bibliography on Professionalization,* American Federation of Teachers, Washington, D.C., 1974.

Pezdek, Robert V.: *Public Employment Bibliography,* New York State School of Industrial and Labor Relations, Ithaca, N.Y., 1973.

Shaw, Lee, and R. Theodore Clark, Jr.: "The Practical Differences Between Public and Private Sector Bargaining," *19 UCLA Law Review 867,* 1972.

Smith, Russell A., Harry T. Edwards, and R. Theodore Clark, Jr.: *Labor Relations Law in the Public Sector,* Bobbs-Merrill Company, Indianapolis, 1974. Annual supplements. This is a useful source book for negotiators as well as for school board labor counsel.

Stanley, David T., *Managing Local Government Under Union Pressure,* Brookings Institution, Washington, D.C., 1972.

Stieber, Jack: *Public Employee Unionism,* Brookings Institution, Washington, D.C., 1973.

Wellington, Harry H., and Ralph K. Winter, Jr.: *The Unions and the Cities,* Brookings Institution, Washington, D.C., 1971. This is one of the better analyses of the policy issues growing out of public sector bargaining.

THE IMPACT OF
BARGAINING UPON
SCHOOL BOARD OPERATIONS

8. The Board's Negotiating Team

The size and composition of the administration's negotiating team is a thorny issue in many districts. Should any board members be on the team? Should the superintendent negotiate? How many people should be on the team? Should an outside negotiator be employed? How much do outside negotiators charge? Questions such as these crop up whenever teacher-board negotiations are discussed. Even administrators who have been through the process are not always sure of the correct answers to these questions.

Since the size of the negotiating team obviously affects who should be on it, size is the first question to tackle. We should refer to *an* appropriate member, rather than to *the* appropriate number, since there is no magic in any particular figure. An "appropriate number" will be a compromise between several factors.

First, the smaller the team, the easier it is to reach agreement, both within the team and with the teacher team. There are several reasons for this. Less time is needed to caucus. It is easier to maintain an atmosphere of informality with small numbers; as the team gets larger on either side, there is more need for formal procedures to govern negotiations. Actually, when you get down to the crunch, often the most effective procedure is for one or two members of the administration team to negotiate with one or two key members of the teacher team. At least two people are desirable, especially if you aren't confident of the good judgment and integrity of the chief teacher negotiator. Mistakes are easy to make in the tension-filled final hours of negotiations. Negotiators may begin to hear what they want to hear, instead of what is actually said. Certainly, you don't want the teacher negotiator to assert that you offered a $20,000 maximum in confidence, when you really offered only to consider such a maxumum if three additional steps were required to reach it.

On the other hand, the smaller the team, the greater the danger of a *serious* mistake in negotiations. Even the most knowledgeable administrators may be unaware of a particular school situation that should affect their response to teacher proposals.

For example, I once negotiated a clause dealing with the board's right to require teacher attendance at evening meetings. This was not a problem in the secondary schools, but there was considerable variation in the 10 elementary schools in the district. The elementary principal on the negotiating team — who was not aware of all the variations — tended to respond in terms of the practice in his school of requiring three evening meetings. Had we followed his advice, we would have undermined programs in two schools where teachers were required to attend five evening meetings a year.

Obviously, every principal can't be on the negotiating team. Yet, again and again, one finds variations from school to school in the lunch program or bus duty or attendance after class or on similar items being negotiated. Sometimes, the variations are not justified and should be negotiated out of existence. Sometimes, however, they are completely justified and may be inadvertently negotiated away because the administration team was unaware of them.

To minimize these problems, two procedures should be used. First, have your negotiating team explore all proposals carefully with the *entire* staff, so any unusual situations are brought out. Second, structure the negotiations agenda so that particular experts are available when their expertise is needed. Thus, you may request administrative payroll and computer personnel to be available only when specific items, such as the number of separate deductions or duration of pay periods, is being negotiated.

Two other important factors, time and continuity, should be considered.

Administrative time is a resource. Boards should not approach negotiations with the notion that such time costs nothing because "it is already paid for." If they do, they are likely to end up spending thousands of dollars to negotiate items whose total costs may not exceed a few hundred dollars. Even worse, they may seriously damage effective administration this way.

Continuity in negotiations and contract administration is essential. When the next contract is negotiated, the board should not have to designate a completely new team because of resignations and retirements.

My belief is that five persons ought to be enough for school systems employing up to 1,000 teachers. I have seen negotiations conducted very successfully by three-member teams, against very sophisticated teacher bargaining teams, in districts employing more than 3,000 teachers. My over-all impression is that board teams tend to be larger than they need to be, if there is adequate communication with the entire staff and effective utilization of non-permanent members of the team.

It is absolutely imperative to avoid permitting the administrative staff, or any segment thereof, to *elect* members of the administration team. For instance, the superintendent should never permit the principals to elect a principal to be on the team. The person so elected may be the most popular principal, or the least busy one, or anything but the most effective negotiator.

It is also a mistake to put persons on the team merely because they hold a certain position in the system. Superintendents naturally like to have a business manager or director of personnel on the administration team. However, this isn't always desirable. Subordinates may be more effective members of a negotiating team than their superiors, *e.g.* an assistant principal may be more effective than a principal at the negotiating table. It is preferable to have a qualified subordinate on the negotiating team than a superior who is simply unsuited for negotiations.

Never let teachers dictate who should be on the board team. The administrator who makes a fetish of getting along with teachers can be a disaster. A sincere desire to have pleasant, civilized, professional relations is an asset in a potential member of the team. Unfortunately, some administrators carry this attitude to the point where they are afraid to say "No" to anything, for fear their real or assumed popularity with teachers will be jeopardized. The negotiators who can't say "No" are bad news on *both* sides of the bargaining table.

If at all possible, board members should not be on the negotiating team. They have to decide whether to ratify the agreement; on the other hand, it would be an unfair practice for a board member to refuse to ratify an agreement he had approved at the negotiation table. Furthermore, if a board member negotiates an agreement that the other board members refuse to ratify, the employees are likely to feel they have been deceived.

In general, the superintendent should not be on the negotiating team either, particularly in medium and large school systems. The superintendent should be informed throughout the proceedings and should provide direction within guidelines set by the board. However, although the superintendent should be available to the board team, he should not attempt to be present continuously as a member. If he does, he will find himself waiting endlessly while teachers caucus, or his schedule will be continuously disrupted because of the uncertain course of negotiations. The teachers are required to negotiate with the board's representatives, whoever they may be. Hence, neither the teachers nor the superintendent should be upset because the superintendent is not a member of the board negotiating team.

Of course, teachers may occasionally have legitimate criticisms of the board's negotiating team. Adamant adherence to the board's position is not, per se, a legitimate criticism. But other things might be: failure to show up on time, repudiation of earlier concessions, and so on. In such cases, the offended party should seek redress in a way that avoids even the appearance of trying to dictate the other party's choice of negotiator.

In many districts, the most difficult question concerning the board team is whether to employ an outside negotiator. Such employment has both advantages and disadvantages. The board pays for the specialized help it needs — no more, no less. Just as boards employ a school architect or attorney to perform specialized tasks at a certain rate, so it may make sense to employ a negotiations specialist in the same way. Furthermore, it is easier to change outside negotiators than to replace a full-time staff member if there is dissatisfaction with performance.

An outsider, employed on an hourly or per diem basis, poses fewer problems than a full-time employee, utilized as chief negotiator. Also, the outsider should have broader negotiating experience than full-time district personnel, who negotiate once a year or once every two or three years. The last point is not so important in larger systems, where administration personnel may be negotiating with several different employee organizations every year.

The main disadvantages are that the outsider does not know the district, and a board may have to pay him to learn what he needs to know about it. This disadvantage is not so great if the same consultant is employed to negotiate subsequent contracts.

Another possible disadvantage of outsiders is that they are not around to administer the agreement. This may influence them to agree to clauses that would be unacceptable to an administrator who had to live with the agreement on a daily basis. However, some outside negotiators also represent or assist the district on grievances, thus mitigating this particular problem.

There is a natural tendency for the consultant to make himself indispensable; on the other hand, this may not be desirable from the board's point of view. Outside negotiators can be desirable, even essential, in certain situations, but the better ones try to reduce, rather than to increase, the board's dependence on them.

The rates for outside negotiators vary from $40 to $100 an hour. Other expenses will not be large if a local consultant is employed, but certain kinds of services usually require additional payment. In any event, this should be clarified at the outset. Many outside negotiators are labor attorneys and tend to bill at their usual hourly rate, with some modifications for all-night or other extended meetings.

Both hourly rates and fixed fees have dangers of their own. If the fee is fixed, the outsider may be tempted to conclude the negotiations by conceding too much too soon. After all, he is, in effect, working for nothing after the fee is fixed and he must continue to negotiate. Realistically, the hourly rate is more equitable and safer, since it is virtually impossible to know how much time will be required.

For example, unit determination issues can require weeks of hard work, including appearances before hearing officers and state labor relations agencies. Employee unions may file charges of unfair labor practices; though frivolous, and filed merely as a negotiating ploy, the charges have to be answered. Internal union politics may render it impossible to negotiate an agreement expeditiously. In general, boards and school administrators greatly underestimate the amount of time required by negotiations, a fact that leads to some unpleasant surprises when the bills come due.

In considering employment of an outside negotiator, boards should talk to board members and superintendents in districts where the negotiator has previously worked. One should be skeptical of consultants who agree with everything the board wants to do; such agreement suggests an overwhelming desire to get the business, rather than sound professional judgment. On the other hand, boards should not automatically exclude consultants who formerly represented teachers in negotiations. Just as in private employment, some of the best negotiators are persons who started out representing employee organizations and were lured over to the management side. In fact, about 20 percent of board negotiators got started this way.

9. Choosing the Management Advocate

The major objectives of a board's labor relations policy should be to achieve a peaceful relationship with employees and with the organization that represents them. These objectives should be accomplished while (1) minimizing cost, being consistent with the need to retain well-trained staff with reasonably good morale, and (2) retaining as much as possible the ability of management to take whatever action it believes necessary to maximize its delivery system. In short, management wants to give up as little as possible while making employees feel that the district is a good place to work.

One way to accomplish this is to pass a resolution that unilaterally implements wages, hours and conditions of work, and also contains a clause that says "employees will be ecstatic." A second method is to be sure your labor relations program is guided by the best labor relations professional you can find.

The district's employee relations program can be guided by a district employee or by an outside consultant. The major advantages of using an employee are his or her full-time commitment to the district and knowledge of the district.

Availability of all parties is always a concern, but especially so during negotiations. Meetings cannot always be arranged to coincide with an outside negotiator's schedule or the day officials usually meet. A district employee, however, is almost always able to rearrange meetings to suit the other officials involved.

The availability problem is compounded by the fact that many elected bodies meet on the same day. This increases the consultant negotiator's difficulties in personally meeting with each group he represents. Not only can an employee be more available to meet with other officials, but he can also be more available to meet with employees in negotiation sessions. This becomes quite critical toward the end of negotiations, especially when there is a threat of

---

This chapter has been prepared by Don Becker, partner, Becker & Bell, Inc., management consultants, labor relations, El Dorado Hills, Calif.

strike or some other type of work action. Once negotiations are completed, an employee negotiator is more immediately available to answer questions of contract interpretation, to respond to grievances, and generally to assist departments in their day-to-day life with the negotiated agreement.

An employee negotiator also knows the district, how it is financed, what the area economics are, what people are earning in comparable jobs within the local area, the district's history of compensation and classification, and other such specific local issues. This knowledge is not only helpful at the negotiating table, but is useful during the year when the agreement is being administered.

Also, a district must develop an "institutional memory." There must be a record of problems that have been discussed during negotiations and of solutions that have been offered; reasons for refusing and for accepting proposals; knowledge of what compromises and exchanges of value occurred in arriving at the final result. If the negotiator is an employee, then he should be able to accomplish these objectives for the district.

What are the advantages of retaining an outside consultant?

The major ones: (1) *the person spends full time in labor relations;* (2) *the consultant has knowledge of many government agencies;* (3) *she/he has more direct access and influence on the elected agency heads;* (4) *she/he has no personal "stake" in the result;* and (5) *the strong feelings generated at the table are directed at the outside consultant rather than at the agency management.*

Labor relations in the public sector are in a constant state of change. An individual who is not committed to labor relations on a full-time basis is unlikely to have the interest or time to keep abreast of these developments. Usually, if the district is even of moderate size, the employees will be represented by an employee organization that has a full-time employee relations professional. If the employees are represented by an AFL-CIO union, then the employer not only faces a professional labor relations expert, but also a back-up organization that is dedicated solely to the field of labor relations.

Often management is not aware of the cooperation between and among local unions. Such cooperation can and does take many forms, *e.g.* a compendium of contract clauses which includes a listing, by subject, of all clauses in contracts with agencies having employees represented by the various union locals. Such cooperation among the employee organizations can be offset by a professional labor relations consultant who devotes full time to developments in the field.

In addition to being acquainted with various labor relations materials, the professional consultant has experience in other agencies; this increases his knowledge of satellite agencies that may affect the district the consultant represents. (An inside negotiator must be aware of the labor relations impact of all comparable agencies. The consultant negotiator must do this for *each* agency he represents. The more client agencies the consultant's firm represents, the more direct knowledge that individual will have of other agency practices, pay, experiments, etc.)

In my opinion, insiders do not have the same ability to impact the local legislative-funding body as the consultant negotiator. One reason for this is that often there is at least one administrative level between the inside negotiator and the key elected officials. Therefore, the employee negotiator often does not work directly with the top legislative funding group. Also, when the negotiator is an outsider, negotiations are less likely to be influenced by personal rather than professional objectives. That is, if the negotiator is a full-time employee, the negotiator is more likely to agree or disagree with a proposal because it will result in an improved benefit for the negotiator as an employee, or because it will be politically beneficial to the negotiator's career. Elected officials who are aware of this potential situation for self-help tend to be wary of employee negotiators' objectivity and, to that extent, may be skeptical about their advice.

In contrast, a consultant negotiator rarely benefits personally from an increase is employee benefits. In fact, usually the consultant will benefit more directly by keeping employee increases to a minimum.

As an outsider, the consultant will not have career ambitions within the district, and, therefore, will not make decisions or recommendations on a basis of how it will affect his promotability. For these reasons, the consultant negotiator can appear to be much more objective than the employee negotiator. Also, since the elected body will undoubtedly have made a special effort to "buy" the consultant's expertise, its members will be more inclined to take advantage of that expertise.

During many negotiations sessions, strong feelings are generated at the bargaining table. This is especially true when a district firmly opposes the union on many issues. Though it is desirable to keep negotiations impersonal, this posture is almost impossible for an employee organization that is facing little or no movement in money matters — especially if the employee organization negotiator is also an employee of the district. Even though the management negotiator is representing a position developed by top management, the employee organization almost always will hold the district's chief negotiator personally responsible. In this situation the scenario tends to go like this:

"We the employees are convinced that our position is true, good and beautiful, and that any reasonable person who analyzed our position would recognize its intrinsic merit. Management doesn't recognize this, probably because its chief negotiator isn't properly communicating our position to the management team. Therefore, he is a bum that somehow we must bypass, and generally discredit. Having done so, we will reach a more reasonable group of people who will see the merit of our position and give us the mere pittance we are justifiably requesting."

For reasons resulting from this common scenario, and since it is too frustrating to "bang your head against city hall, " employee organizations need a symbol upon which to vent their wrath. The obvious choice is management's chief negotiator. When this happens, it is extremely difficult for a normal relationship to be re-established so that business as usual can be carried out subsequent to negotiations.

The hard line taken by the management negotiator often has a direct impact on the number, kind, and type of grievances that arise during the contract. To minimize this impact, the bargaining frictions generated should be deflected from the individuals who must live with the agreement during its life. A very effective way to accomplish this is hiring an outsider to handle negotiations and to absorb the heat. This allows the district employees who administer the agreement to be somewhat sympathetic when the employee representative says what a hard-nosed, unreasonable person the consultant was. Since the negotiator is an outsider on contract, it is easier to change negotiators if such an action should become advantageous.

In considering the advantages of a consultant *versus* an employee negotiator, cost comparison is an important factor. When totaling the cost of an employee's handling negotiations, one must include the salary of the negotiator as well as the clerical and administrative staff that assist the negotiator. One must also consider space, equipment, supplies and general overhead costs for each of these individuals involved. Negotiations almost always generate substantial overtime, which is normally compensated in some manner.

Of course, most districts use their negotiator for other things. When negotiations are over, there are other functions to perform. But a problem is that these other job functions overlap the negotiation period. Either these jobs are ignored during negotiations, or the negotiator cannot give full attention to negotiations. This is especially true if the employee is also involved in the budget planning, personnel recruitment, and/or general administration. Of course many of the benefits derived from having a full-time professional negotiator are lost in this situation; for example, the part-time negotiator normally will not have the time nor the incentive to stay abreast of the state of the art.

If a district decides to hire a consultant negotiator, what should it look for? Here are some factors to consider:

Experience: The consultant should have experience in actual negotiations. The number of years in the business is important, but seven consecutive years with one bargaining unit in one district is probably not as helpful as three years with four different districts, each having one bargaining unit. Also, the consultant should have had experience in the other aspects of labor relations, *i.e.* classification, compensation, grievance handling, presenting arbitration, unfair practice charges, and fact-finding. In addition, the prospective consultant should preferably have had experience with a district of the size and type considering the consultant for employment.

Availability: The consultant should be able to commit a certain amount of time in days or hours per week or month. The consultant should provide or be able to provide other negotiators with similar experience, who will act as backup in case of emergencies or provide quick telephone information when the consultant is not immediately available.

References: If possible, get feedback from several agencies listed; the more, the better. Talk to the person or persons who were at the table with the consultant. Find out how the consultant handled operations there. Did the consultant seem organized? Did he have meeting objectives laid out? Were they reached? Were meetings canceled? If so, why? Were commitments kept? Were over-all objectives reached? Will they use the consultant again? And so on.

"Chemistry": Is the consultant someone with whom the people in your district can work?

Once the selection of an outside negotiator is made, the district should consider the following items for inclusion in the contract:

1. Specific listing of services including termination dates, if any;

2. Person who administers contract for agency;

3. Name of consultant or consultants who will provide service to agency;

4. Specifics on how and at what intervals or after what services are provided will the contractor be paid;

5. The ability to audit contractor's record concerning performance of services to agency;

6. What assistance the agency will provide, *e.g.* place to negotiate, management team, supplemental clerical work; and

7. Whether either party, or both, can terminate the contract, and if they can, under what circumstances and conditions.

10. When and How To Ratify a Contract

At last, your negotiating team has reached the end of a long bargaining session with the teacher union, and presents a contract to you for ratification. But you really don't like the contract, and most other members of your school board don't, either. Too many clauses are unacceptable.

But you feel locked in by circumstances. If you refuse to ratify the contract, the consequences may be severe. The teachers will allege bad faith. Your negotiating team will appear to be discredited. And worse, the team will have to return to the bargaining table for another round of talks in a not-very-pleasant atmosphere.

Deciding whether to ratify a contract can be one of the most difficult problems a school board has to face. There are no rules and few guidelines to help you make the right decision. You'll have to examine all the circumstances coolly and rationally, and keep in mind these specifics:

The alternative to the proposed agreement is likely to be a bruising battle that ends in the same — or virtually the same — agreement. You'd better be certain that the basis for your refusal is serious enough to justify the battle that may follow. Consider carefully the long-range consequences of a refusal to ratify and its impact upon future bargaining. Those consequences are not always bad. The union may become more realistic once it realizes that the board has no more to give. But a refusal to ratify also could lead to union demands to bypass your negotiating team and bargain directly with the board.

Your chief negotiator should be a key person in helping the board make its decision about ratification. It doesn't make sense for a negotiator to recommend acceptance or rejection of each specific item, and then be *unwilling* to recommend acceptance or rejection of the entire package. That usually happens when the negotiator doesn't like the contract but is convinced that he can't get a better one. So he outlines the pros and cons, then disappears when the votes are taken. But you shouldn't let your negotiator slip away. Ask him to make a recommendation. You don't have to follow it, of course, but you'll have heard the opinion of the person closest to the actual bargaining.

The timing of ratification can be extremely important. As a rule, the board should ratify *after* the teachers do so. Prior board ratification leads to all kinds of problems if and when the teachers reject the contract. An example: One board ratified the contract in July, even though the teacher association said that its constitution required ratification when the teachers returned in the fall. The board, unfortunately, began implementing the benefits under the contract. In the fall, however, the majority of teachers voted against ratification. When the union tried to reopen negotiations, the board refused. Both sides filed unfair labor practice charges that were later dismissed, but the entire hassle could have been avoided had the board waited until the teachers had voted on the contract.

So, wait until the teachers ratify, but don't wait too long after that. That's especially true if the teachers have been divided over ratification. Some union members may want time for a recount or a challenge. If the board ratifies promptly, however, the contract is a *fait accompli* and further opposition is futile.

One difficult problem boards may face is a member who wants to ratify some but not all of the contract. If you can't conscientiously ratify an agreement, then don't. But if only one clause is unacceptable, you may be able to modify or eliminate it. Give your negotiator authority to make a compensating concession. Otherwise, even if the board is able to ram through the change, the taint of improper practice may remain. Bear in mind, though, that trying to change one item in an agreed-upon package usually is costly. The other side knows you are eager to change the item and may insist upon a great deal in return. Make sure your negotiator has some "goodies" available just in case they are needed to achieve agreement on a last minute change.

Finally, you should be able to avoid difficult and controversial ratification decisions if you're careful to communicate well with your negotiating team. Often, it's hard to do that: An agreement may be negotiated under such intense time pressures that it's impossible to maintain full communication when crucial decisions are made. But if you work closely with your team, you'll usually be able to avoid surprises — and controversial decisions — at ratification time.

11. Board/Superintendent Relations in Bargaining

Few, if any, situations generate more stress than bargaining on board-superintendent relations. Thus, it is essential that both board members and superintendents be sensitive to the pressures each must face in the negotiations process.

Intimidation sometimes works, and teacher unions know it. An assault on job security can render even the boldest school official docile. And the tactic works as well on school board members and principals as it does on superintendents, although for somewhat different reasons in each case.

Politics is what separates public sector bargaining from private sector bargaining. Teacher organizations try to intimidate board members by playing an active part in school board elections. Most board members naturally want teacher support. Failing that, they want at least to avoid teacher opposition.

If the board has stuck its neck out lately with controversial decisions on integration or new bus routes or sex education, members facing re-election may be especially loath to find themselves on the teacher union's enemy list. Board members who dug in their heels on teacher demands six months ago may demonstrate surprising flexibility as election day draws nigh. Suddenly they find merit in proposals that would have been rejected out of hand earlier in the year.

If a school board member *should* decide he'd rather be right then re-elected, the teacher union always can find an ambitious soul to challenge the incumbent. A host of challengers, in fact, is often waiting in the wings, lacking nothing but a campaign organization. The teacher union can provide one — all in the name of "the children," of course. Just coincidentally, teacher-backed winners are inclined to be more considerate of teacher demands at the bargaining table.

Of course the election calculus varies enormously from one school district to another. In some communities, teacher union support is the kiss of death for election hopes. In those communities, school board members are virtually immune to teacher intimidation. But elsewhere, teacher support counts, and school board behavior shows it.

This reality often is overlooked because the pressures teacher bargaining puts on school board members differ from the pressures unions put on management in the private sector. Board members cannot be intimidated economically, but they *can* be intimidated politically.

In the real world, the alternatives may be to make salary and benefit concessions and remain a school board member, or to reject teacher demands and lose one's seat on the board.

Similarly, the unions know that working over the superintendent — especially one who is insecure about his job — can be remarkably effective. Thus the teachers may zero in on the superintendent's expense account or the convention trip to San Francisco last winner. Or they may take a vote of "no confidence" in the superintendent. The effectiveness of such tactics depends upon whether board members realize that such teacher maneuvers are designed to gain concessions in matters that have nothing *per se* to do with the superintendent.

A popularity contest among employees is not, in any case, the way to gauge a superintendent's effectiveness. Clearly, it should not be necessary for the superintendent to explain that teachers are painting him as a plantation overseer for tactical purposes. Regardless, the school board is begging for trouble if it encourages teachers to think they can control the destiny of the superintendent. That's the board's responsibility, and teachers had better be so advised — the sooner, the better. If teachers control the superintendent evaluation process or win veto power over it, management worries more about how it stands with teachers than about the good of the school system.

It is futile to say administrators should not act as though they are under attack. They do, and they will as long as they're uncertain about how board members perceive the management-labor relationship. Many a bargaining-table Waterloo has been preceded by the erosion of administrator confidence in the board. Lacking confidence in the board's ability to distinguish intimidation from justified complaints, some superintendents begin to make harmful concessions to teachers. Since these concessions must be presented to the board as reasonable management decisions, board members may never be aware of the underlying circumstances or of the harmful consequences for the schools.

Potent as teacher intimidation can be when applied to board members and superintendents, it nevertheless often manifests its most effective force at the building level. Suppose one school has more than its share of litigious, aggressive teachers. The principal may begin to worry: "If more grievances pile up in my school than in the others, I'm going to look bad." Humanly, he starts to overlook certain teacher actions that merit disciplinary measures. Rightly or wrongly, the principal has become intimidated because he lacks confidence in the understanding of his superiors.

All this is not to say that teacher views are irrelevant and that school administrators are always right. The point is that school board members should support administrators more frequently than they do — particularly during bargaining sessions when management is under attack for tactical reasons.

Often, teachers submit numerous detailed proposals, ostensibly to provide "due process" for teachers suffering from administrative abuse. When school board members demand specifics, the union representatives often demur, pleading a need for anonymity on behalf of the accusers. This is often a good time for the board to express its vigorous support of the principal or superintendent being maligned. Frequently, the contrast between alleged teacher concern for due process, and their willingness to engage in anonymous attacks upon administrators is a very sobering experience for all concerned.

12. Intra-Board Conflict During Bargaining

If bargaining places a strain on board-superintendent relations, it sometimes places even more strain on the relations among board members. Disagreements within, rather than between, bargaining teams can be one of the greatest difficulties of collective bargaining. Every experienced negotiator — whether for management or a union — can cite cases in which the disagreements within his team were more difficult to resolve than the disagreements between the two teams.

Usually the disagreements between members of the union team, whether they be teachers or members of any other group, become obvious during the course of negotiations. Teachers on maximum want the salary package to stress higher maximums; those in the middle or beginnning years may want a reduction in the number of steps. Single teachers may prefer individual employee health coverage to more funds for sabbaticals; married teachers with families may want the priorities reversed. Dozens of conflicts like these may emerge during negotiations. Typically, they are resolved — in fact, they must be resolved if there is to be an agreement — after some "negotiations" within the bargaining team.

The management negotiators may not be aware of these conflicts, or of their intensity, particularly if there is good discipline on the union negotiating team. For both sides, it generally pays not to let the other side know about your internal divisions. The reason is that these divisions can often be exploited by a skillful adversary. Suppose, for example, that the board team perceives that a particular group of teachers has achieved its major objective in the negotiations. In that case, these teachers will probably not be greatly interested in holding out for benefits that would go chiefly to other teachers. On the other hand, the teachers who have not yet achieved their major objectives are much more likely to be adamant on the remaining items that pertain especially to themselves.

Problems arise when it becomes clear that a benefit granted to some teachers will reduce the benefits granted to others. It is easier for both sides to agree upon items that affect all teachers equally. This is why clauses relating to sub-groups within the negotiating unit are often troublesome to both teams of negotiators.

The interests of individual members of the management team also may be affected by a proposal. Suppose the teachers propose that teachers be paid for unused sick leave upon resignation or retirement, up to a maximum of the annual salary received when leaving the system. In most systems, routine practice is to give the administrative staff the same sick leave benefits granted to teachers. For this reason, members of the administration bargaining team may react very differently, depending upon their own situation. An administrator on the verge of retirement may be much more receptive to the teacher proposal than a first year administrator. The latter might prefer to see board funds spent for items that would provide immediate benefits to himself as well as for most teachers.

In the example just cited, it is very unlikely that the members of the administration team would state their motivations candidly, even to each other. The administrator about to retire is not going to say, "I favor the teacher proposal, because I'll get a year's salary in unused sick leave if the teacher proposal is accepted." In the real world, he is more apt to give other reasons for favoring the proposal.

Many strong disagreements are camouflaged this way. It is extremely difficult to resolve such disagreements when the real reasons, interests and motivations are not discussed frankly; since those that are discussed are rationalizations, not reasons, controversy over them is futile. Furthermore, sometimes negotiators only make matters worse by referring to the underlying motivation, since nobody likes to be shown as profiting personally from a position he allegedly espouses as a matter of principle.

These comments are not meant to suggest that a management position should be resolved by nose-counting the administration team. The chief negotiator should solicit views from team members and try to get a unified management position, but he should not be bound to any ratio of support. Ordinarily, the chief negotiator would be foolish to negotiate a clause strongly opposed by most of his team, but this is necessary in some situations. Of course, disagreement at the board level is another matter; even individual opposition cannot be easily ignored at this level.

Even at the board level, however, conflicts of interest disguised as differences of principle arise occasionally. A board member may feel that approval of a proposed agreement would be fatal to his re-election. As a result, he may oppose the agreement on the flimsiest grounds. He may even hope secretly that the board adopts the agreement despite his opposition. Then he can run as the taxpayers' hero while avoiding the responsibility for sabotaging an agreement and negotiating another one that is likely to result in a strike.

Dealing with disagreement at this level may require the bluntest kind of talk with the board. On occasion, either board members or teacher negotiators try to renege on an agreement for political reasons. Such cases are not frequent but they do happen. A negotiator who can't get his principals to abide by their agreements is often replaced, which causes even more complications if the new chief negotiator needs to be briefed on the negotiating history.

The reason for the disagreement can be very important. It is one thing to try to rectify an honest mistake, *e.g.* where board members have approved something because of an honest misunderstanding. Deliberate efforts to repudiate an agreement because one fears the political repercussions are something else. It's not that boards have no right to try to change something they have agreed to. The point is that they should be prepared to offer the other side something in return for such a change. Offering someone an inducement to change a *bona fide* agreement is much different from offering spurious reasons for not living up to the agreement or simply refusing to abide by it.

Usually some palatable way can be found to resolve internal disagreements whenever they arise. For example, consider a board disagreement in a district where the board was able to pay the highest salary schedule in the state. The board's reluctance to do so was strictly political. Some board members up for re-election were afraid that if the system was paying the highest schedule in the state, opposing candidates for the board would make a big issue of the fact. Substantively, these board members had no real objection to the proposed schedule. This became evident by their efforts to reduce the schedule by $50 or $100 at certain points. The reductions involved were very small but they would keep the district's schedule from being the highest in the state.

This might not have been a problem except that the teachers had the same problem in reverse. Their leadership was under pressure to achieve the best schedule in the state. For the teacher leadership also, the dollar amounts involved were not so important substantively, but their organizational impact was crucial.

This particular problem was resolved by an increase in the board contribution to a tax deferred annuity. This contribution was virtually as good as a salary increase since the teachers could take out the contributions at the end of the year if they chose to do so. This enabled the teacher negotiators to claim that they had negotiated the best package in the state; the salary schedule plus the board's contribution to the tax deferred annuity (unique at that time in the state) was more than any other schedule. At the same time, the board members felt that their political flanks would not be exposed; the salary schedule was among the top, as the community expected, but it could not be clearly identified as the highest.

Although he should make every reasonable effort to get the agreement his side wants, the chief negotiator must be prepared to tell his principals if they are adhering to an unrealistic position. Otherwise, he will find himself in an impossible position at the table. It is one thing to have a board set forth unrealistic objectives at the beginning of negotiations. If the board's bargaining position is an unreasonable one, the fact that it is will become evident as negotiations are carried on.

What do you do, however, when a board or board member insists upon a final offer that the teachers reasonably cannot accept? At this point the negotiator has to be ready to take drastic action. One way out is let an impasse develop, and have some third party come in and educate the board about the facts of life. Chief negotiators on both sides frequently adopt this course of action if they are afraid of the repercussions of a realistic discussion with their principals.

Sometimes unrealistic boards can be moved to agreement by a two-stage process. In the first stage, the board is persuaded to improve its offer, to weaken teacher determination to utilize impasse procedures. Here the negotiator can emphasize the long-run dangers of teachers' getting a significant improvement by third-party intervention; if this happens, they will be much more reluctant in the future to settle before such intervention. If appropriate, it should also be emphasized that the board's position is building militancy among teachers.

If the negotiator can get the board to accept these possibilities, he can usually persuade it to make an offer that is sufficiently close to the final teacher position. Suppose the parties are officially $750 a teacher apart, but the negotiator believes the teachers will accept $250 more per teacher. Suppose, also, that the negotiator believes that the board should come up to this figure, but that it would be unwilling to present the figure as a board offer. In that case, his strategy would probably be to get the board to move closer to the settlement figure, so that the final figure comes as an offer from the teachers, *e.g.* he tries to get the board to offer $200 more, so that the teachers can make the last move. With the board, emphasis is placed on the foolishness of going to impasse for so little more money and for such a loss in morale among the "defeated" teachers. The negotiator does not and cannot, make a "final offer" of such and such to teachers: instead, he tries to find out if, assuming that by some miracle he could improve the offer, the union negotiator could sell such and such a deal to his constituents. At this point, the parties should get their agreement. If they don't, they have problems!

13. Maintaining the Confidentiality of Board Positions

A school board and a teacher union are down to the wire on collective bargaining. The next move of the opposition can spell the difference between costly concessions and a decent settlement. The teacher union *may* have a pipeline— a *one-way* pipeline—into the school board's inner and confidential deliberations.

Having board members allied with teachers does not, of course, always result in union access to board strategy, tactics, and final offers; nor are board members the only possible sources of leaks during bargaining. But board members often are — or can be — defeated in the next election by teacher votes, and that makes them more vulnerable to teacher interests.

Because collective bargaining is an adversary process, it is essential to maintain the confidentiality of board positions, including strategy and tactics. A board member who cannot be trusted at bargaining time puts the board negotiator or negotating team in a no-win situation. The board must recognize that the problem exists, distasteful though that may be.

A few states provide some protection against the most obvious conflicts of interest by prohibiting board members who are also union members from participating in negotiations with their union. Unfortunately, the most obvious conflicts are not the most difficult situations; the latter do not involve formal board member affiliation with a union but do involve a political relationship that leads to breaches in confidentiality. Such laws are not perfect and are not applicable in every state, but the precedent they establish may help board members feel more objective as they approach the problem in their own school system. So start with the laws relating to conflicts of interest and make sure all board members and staff are aware of what they are.

Next, board members can remove a burden from any staff member who might *seem* to be in conflict with the board's position. A top level administrator may be married to a teacher and union member; or the superintendent's secretary may have a daughter-in-law on the union's bargaining team.

To take some precautionary measures concerning such individuals is not to indicate that they are unethical, and it can be a kindness. If it is done as a matter of policy and with an even hand, the board is protecting the individuals as well as the district. After all, federal officials are required to sever their business connections and put their investments in a blind trust, not on the assumption that they will be dishonest in office — else why appoint them in the first place? — but because they must not even *appear* to have a conflict of interest. The same principle should be applied to collective bargaining situations and relationships.

Guarding against leaks by board members themselves is a much more difficult problem. Suppose you believe or even know that Board Member X is leaking board positions to the teachers; you might have received the information confidentially; regardless, you can't prove it publicly. In such cases, it is awkward to suggest that board members refrain from talking to teachers. Board members are apt to bristle at any such suggestion, especially if it is impractical to discuss the real reason for the request.

One alternative is for the chief negotiator to consult key members informally about strategy and bottom lines. This is probably the easiest solution, since it is common practice even in the absence of leaks. But the negotiator needs to know the board and must be confident that those consulted can deliver a majority of school board votes when final decisions must be made. Another way to protect against leaks is for the board to appoint a bargaining sub-committee among its own members. If necessary, everybody except Member X with ties to the teacher union can be on it. This may be too bloody a solution for the squeamish school board member, but there may be no easier way. However, a smaller sub-committee could have a less controversial rationale: the need to avoid tying up the entire board. The operative word here is *appoint;* if the request is for volunteers and the leaking board member volunteers, creation of the sub-committee solves nothing.

As long as there are school board members who believe their position requires them to talk to teachers about matters subject to negotiation, there will be a double standard that works to the teachers' advantage. Unless and until legislation resolves the problem, it will be up to alert board members to neutralize the advantages the teachers have. It may not be pleasant to do so, but the alternative — like cutting your own throat — is considerably less agreeable.

14. The Case Against Due Process for Superintendents

Due process for superintendents is a plausible but erroneous idea. Nevertheless, it *is* being considered — and at great length — by superintendents and school boards. Unfortunately school board members and administrators appear to be overlooking a crucial fact: Principles that are applicable to employees are not necessarily applicable to management — and even may be contrary to public policy when so applied.

To illustrate the point: Suppose you need an attorney. You've been hit by a truck or need to draw up a will or your wife has run off with the milkman. Whatever your reason, you go out and hire McDonald, Burger and King, attorneys at law. They become your legal representatives for as long as you choose for them to be.

The time may come, however, when you want to change attorneys. If you do, "due process" is almost always irrelevant. You may want to hire your brother-in-law, who just passed the bar exam and charges only $5 an hour rather than $125. Or you may not like M.B.&K.'s style, or dress, or speech. Whatever your reasons for wanting to change, except in special circumstances, you don't need to justify your decision or afford due process to the attorney you terminate. Even if you have a contract with such an attorney, it probably doesn't require *or* provide due process. It may contain a clause that spells out how much you have to pay to terminate the services of the firm and an understanding that you will pay for whatever expenses have been accrued on your behalf and for any actual legal work that has been done. But you don't have to justify or explain your *decision*. I'm not suggesting you *shouldn't*, only that legally you don't *have* to.

This example is not intended to encourage or condone the act of replacing attorneys regardless of the circumstances. Instead, it is to stress the importance of representation — particularly the right to a representative *of your choice.* As an individual who is paying for a job or service, you cannot be forced to accept someone you do not want as your representative.

This leads us to the dilemma facing school board members: Why should a school board be represented by someone it doesn't want? The superintendent is its representative. My argument is that we should not force a school board to accept an unwanted representative, just as we would not force an individual to do so.

In my opinion, it is absolutely crucial that boards *not have the right* to break a contract. They should, however, have the right to change superintendents at any time. The contract should guarantee this right. Superintendents have a right to demand — and boards have a responsibility to provide them with — a contract that clearly states what will happen if the board wants to change superintendents. (Indeed, because it is awkward for most job candidates — superintendents included — to demand terms of their dismissal, it is up to fair-minded school boards to take the lead in ensuring that such terms are spelled out in the contract.) I have no problem with contracts requiring a board to pay off in full, or even more, whatever both parties agree to. Such a contract enables a board to say to its superintendent: You are doing an excellent job, but we want someone else. And for that right, the board is willing to pay liberally, if need be.

Community controversies over whether a superintendent should be fired usually are devoted to the issue of competency. This is or should be irrelevant to the legal issue. Firing a superintendent may be extemely unfair; it often is. But equally unfair is a policy that forces a school board to retain a superintendent it no longer wants or thinks is best for the job.

A contract should spell out an acceptable course of action should the board want to employ a new superintendent. Such a contract can deter unneccessary squabbles and cries of foul play by either party. In many cases, the board's decision to replace a superintendent could cause him financial disaster. For this reason alone, it is imperative that the superintendent be provided contractual protection, but not in the form of tenure or due process. Instead, the board should guarantee the superintendent some sort of financial security to compensate for his existence at the razor's edge.

A likely misinterpretation of this argument is that it will encourage school boards to treat superintendents arbitrarily and capriciously. In fact, if the superintendent's buy-out price is high enough, the board isn't likely to act in such a way. The buy-out not only protects the superintendent, but it emphasizes the need for conscientiousness and thoroughness on the part of the board in the superintendent-selection process.

The crucial issue is board accountability. In every action it takes, especially the employment or termination of a superintendent, the board is accountable to the community. This is another reason not to limit the board's right to a representative of its choice. Is it fair to hold a school board accountable if it does not have the right to designate its representative at any time? Realistically, the more you restrict a board's right to act, the less accountability the public has a right to expect. Sympathy for superintendents unjustly fired (and there are many) should not lead us to overlook this fundamental fact.

15. The Policy/Administration Dichotomy

According to the conventional wisdom, school boards formulate educational policy and the administration carries it out. Unfortunately, the conventional wisdom is out of touch with the realities in most districts. Indeed, the practice of collective bargaining illustrates why this tidy division of labor does not work in many districts, and probably cannot be made to work in the largest and smallest districts. The dichotomy was and is impractical in many districts regardless of the impact of collective bargaining.

As a general rule, the larger the school system, the more likely the board will be controlled by the administration. Many board members in big school systems may not agree, but the point is hardly debatable. After all, even *full-time* elected officials who are paid have trouble keeping their staffs under control. Thus, what kind of control is exercised by school board members who are *part-time,* unpaid individuals? The answer is "Not much." School systems, big ones in particular, exercise little effective control over administrative employees.

Staff control of information is a crucial factor. In a large district, the staff controls virtually all information that flows to the board. If, for example, the staff is opposed to a board policy, it can emphasize or even generate negative reactions to it. On the other hand, if the staff favors a policy, its approval probably will be accentuated in administrative memorandums that omit — consciously or otherwise — any negative aspects. The Bible may or may not require interpretation or clarification but board policies usually do. This automatically leads to a measure of staff influence or control. By the time issues and policies reach the board's attention, its members have little room to maneuver. In fact, many important issues never even gain the board's notice in a large district.

In small school districts, control over administration is within the realm of reality. Board members are more familiar with issues and individuals. They are less subject to bureaucratic control. They have fewer problems to process. To illustrate, let's compare demands imposed upon the board of education in Boondock (25 teachers, two administrators) with those of Big City (2,000 teachers, 200 administrators). Boondock automatically has fewer worries over maintenance and renovation. In addition, it probably has a student-teacher population that is homogenous, hence fewer headaches over such thorny issues as integration and discrimination.

Boondock's education program is bound to be less complicated than Big City's. Feedback to the board on virtually everything that's happening is likely in Boondock; not so in Big City, where most board members have only cursory information or none at all about how things shape up in each school building.

Bargaining practices provide another measure of the wide disparity in board control that exists between large and small districts. In large school systems, bargaining invariably involves several complex and interrelated issues; it is very difficult for board members to keep current on the ramifications of these issues. In contrast, matters in small districts are less complex. Moreover, the board is often able to handle them directly. For example, the grievance procedure in a large district may include questions of level, such as whether grievances above the building level should be directed to an area superintendent or to an assistant superintendent for personnel. After this has been resolved, it must be determined whether the grievance will go to the superintendent or to arbitration. In districts with only 50 teachers and a couple of administrators, levels are clear-cut and follow the obvious rungs within the administrative structure.

As the size of the district increases, the control exercised by the board decreases for external and internal reasons. In cities, the board must coordinate its program with other public services and officials. This has the effect of diminishing school board control. Agencies such as police, fire, sanitation, transportation, and recreation tend to develop a measure of control, or strong influence, over board policies, and rightly so. Schools in communities outside large cities often represent the largest public entity in town; integrating school programs with other services presents fewer problems.

Clearly, the division of labor between school boards and administrators is different, depending upon district size. The distinction between policy making and administration is relatively minor in small districts. In a small district, a teacher transfer often constitutes an item of business for the board. The actual transfer is the item for consideration, not the policy covering transfers. Meantime, in larger districts, the board doesn't have time to consider individual transfers, even if it wanted to.

Textbook approaches to administration lack credibility partly because they fail to take into account district size. In any case, the policy/administration dichotomy hardly makes sense, in small districts *or* large ones. Boards in big districts have very little time to consider individual situations in which policy is applied; whereas, small districts tackle these individual situations routinely.

As often happens, words are juggled to achieve a desired result. That which is labeled policy in District A is called administration in District B in order to rationalize the board's inability in B to consider it. In the real world, what seems to be happening is this: In small districts, boards do the total job. In medium-size districts, the distinction between policy and administration is or can be a good working guide. In large districts, boards simply lack the time to develop policy in many areas; their problem is which policies will be resolved by the board and which will be delegated to the school administration.

Collective bargaining illustrates the relationship between size of district and delegation of board authority. In most large districts, boards delegate a considerable amount of this power to administration. Bargaining does not involve a new delegation of authority as much as it requires a new environment for exercising appointed authority. In small districts, boards manage and make policy. They do the negotiating as well. Unfortunately, such boards find themselves in deep water when the bargaining begins. Teachers often use the services of a full-time negotiator who is employed by 15 or 20 other teacher groups in the area. Board members can't specialize this way. For this reason, bargaining is often a threat to board authority in small districts, despite the board's preeminent role in most district affairs.

In the long run, the pressure of bargaining will be a major factor in the nationwide trend toward larger school districts. While bargaining must be accommodated initially to the size of the district, district size eventually may be altered to conform to bargaining needs. This progression most likely will gain momentum if small districts prove vulnerable in bargaining — as indeed they are with increasing frequency.

16.   The Administrative Team:
A Step Forward
or Backward?

During the past few years, there has been considerable discussion of "the administrative team" or "the management team" in education, a district-wide group responsible for district-wide operations. It is no accident that the administrative team concept has received increasing attention as collective bargaining in education has increased. Successful bargaining requires unity, and the administrative team is perceived as a way to achieve and maintain administrative unity. This chapter presents two views of the concept.

A Step Forward

Team management of a school district is not a concept to read about and brood over. It is a thoroughly practical technique that deserves immediate and widespread application. It is essential to maintaining and improving the quality of education in your school district.

An effective administrative team includes the superintendent and the certified and uncertified management staff at both district *and* building levels, and serves as an effective resource the board of education. Here is how and why the concept of the administrative team works.

Initially, the team approach is written into board policy. Team members must be chosen carefully and include all administrators in the district (both certified and classified). A team job description should be developed that outlines the relationships between and among team members. It also designates the duties to be accomplished, the cooperative ventures to be undertaken, and the responsibility and authority of team members.

The first part of this chapter was prepared by Paul B. Salmon, executive director, American Association of School Administrators, Arlington, VA. (It appeared in a slightly different version in *The American School Board Journal,* June 1977.)

At the same time, ground rules should be spelled out. For example:

• The team is the officially designated leadership unit for developing, recommending, implementing, and monitoring board policy and administrative regulations.

• The team must be recognized by the board as a storehouse of seasoned counsel that operates on the scene, where the action is; this reservoir should be tapped regularly and consistently for information and advice.

• The team functions through the superintendent.

• The team must be protected and rewarded. The board must recognize that team members need protection from unwarranted attack and from having its actions and decisions reversed by higher authorities. (Nevertheless, agreed-to procedures should be open to review and reversal at a higher level, but such arrangements must be understood and condoned before an incident occurs that could cause reversal.)

• Team members are compensated through a process that guarantees members fair and just reward for the time they work and the responsibility and skill they must exercise in their tasks.

To help assure that the team makes sound decisions from the outset, the board of education should let team members have a say before any policies are adopted. This amounts to a debugging device before final action is taken by the board. The procedure requires that each member of the team review proposed policies and file with the superintendent an *Educational Impact Statement,* essentially a statement that sets forth the likely consequences of any given management decision in terms of its effect on the program and operation of the school district. The justification for this process is twofold: First, it assures that each member has both the opportunity and responsibility to analyze proposed policies from his or her respective point of view; he or she can assess proposals on the basis of his sphere of operation and offer observations concerning the administrative consequences if given policies were adopted and implemented. Second, it requires responsible and continuing participation by each member of the team.

As you might suspect, leadership qualities exhibited by the superintendent cast long reflections over the team. Each superintendent must recognize and comport himself as a leader in a power-sharing situation. Superintendents need to realize that power is not a finite quality; rather, it is infinite, and additional power often can be gained by according a certain amount of clout to others.

Superintendents who are seen as effective team leaders carrying out the will of the board while functioning as members of their teams will be more powerful than superintendents who act unilaterally without concern for their middle managers. It's reasonable to assume that the middle management group will support the team-oriented superintendent over and above the superintendent who usually ignores those at the central office or building level.

From the ground rules for the team listed in the foregoing, let's turn to some imperatives:

● Total commitment to the team concept must be felt and demonstrated by the superintendent. He cannot structure the group so that there is one-way communication and power emanating from him.

● A mechanism must be developed whereby team members have representation. If the school district is small, such representation can be direct; in a large district, representation by level might work best — that is, representation from various levels of middle management. Area representation functions nicely in some districts. And in others, position representation does the job (individuals from various positions established within your organizational chart).

● All administrators must be active participants in team activities. They must perform individually (through the Educational Impact Statement, for example), as well as collectively.

● Job descriptions should be written that include responsibilities, duties, and authority.

● The team must have adequate time for decision-making. Board agenda should be distributed to the team at the same time such schedules are given to board members. In like manner, the team must receive copies of unadopted board minutes, followed by adopted minutes, after each set has been prepared for distribution to the board members.

• The board of education should endorse the Educational Impact Statement system of policy development and ought to arrange to have statements and accompanying recommendations submitted to the board before any policies are adopted.

• Communication is the key to success in team management. Individually and collectively, team members must work on analyzing their responses to proposed policies and take time to develop a consensus concerning any controversies that arise.

It's reasonable to assume that sometimes team members will disagree with the superintendent's position on an issue. To prepare in advance for these inevitabilities, a method for coping with impasses must be established when the team *first begins its work.* These procedures, in fact, must be written into the policy statement that governs the team.

In dealing with disagreements, some superintendents will go no further than allowing the team to have input. As such, the superintendent remains a "majority of one." If the team and the superintendent do not agree, the superintendent attempts to explain his own position, but then makes a recommendation to the board for consideration without giving the board members information about the team position.

Other superintendents are willing not only to receive the team's recommendations, but, if they are counter to the superintendent's own position, to advise the board that the team has considered the issue and that the superintendent and team are not able to resolve differences. Often the superintendent will present the team's position, and then his own recommendation for action.

Still other superintendents permit team representatives to appear before the board to argue their case as the superintendent presents a recommendation for action.

And still other superintendents seek mediation on the differences by having a mutually-agreed-upon third party intervene to explore ways in which differences can be resolved before a recommendation is presented to the board of education.

(It is important, to reiterate, that a policy governing the resolution of an impasse be developed and agreed upon *prior* to the occurrence of the first dispute.)

Another mainstay of the team concept is a central disciplinary mechanism. It requires that a person monitor team operations at all times to ensure that members are complying with the rules as they have been laid down. If someone does not comply, that individual should be criticized privately by the disciplinarian.

The marked increase in collective bargaining activities within school districts is ample proof that boards of education and superintendents should look twice at the team management idea. It stands to reason that subordinate administrators who are not involved substantially in both the development and administration of school district policy may decide that the only way to put muscle into their convictions is to sit across from top management at the bargaining table. On the other hand, if middle managers are involved with and respected fully by the board and superintendent, they will develop loyalty to the high echelons and help the school district make aggressive progress toward improved education.

A Step Backward

Education is well known for providing solutions that are more troublesome than the problems they seek to solve. An example is the administrative team. As is true of most "solutions," this one has elements of plausibility, even logic. But in practice the administrative team is creating more problems than it solves. It may be useful to see why the idea has initial appeal, as well as why its practical value isn't clear or very convincing.

For one thing, the meaning of "administrative team" is neither clear nor commonly understood. Efforts to define the concept invariably turn out to be the general canons of school administration. The main difference seems to be that the canons actually are *applied* when they carry the label of "administrative team."

While fuzziness surrounds the meaning of administrative team, this much is evident: Collective bargaining requires unity on management's side. At the bargaining table, a school district must present a solid front, regardless of differences that exist within the management negotiating team. The reason is obvious. A district cannot afford to let the union exploit its internal conflicts. Hence, if a district avoids revealing those differences, the union cannot use them as a wedge. If a district negotiator regards a union request as unjustified, he therefore cannot tolerate having someone on the team say that it *is* justified. When an administrative team is involved in bargaining, the odds are that someone will express sympathy for the union's point of view. Such sentiments will only stiffen union determination to get concessions on the item.

Occasionally, of course, a district wants to make concessions. Under these circumstances, differences of opinion stated by management at the table become part of an agreed-upon strategy. Furthermore, to express disagreement in the management caucus sessions is one thing; in fact, it's desirable. But once a district position is adopted, everyone on the management side should support it publicly and at the table regardless of private doubts.

The same principle applies to management action away from the bargaining table. If some administrators demonstrate support for teacher salary demands, it becomes more difficult for management to oppose them. This is not to suggest that administrators must adopt a management-can-do-no-wrong philosophy. It means that individual administrators should not be allowed to undermine management's position before, during, or after negotiations. This guideline is particularly crucial if supervisors or principals or other administrative personnel have bargaining rights. The full cooperation of staff-is essential in bargaining and administering teacher contracts.

To build a cooperative spirit, school boards and superintendents typically slip a friendly arm around middle management and say, "Hi, team member. From now on, we're going to fight the battles *together*." Frequently, this sweet talk is without follow-up; middle management is signed on, but thereafter nothing happens. If such rhetoric helps keep middle managers from flirting with unionism, it has served its purpose. The difficulties arise when management goes beyond the rhetoric.

Sometimes, the district administration perceives a need to provide more tangible support for middle management to keep it on top management's side. To achieve this objective, the district offers long-term contracts for middle management. The assumption is that if principals have long-term contracts (meaning job security), they will be less likely to support unionism. Whether one agrees or not, this approach is highly suspect as a solution to unrest among middle managers. In fact, the way to encourage teamwork is to make job security for middle managers dependent upon their adherence to the policies of the board and top management. In some circles this point of view is perceived as "undemocratic," but it is nothing of the sort; the notion that it is illustrates the extent to which education is permeated with anti-management philosophies.

Another unfortunate result of the administrative team fiasco is the notion that management personnel should be treated as a legislative body. The usual reaction of appointees to an administrative team runs thus: "If we're in this together, we must have something to say about how schools are administered." Team members are convinced, in other words, that they have a right to *legislate* in the development of school district policy. The fuzziness of the concept of participation notwithstanding, staff members *ordinarily* should have an opportunity to express an opinion before top management adopts a policy. Unfortunately, as a result of confusions associated with the administrative team concept, staff members tend to regard their advisory role as a legislative one.

To illustrate: Suppose a superintendent solicits principals' opinions concerning student smoking regulations. For various reasons, these opinions may be in direct opposition to the ultimate consensus of top management. Of course, eventually the principals will learn that their opinions ran counter to the final policy decision. When this happens, they probably will allege that being on the administrative team is a sham. Board members and superintendents, meanwhile, tend to compound the confusion by vacillating and saying that perhaps middle management really didn't "participate" since the policy adopted was not supported by principals. Immersed in guilt over the thought that middle managers now consider the team concept a flakey operation, board members may be tempted to reverse themselves and give in to the collective opinions of principals. Nothing would be wrong with such a concession if it represented action based upon the board's assessment of the merits of the issue. But when, as is often the case, the recommendations of middle management are adopted merely to avoid the appearance of sham participation, the effectiveness of management is impaired.

An administrative team is a group of individuals whose cooperation and coordination are essential to the effectiveness of an enterprise — in this instance, a public school system. It is unreasonable, however, to assume that cooperation and coordination accrue when such a group is accorded the rights of a legislative body. Normally, top management should seek the views of team members on issues that affect everyone. Even so, the basic decisions must be made by top management, and often they will conflict with the recommendations of middle management. In many situations it would be a mistake to collect opinions from every manager; for reasons of security or confidentiality, discussions with management personnel may need to be limited.

The weak intellectual foundations of the administrative team concept are particularly evident in bargaining. Somewhere along the line in bargaining, someone must exercise decision-making authority. To be sure, that person must be well prepared with information from a variety of sources; nonetheless, it would usually be disastrous to make these decisions by majority vote. Any such procedures would undermine managerial accountability for the outcome of bargaining. In fact, the administrative team concept is an outgrowth of the same fallacy that often underlies the teacher union approach to collective bargaining. The fallacy is that a democratic school system is one run by the employees or one that maximizes employee participation in management — regardless of circumstances. In my opinion, employee participation in the policymaking process is a means to an end. Like any other means, it has limits and conditions that should be subject to managerial discretion. Whether such discretion is exercised "democratically" depends as much on its relationship to the community as it does to its acceptability to middle management or other employees.

17. Joint Bargaining as an Alternative

A growing number of school boards and school administrators are pondering the advantages and disadvantages of joint bargaining. That is, they are debating whether to join with other boards in the employment of a single negotiator who would then bargain for the entire group. Unfortunately, despite the obvious advantages of joint bargaining, it must overcome several difficult practical problems in order to succeed.

It is not difficult to see why so many boards are considering the idea. Bargaining requires tremendous amounts of time and energy. If one-year contracts are in effect, boards no sooner finish negotiating one contract than they must begin preparing to negotiate the next one. If groups other than teachers are involved, negotiations become one big unhappy merry-go-round.

Another reason for considering joint bargaining is the fact that in most districts settlements are based upon what neighboring districts settled for. This does not apply to pattern-setting districts, but few districts set, rather than follow, the pattern of settlements. Furthermore, most boards operate at a disadvantage under present arrangements. Board members have trouble keeping informed about bargaining settlements or developments in their area. Sometimes they lack information about the specific factors underlying a specitic item of agreement in a nearby district. The result is that they are unable to evaluate the applicability of the item to their situation. When teacher negotiators in district Y argue, "If district X can make this concession, why can't you?" the administration in Y may have no answer. Nevertheless there may be good reasons why the concession could be made in district X but not in Y. Or it may be that teacher negotiators in district X dropped many demands to get the item in dispute, demands which are still on the table in district Y. Lack of information can thus be a severe tactical handicap to administration negotiators.

In contrast, having a single negotiator for two or more districts eliminates or minimizes problems of inter-district communication during negotiations. This is especially helpful where the employee groups are represented by the same organization or the same individuals or both. (Such situations, which are getting to be quite common, give the employees a significant tactical advantage in negotiations. They can coordinate their strategy and secure the most advantageous agreement first. Then they use the first agreements to whipsaw other school districts that have been holding out.)

Despite enormous expenditures of time and resources, many districts end up with an agreement that is substantially similar to the agreements reached in nearby districts. To many administrators and board members, it seems pointless to expend so much to achieve so little that is different from the agreements that neighboring districts have negotiated.

Furthermore, as a practical matter, many districts have relatively little discretion in negotiations. The teachers will not allow districts to fall too far behind, and the public will not permit them to get too far ahead of other districts. As a result, discretion is more apparent than real, and applies mainly to peripheral issues. At least, it does so if the board and the administration wish to avoid a major fight with the taxpayers or the teachers in their district.

One additional advantage of joint negotiations should be cited. Typically, all the participating boards share in the cost of the joint negotiator. As a result, the negotiator could make more than if employed by a single board, yet the cost to each board would be less than the cost of a separate negotiator for each board. These factors enable a group of boards to employ highly skilled negotiators at minimal cost to the boards.

Although the advantages of joint bargaining seem clear enough, its disadvantages are not always so obvious. Suppose a board agrees to initiate joint bargaining with neighboring school districts. Wealthier districts might be opposed to the idea, feeling that they would lose their competitive advantages if their bargaining were tied to poorer districts. The latter would like other boards to share their costs (which is usually not possible) but fear that they might agree to concessions they cannot afford. Hence poorer districts too may be reluctant to participate in joint bargaining.

Suppose that one way or another districts overcome these obstacles. Perhaps they do so by getting districts with very similar resources, problems and conditions of employment to join together for bargaining. Suppose further they manage to get agreement on a negotiator and his fee. The negotiator must now get his negotiating guidelines from the districts involved. It is virtually impossible to do this while meeting with only one board at a time; issues arise with board C that will affect the guidelines of boards A and B. Thus joint bargaining introduces a new layer of decision-making that can be more complex and time-consuming than the relations between a negotiator and a single board.

The negotiator who will be representing more than one district has to get some common agreement on how far he can go in offering concessions, both economic and non-economic. Substantive offers and tactics that make sense in one district may not in another, so negotiations between the cooperating school districts are often required merely to achieve agreement on guidelines. During negotiations, there is the constant danger of making a concession that is acceptable in most districts but unworkable in one because of special factors overlooked by the joint bargaining team. After all, when it bargains for only one district, the administration team can be thoroughly knowledgeable about the district. Under joint bargaining, the administration team would become too large and unwieldly if it included knowledgeable members from every school level in every participating district.

Troublesome as they are, these problems are probably not so difficult as the problems of ratification. In the first place, the cooperating boards must agree informally beforehand to be bound by the agreement negotiated. On the other hand, such an agreement could be interpreted as an illegal delegation of authority to a third party not responsible or accountable to the public. Therefore, each board has to ratify the agreement separately. Imagine the teacher reactions if one or more boards refuse to ratify the agreement negotiated jointly. The teachers would be outraged and probably refuse to engage in joint bargaining again, at least with the non-ratifying school board.

Note that the analysis has omitted any discussion of the problems raised on the teacher side by joint bargaining. For example, what if one particular teacher organization refused to ratify the joint agreement? In that case, the school boards might conclude that there is no point to joint negotiations. In short, if each school board or teacher organization is free to go its own way after an agreement is reached, it is likely that one or more will refuse to ratify the agreement, with disastrous consequences for the future of joint bargaining.

This problem highlights one of the most important ways in which public sector bargaining differs from private sector bargaining. In the latter, employers are freer to accord bargaining authority to negotiators representing a group of employers. Private companies do not have to worry about an illegal delegation of authority, hence joint bargaining can proceed on a much firmer basis in the private sector.

Another knotty problem in joint bargaining relates to inter-district differentials in conditions of employment. Some districts have more liberal policies than others relating to sick leave, transfers, sabbaticals, and so on. The dilemma is obvious. Teachers who are currently enjoying the most liberal policy are extremely reluctant to give it up. At the same time, the boards cannot simply accept the most liberal provision existing on each item and apply it to all districts. Of course, this is what the teacher negotiators will try to achieve, but it would normally be impossible for boards to accept such an outcome. It would be as unrealistic as expecting the teachers to accept the least liberal provision existing in all the districts. In other words, the extreme positions are very troublesome in the transition to joint bargaining.

One possible solution is to have "two-tier" bargaining. At the regional level, bargaining could proceed on items that are or could be relatively uniform throughout the region; bargaining at the local level would still be used to resolve other issues. While this approach has merit as a way of initiating joint bargaining, its long-range viability is doubtful. It would not materially reduce the cost or the time to individual districts and might inhibit needed flexibility on items negotiated locally. Bargaining issues do not stay

93

categorized very neatly; a proposal that seems relatively discrete and amenable to uniform treatment throughout the region may involve quite different issues from district to district.

This discussion has been devoted largely to the merits of joint bargaining from the employer viewpoint. For teachers, joint bargaining is much easier to achieve legally, but it is likely to lead to severe organizational problems, especially in the transition period. State and national organizations tend to be favorably disposed toward joint bargaining because it leads to more efficient use of state and national resources. Local teacher organization leaders, on the other hand, may be just as reluctant as are local boards to give up the prestige and autonomy associated with the individual district approach.

In this author's view, joint bargaining will sometimes overcome the legal and practical obstacles discussed in the foregoing. The most desirable approach from a negotiations standpoint would be fewer but larger school districts. Such a development would tend to maximize the advantages and minimize the disadvantages of joint bargaining for most districts. Of course, any move in this direction should not be based solely upon bargaining considerations, important as they are. Nevertheless, it seems fair to say that bargaining considerations add to the widespread demand for fewer but larger school districts wherever a multiplicity of small districts in the same area are forced to bargain every year.

18.   Additional Questions and Answers, Suggestions and Sources

The following seven questions about collective bargaining with teachers are frequently asked by school board members and school administrators. Each question is related to a standard tactic employed by teacher unions, and each response is one that generally has proved effective when school board negotiators have employed it.

1.   Our board already knows what its best offer to the teachers will be. Can't we make our offer right now at the start of bargaining? Why waste time in a lot of meetings?

No effective union negotiator is going to snap up your first offer — ever. Were he to do that, his union members would begin to wonder why they need him. And, for that matter, neither would your board want to agree immediately to the initial demands of the union. The *essence* of collective bargaining is discussion and compromise. Both parties to negotiations need to feel that they have gone through the whole process. If you try to skip steps to hurry things along, you won't reach a settlement any sooner. In fact, a skilled union negotiator will use your best offer as a take-off point to extract concessions you didn't intend to make.

2.   Every time we renegotiate our contract, the teachers bury us in paper with more and more proposals. Must we negotiate on every item?

Naturally, the teacher negotiator will come up with ever-increasing demands; that's his job, and it is the way a union justifies its existence to its members. Upping the ante every year is standard practice. Not all (and sometimes very few) of the union's proposed items are serious; your job is to ferret out those that truly *are* rock-

The first seven questions and answers in this chapter were prepared by Alfred T. Riccio, negotiations specialist with the labor relations firm, Thealan Associates, Albany. NY. (They were published previously in *The American School Board Journal,* November 1977.)

bottom demands. You should require the union representatives to justify every proposal they make. That, of course, is an impossible task for them, and, as a result, their list will shrink rapidly.

Deal with blockbuster proposals in packages; do not negotiate item by item in piecemeal fashion. The package method will force the union to focus on its priority items and help the board to smoke out featherbed proposals.

3. What kind of proposals should our board make? Is our bargaining position weakened if we don't make any?

Just as you require a union to clarify its demands, your school board must be sure that its own proposals are realistic and can be justified to the teachers and to the public. Otherwise you will injure your credibility. One of your priorities ought to be to correct any clauses in your previous contract that made the contract difficult to administer.

Before negotiations begin, your school board should meet with all or many of your district's administrators to discuss problems caused by the current contract (in large districts, a representative committee should suffice). In addition to soliciting comments from administrators, you should have all employee contracts and the new union proposals reviewed by a labor relations expert to determine what should be eliminated, added, or amended. Your proposals can then be structured to meet these needs. Above all, do not offer to negotiate managment rights, or you will be bargaining away your own function.

If, after review, you find your current contract is basically "clean," your school board seriously should consider making *no new proposals*. This strategy can be especially effective in states that have "sunshine" bargaining laws. The effect of your posture will be to suggest that the teachers are bargaining out of greed, not out of need.

4.   Our teachers want to hold bargaining sessions at least twice a week. Should we meet that often? Should we meet whenever the teacher union requests a meeting?

Teacher bargaining teams often request frequent meetings, hoping to wear the board down. This is a union tactic that has weathered well. Human flesh and blood can stand only so much. Endless sessions, hard seats, air blue with smoke and hot with blather has caused many a management team to give in out of frustration and fatigue.

You may have to stock up on aspirin and restoratives, but stand fast. Your strategy should be to use the timing and frequency of meetings to your advantage. To meet strictly according to the union's schedule will be construed as a sign of weakness, and can only prolong the agony. Instead, show from the beginning that you are not in a hurry to settle. The union needs the contract; you do not. If the teachers show a willingness to move, then you should be prepared to meet and negotiate, but be sure there is a purpose to be served. Your firmness places the burden upon the union to seek alternatives or to modify its last position before you return to the table.

5.   One of our board members knows several teachers. He feels he can talk to them privately and arrange a settlement. He's not a member of our negotiating team, but shouldn't we let him try?

Not unless you are willing to turn over all future negotiations to amateurs. If you let your man meet separately with teachers, you are allowing the union to divide and conquer (a technique unions devoutly love), and you will be obligingly undermining your own team for years to come. Future contract negotiation will be that much harder; the teachers will go straight back to Mr. Fixit or wait until he comes around again, while your bargaining team sits mute with hands tied. Your school board must speak, publicly and at the bargaining table, with a unified voice. Stick to that and let the teachers speak through their representatives — to you.

6. Many of the clauses in our first contract cover areas that have since been defined as management prerogatives by our state labor board. Because we conceded them once, are we stuck with these clauses in our contract forever?

As long as the areas are included in your current contract, you are obligated to uphold them, but you can legitimately refuse to bargain on these items the next time around. Be prepared for flak, however. No union ever will give up a gain willingly. Since the areas were included in one agreement, the union will argue that they remain forever subject to negotiation. Not true. You have your state labor relations board and the courts to back you up on your stand.

7. Once a contract is signed, isn't our management obligation fulfilled until it's time to renegotiate?

Not by a long chalk, and if you don't think so, you are flinging the door open to the union grievance committee and to plenty of grief. The term collective bargaining includes the interpretation and administration of the final contract, as well as negotiation. It is the responsibility of both parties to ensure that the integrity of the agreement is not lost and that the terms of the contract are properly administered.

Here is where the management team concept can be used to develop an effective and consistent method of administering the contract and of handling grievances. The team approach assures the first line administrator that he has the support of middle management and the board. It also will spread the terms of the contract systemwide and help to reduce grievances — your main responsibility until the next time your contract is to be bargained.

8. A union represents employees who occupy certain positions, *e.g.* teachers, counselors, psychologists, school librarians. But what employees in what specific positions are represented? Are substitutes? Part-time teachers? Temporary teachers? Paraprofessionals?

Before bargaining begins, there must be a unit determination, *i.e.* a determination of what positions will be covered by the contract.

Unit determination is a complex subject, and boards should avoid decisions or policies on the subject without expert advice.

The following references will help those who want to learn more about the foregoing subjects:

Lieberman, Myron, and Michael H. Moskow: *Collective Negotiations for Teachers: An Approach to School Administration,* Rand McNally and Co., Chicago, Ill., 1966, pp. 121-91.

Midwest Center for Public Sector Labor Relations: *Questions and Answers on Unfair Labor Practices,* Indiana University, Bloomington, 1977. In states that have enacted bargaining laws, school boards and administrators must avoid committing unfair labor practices. Such avoidance typically requires several significant changes in board operations and school administration. This reference is an excellent summary of this important topic for all district personnel.

Newby, Kenneth A.: *Collective Bargaining Practices and Attitudes of School Management,* Research Report 1977-2, National School Boards Association, Washington, D.C., 1977.

Schwartz, Philip J.: *Coalition Bargaining,* School of Industrial and Labor Relations, Cornell University, Ithaca, N.Y., 1970. Although coalition bargaining has made little headway in education, it may increase rapidly in states or school districts where various public employee unions believe they can achieve more by bargaining together than by bargaining separately. This publication describes experience with coalition bargaining in the private sector.

Summers, Clyde W.: "Public Employee Bargaining: A Political Perspective," *Yale Law Review,* Vol. 83, 1974, pp. 1156-1200. This is an insightful analysis of how some of the differences between public and private sector bargaining impact public management.

When Management Negotiates, National Association of Manufacturers, New York, N.Y., 1967. This publication provides useful suggestions for preparation. Although oriented to the private sector, many of the issues raised are relevant to public sector bargaining.

THE DYNAMICS
OF BARGAINING

19. Strategy and Tactics in Negotiating with School Employee Unions

In negotiating, the first collective bargaining contract is particularly important. In terms of contract substance, the first contract sets the pattern for all later contracts. Inertia is an important factor in labor relations and the burden on the party seeking to get a certain provision in the contract is much greater when that provision will change one that is already in the contract. The first negotiations also establish the pattern for the parties' future relationships on a personal level. Firmness, intelligence, candor and hard work at the bargaining table will translate into respect, which will be invaluable in helping you to achieve future goals. By the same token, weakness, sloppiness, or dishonesty the first time around will cripple you in future dealings with the union.

One of the central differences between collective bargaining and other kinds of negotiations is that there is an elaborate legal structure regulating the conduct of labor negotiations. This legal structure is the most important single determinant of negotiating strategy and tactics in collective bargaining.

The statutory basis for the legal regulation of collective bargaining by public school employers is usually a statute that makes it unlawful for a public school employer to "refuse or fail to meet and negotiate in good faith with an exclusive representative." Closely related to the duty to meet and negotiate in good faith is the provision that it is an unfair practice for an employer to "refuse to participate in good faith" in the statutory impasse procedures. Most state public employee bargaining laws impose similar obligations upon employee organizations representing public school employees. Despite differences in language, these provisions are frequently the same in substance as Section 8(a)(5) of the National Labor Relations Act, which imposes on private sector employers

---

This chapter was prepared by Joseph Herman, senior partner in the Los Angeles office of Seyfarth, Shaw, Fairweather, and Geraldson.

the duty to bargain in good faith. Indeed, many state laws define "meeting and negotiating" in terms that would be equally applicable to the duty to bargain in the private sector. For example, the definition in the California statute provides that:

> "'Meeting and negotiating' means meeting, conferring, negotiating, and discussing by the exclusive representative and the public school employer in a good faith effort to reach agreement on matters within the scope of representation and the execution, if requested by either party, of a written document incorporating any agreements reached."

While this definition is helpful, it does not address itself to many important questions. First, it does not deal with the selection of the parties' representatives. However, Section 3543 of the California statute guarantees to public school employees the right "to form, join, and participate in the activities of employee organizations *of their own choosing.*" Similar language in other public sector statutes has been interpreted uniformly to mean that the union has the right to select the individuals who will negotiate with representatives of the employer and that interference with this right by an employer is an unfair labor practice. Thus, the fact that an employer finds one or more of the union's representatives personally objectionable does not ordinarily justify an employer's refusal to negotiate. In this connection, the Wisconsin Employment Relations Commission made the following comment:

> "Personal differences arising between the representatives of the parties engaged in negotiations with respect to wages, hours and working conditions of municipal employees do not constitute a valid reason for refusing to bargain in good faith. Both municipal employers and representatives of their employees have the right to designate whomever they choose to represent them at the bargaining table. To allow either or both parties to refuse to bargain with each other because of alleged or actual conflicts between their representatives would be contrary to the intent and purpose of (the Act). *City of Superior,* WERC Decision No. 8325 (1967).

While both parties thus have broad rights in terms of selecting their bargaining representatives, the selected representatives must be clothed with sufficient authority to engage in meaningful negotiations. The use of representatives who do not have any power to agree and who must continually check back with their principals constitutes bad faith bargaining. This does not mean, however, that a party's representatives must have authority to reach binding agreement without any need for ratification. To the contrary, both parties in the public sector typically take any tentative agreements back to their principals for ratification.

Another dimension of the employer's duty to negotiate is the duty to furnish relevant data and information to a union representing its employees. The courts and the various labor boards have uniformly held that employers are required upon request to furnish unions with sufficient data with respect to wage rates, job classifications and other related matters to permit the union to bargain intelligently, administer the contract, and prepare for negotiations. In this regard, it should be noted that the "union is not required to show the purpose of their requested data unless the data appears to be clearly irrelevant." Rather, the burden is on the employer to show that the requested data is not relevant. An employer is not required to necessarily supply the information in the same form requested as long as it is submitted in a manner that is not unreasonably burdensome to interpret.

Another constituent part of the duty to bargain in good faith is the requirement that an employer not make unilateral changes in wages, hours or working conditions that are subject to negotiation without first negotiating with the union. Thus, the Connecticut State Board of Labor Relations observed that "it is well recognized that unilateral employer action upon a matter which is the subject of current collective bargaining between parties constitutes a failure and refusal to bargain in good faith upon the issue in question." In one case, for example, the Connecticut Board held that an employer acted improperly when it unilaterally adopted a new classification plan while negotiations were in progress. However, once an employer has given the union an opportunity to negotiate over a given proposal and it appears that the parties are at impasse, an employer is permitted to unilaterally implement such proposal.

Although the courts and the various labor boards are not supposed to sit in judgment concerning the results of negotiations, they do review negotiations to determine whether the parties have, in fact, negotiated in good faith. What constitutes good faith bargaining has been variously defined. The Connecticut Supreme Court summarized it as follows:

> "The duty to negotiate in good faith generally has been defined as an obligation to participate actively in deliberations so as to indicate a present intention to find a basis for agreement.... Not only must the employer have an open mind and a sincere desire to reach an agreement, but a sincere effort must be made to reach a common ground."

In determining whether there has been good faith bargaining, the courts and labor boards consider the *totality* of the parties' conduct throughout the negotiations. Thus, while an employer has a clear right to insist upon a management rights clause, it has been held that an employer's good faith is suspect if it insists on retaining such absolute unilateral control over wages, hours and working conditions that it, in effect, would require the union to waive practically all of its statutory rights.

Finally, it should be noted that it is not ordinarily illegal for an employer to advise its employees of what is occurring at the bargaining table. As one court noted in construing another public sector labor relations law:

> "The act does not prohibit an employer from communicating in noncoercive terms with his employees while collective negotiations are in progress.... The element of negotiation is critical. Another crucial factor in these cases is whether or not the communication is designed to undermine and denigrate the union."

There are many refinements to these legal principles, but taken as a whole, they suggest nine general guidelines which may be helpful in applying the law to the actual conduct of negotiations:

1. Select negotiators with meaningful authority to engage in the give-and-take of negotiations.

2. **Provide, upon request, relevant information** in a timely fashion.

3. **Don't take unilateral action on matters that are subject to negotiations** unless and until such matters have been presented to the union's bargaining team and the parties are at impasse on said matters. It should be noted that this prohibition does not apply during the term of an existing collective bargaining agreement under which the employer has specifically or implicitly retained the right to take the action in question.

4. **Don't make proposals on a take-it-or-leave-it basis.** This does not mean, however, that, after a reasonable period of negotiations, an employer cannot legitimately state its final position.

5. **Don't communicate proposals to employees until after they have been presented to the union's bargaining team** across the bargaining table.

6. **Avoid categorical statements** such as, "We will never sign a contract."

7. **Take good notes at bargaining sessions.** Good notes serve three purposes: First, they provide a good means for keeping board members informed as to what is going on in the negotiations; second, they are helpful in reconstructing what actually occurred in negotiations in the event it is ever necessary to defend against a charge of refusing to negotiate in good faith; and third, negotiating notes are often useful in terms of ascertaining the intent of the parties in agreeing to given provisions in the contract. As such, they can be extremely useful in administering the contract and in presenting evidence of the parties' intent in arbitration proceedings. (It is generally indicative of bad faith bargaining for one party to insist that there be a verbatim transcript of negotiations or that negotiations be tape recorded. As the NLRB stated, "...many authorities and practitioners in the field are of the opinion that the presence of a stenographer at [bargaining] meetings has an inhibiting effect. The use of a stenographer or mechanical recorder to create a verbatim transcript does tend to encourage negotiators to concentrate upon and speak for the purpose of making a record rather than directing their efforts toward a solution of the issues

before them." However, nothing prohibits *both* parties from agreeing to have a verbatim transcript of negotiations.)

8. Make proposals of your own and counterproposals. While the law does not require either party to agree to a proposal or to make a concession, proposals and counterproposals are the common practice in collective bargaining, and the willingness to make them is evidence of good faith.

9. Don't delay unnecessarily the start of negotiations. State laws frequently tie negotiations to the district budgetary process, *e.g.* California law provides that negotiations begin sufficiently before the adoption of the final budget for the ensuing year "so that there is adequate time for agreement to be reached or for the resolution of an impasse."

As to strategy, there is no single, right way to negotiate. There is no fixed, magic formula that is guaranteed to produce the result you want. If you talk to experienced negotiators you'll find a variety of approaches and styles. A successful negotiator must be *himself;* he must use an approach that is consistent with his own personality, experience and background. Some highly successful negotiators are table pounding bulls; others are quiet and reserved. Each can be equally effective if he uses his own personality to advantage. But no negotiator should try to copy the technique of someone whose personality is completely different.

How do you determine the composition of the employer's negotiation team? Like employee organizations, public school employers have the right to determine who is going to represent them at the bargaining table. The Tennessee statute, which prohibits outside negotiators, appears to be the major exception, but it has not been in effect long enough to evaluate the impact of prohibition.

The primary object in selecting the school board's bargaining team is to bring administrative knowledge and experience to the bargaining table. The team should be able to discuss accurately and intelligently all relevant problems that may arise in the meetings. While it is not necessary, or even advisable in most cases, to make instantaneous decisions, it is equally inadvisable and unnecessary to be laggard in the discussions because management representatives lack sufficient knowledge and information to discuss the problems at hand.

The team should be fully advised of the attitude and policies of the school board. While it is not impossible to retract a statement or a tentative agreement made by the spokesman of the administrative representatives, it will be difficult in practice and may be labeled an indication of bad faith. To ensure that school board attitudes are being correctly communicated, there should be a continuous interchange of views between members of the board and those who represent it at the table.

A unified approach should be developed. Members of the school board should be in agreement among themselves and with members of the administrative team. Also, members of the team should agree with each other and with the board. Dissension among members of the administration can be disastrous.

The chief negotator should be someone who has had firsthand experience in negotiating a labor contract. Someone on the bargaining team should be familiar with the district's personnel and budget policies — often the superintendent. In addition, the team should have someone who is familiar with the day-to-day operations on the school level and can evaluate the impact of particular provisions on operations — in many cases, a principal.

While it is lawful for a school board member to participate directly in the negotiations, practical considerations make it unwise generally for board members to do so for several reasons: (1) Board members rarely are trained in personnel matters; (2) they are subject to direct political pressure from the unions they would be negotiating with; (3) continuity between one negotiation and the next is important and a board member may not be elected the next time around; (4) negotiations are time-consuming, and board members may not be willing or able to devote the required amount of time; and (5) the school board must ultimately approve or reject the contract, and it will be awkward for a board member who has directly participated in the negotiations to objectively review the resulting contract.

After you have selected the members of your negotiating team, you should begin to prepare for negotiations. It is a cliche among trial lawyers that preparation is 99 percent of trial technique. No good trial lawyer would attempt to present a case in court without full knowledge of the strengths and weaknesses of his case, the facts he intended to prove, the arguments of the other side, the facts with which to counter those arguments, and a thorough knowledge of the law involved. The same is true of collective bargaining. Contrary to popular belief, rhetoric is not the central ingredient of hard bargaining. Hard bargaining requires having the facts with which you can convince the union (and perhaps later a fact-finder or the faculty) of the validity of your position. The effect of showing a union negotiator who has been decrying the poor salary scale in your district that your salaries in fact rank high in your area can be devastating. Moreover, when the union recognizes that you are armed with the facts, it is less likely to continue with exorbitant demands and conversely is more willing to come to a reasonable position earlier in the negotiations.

Begin the preparation for negotiations by thoroughly reviewing existing personnel policies, both written and unwritten, and existing methods of operation. This review should include contacting each administrator and supervisor about the problems they have encountered in the day-to-day administration of present policies. Get their comments in writing, so that if you're called upon later to substantiate your position at the bargaining table, you'll be in a position to do so. Key suggestions to your policy manual.

Next, attempt to anticipate the union's demands. The more time you have to review and evaluate the union's demands, the better off you'll be. In many cases, this should be easy since the unions will have a standard initial proposal.

Then, analyze each of the anticipated union demands from the standpoint of cost and of its effect on your district's ability to fulfill its legal responsibilities.

One way for the employer to look at a labor negotiation is that it's a process of bringing the union and the employees it represents down to earth. The way to facilitate this process is to get the union to set priorities on its demands. This is a continuous process throughout negotiations. You begin it by getting the union to submit its proposal first. This establishes a ceiling for the union, and, in developing a proposal, the union necessarily will have to make some preliminary judgment as to what its priorities are. Of course, the union's initial demands will be extravagant, but forcing the union to put down its demands in writing usually has some restraining effect. On occasion, a union will attempt to avoid this restraint by holding back some of its demands initially. For example, the union might present a complete proposal on all items except salaries and simply state in the salary part of its proposal that it wants a "substantial" salary increase, leaving to some time in the future the definition of "substantial."

When the union presents its proposal, go through it carefully, section by section, word by word, first with the union and then on your own. Get the union to explain the reason for each provision, since much of the language probably will be "boilerplate," *i.e.* standard language that the union is proposing everywhere. It may have nothing to do with the situation in your particular district, and the negotiators you're dealing with may not fully understand the purpose for the provision. Thus, where the union's proposal would change your existing practice, ask the union negotiators: "What's wrong with our present way of operating?" "What actual problems has our present practice caused the employees?" In many cases, the justification given by the union for its demands will be much narrower in scope than the provision. This helps you to begin the process of separating the wheat from the chaff, of assigning priorities to the union's demands. It will give you a basis for counterproposing a more limited provision, which will meet the asserted justification without the cost of the union's original proposal. Many times the actual problem that gives rise to a proposal is very different from the proposal that is made to cure it. In addition, questioning pins down the meaning the union gives to the language and, thus, gives you the information necessary to draft a counterproposal.

What if management is adamantly opposed to any concessions, however watered down, to a particular proposal? Some negotiators argue that the negotiator should not even probe the area with questions, on the theory that such questions will dignify the proposal. To me, this argument is fallacious. Few union representatives today are that unsophisticated. Moreover, it is too difficult for the negotiator to know for certain that he will be able to hold his position throughout negotiations. It is not unusual for clauses to be agreed to in final contract settlement following a strike, with no bargaining history.

If some proposals are ludicrous on their face, refrain from overreacting when you ask questions. Somewhere in the background of the proposals is probably serious intent. Your purpose isn't to display your superior wit or engage in ridicule.

After you have reviewed the union's proposal with the union, go through it with the other members of the board's bargaining team to make sure you fully understand the proposal and haven't missed anything. After this review, you may want to go over certain portions of the union's proposal again, to clarify points that were missed or obscured in the first review. The whole process of reviewing the union's proposal may take several sessions, but it can be the most important part of the negotiations because it pinpoints what the real issues are and helps you to set up the various tradeoffs that will be necessary to reach an agreement later on. Also, it demonstrates to the union that you are taking its proposal seriously. This does not mean, however, that you should try to cover in your counterproposal every item or subject covered in the union's proposal. There will be many subjects dealt with in the union's proposal, such as class size, which you omit from your response because you don't intend to agree to any provision relating to that subject. Some areas covered by the union's proposal may be outside the scope of the negotiations. Some subjects encompassed by your counterproposal might be omitted from the union's proposal. Both sides have the right to submit proposals. You don't want to simply be in the position of responding defensively to what the union has proposed. You should take the initiative in those areas where it is incumbent upon you to do so. For example, it is unlikely that the union's proposal will have included a management rights or no-strike clause, and yet, these are subjects you might want to have included in your contract. There may be certain fringe benefits that you feel have got out of control or a sick-day plan that is subject to abuse. If this is the case, you may want to propose certain cutbacks in these areas. If you later go into fact-finding, you will find it very helpful to have some of your proposals on the table so that the fact-finding isn't just a one-way street with the union having everything to gain and nothing to lose.

After the process of reviewing and analyzing the union's initial proposal, it's usually a good idea to take one or two weeks to develop a complete counterproposal, covering all items in the final contract, from the preamble to the termination clause. (To a large extent, your initial proposal may be a restatement, in contractual language, of the district's present policies.) In the counterproposal, try to include agreement on two or three items the union had proposed. These should be minor items, such as a savings clause or a termination clause. Movement on major items should be saved until later in the negotiations, after the union has indicated that it is ready to make corresponding movement on its side. By agreeing to a few items, you get the ball rolling and establish a climate of reasonableness. If the other side perceives you as being completely inflexible and unreasonable, it won't have any incentive to change its position, so it's important that you hold out from the beginning the carrot of possible movement.

Limit the counterproposal to non-economic items, that is, language matters not relating directly to wages or fringe benefits. This is in line with the general practice in labor negotiations of trying to reach agreement on all non-economic items before discussing economic matters. This procedure generally is considered advantageous to management because the union frequently will make concessions in the later stages of negotiations to get to the economic part of the discussion. However, in some cases, it is not possible to adhere completely to this procedure because the union is holding firm on one or two non-economic items, and the only way to get it to move is to "buy" movement through the economic provisions of your proposal. Also, there may be economic issues that are so complicated or so intertwined with other portions of the contract that discussions must necessarily be started on these issues at an early stage of negotiations.

As the negotiations proceed, it is customary to reach agreement upon items one at a time, to mark agreed-upon provisions as "OK," and to initial and date the language. In reaching these agreements on particular items, it is important to agree upon *specific language*. Don't be satisfied with agreements "in principle," because such agreements have a way of evaporating when it comes time to approve specific language. When the parties can't reach agreement on an item, it is marked "pass" or "hold" and returned to in later sessions.

The objective in making a complete management counterproposal is to get the union off its initial proposal. This is a gradual processs. It doesn't happen overnight. Try to give the union bargaining committee an opportunity to get everything off their chest by reviewing their proposal carefully. Then focus subsequent discussion on your counterproposal. As the negotiations progress and agreement is reached on particular items, try to incorporate that agreement into a subsequent redraft of management's counterproposal and indicate on the redraft that a particular item has been agreed to and the date of such agreement. This is a continuous process. After each session, update the counterproposal, adding all items agreed to at the last session. After awhile, both sides are working from your document. By structuring the negotiations in this way, you get control of the writing of the agreement. Some union representatives are happy to have you assume this responsibility for what they dismiss as mere "paperwork." But control of the writing of the agreement is vital. It means control of substance and outcome as well as process.

This constant redrafting serves two functions. First, it keeps the parties up to date as to where they stand and what has been agreed to. Second, it constantly resubmits and keeps on the table those proposals you have made. What about the big stack of proposals that the union originally submitted? Don't make reference to them. If the union wants to bring up a particular proposal, it will do so on its own, without the need for any reminders from management. You should give the union a way to drop proposals gracefully, which means not asking directly whether it has dropped a particular proposal. The way to find out where you stand on these loose ends when you get down to the final stages of negotiations is to say: "I've reviewed my negotiation notes and it appears there are three remaining issues: salaries, length of contract, and the amount of paid vacation. Are your notes in agreement?" If the union agrees that these are the only three remaining issues, you will have confirmed that it has dropped the other parts of its initial proposal. Even if it adds one or two items, you still will have facilitated the tacit withdrawal by the union of a great many of its original demands.

Generally, it is inadvisable to try to write contract language in the heat of a negotiating meeting; a much better practice is to reduce agreements to writing and, after careful review, submit them at a subsequent meeting. Careful draftsmanship of a collective bargaining agreement will avoid disputes over the meaning and application of the contract in the grievance procedure. Hasty or thoughtless draftsmanship almost inevitably results in future difficulties. In terms of language, simplicity and brevity are valuable. A collective bargaining agreement is essentially a statement of limitations on the power and authority of the school board and its officials to administer the school system unilaterally. Every "right" conferred by the agreement upon the employees and their representative means a corresponding "duty" is imposed upon the employer. The more lengthy and complex the agreement, the greater the limitations, and the greater the possibility of disagreement over the meaning and application of its terms.

On making concessions: Don't make them too quickly or on the spur of the moment. If concessions are made too quickly, the union negotiators will feel they should have asked for more, which only promotes intransigence on other subjects and extravagance in the next negotiations. Unions, particularly teacher unions, are highly political organizations that have to justify their existence to their members by proving that they won increased wages and benefits that the employees would not otherwise have received. If the employer agrees too easily, the union is precluded from taking credit, and, even worse, it may be accused of not asking for enough.

Timing also is important in making concessions. Just because you are willing at the outset of negotiations to agree to a union demand doesn't mean you should express your willingness at the outset; make sure the union pays a high price for it. Also, don't make a concession on an item that was left unresolved after the prior session without first ascertaining the union's present position on that item. The union may have changed its position in the period since the last meeting, so that if you begin the session by announcing a concession on your part as to that item, you may be giving away more than you have to. One of the few absolute rules of negotiations is never to give away more than is necessary because there will be other rounds of negotiations in future years and you'll need all the credit you can muster for those negotiations. Don't squander your resources now.

Try to get the union to make counterproposals that are acceptable to you. It's always better to say "Yes" to a union demand than to try to get them to accept your proposal. This is particularly important in the final phases of negotiations. Try to structure things so that the final proposal is the union's and you're accepting it.

If you can't get the union to submit a final proposal that is acceptable to you, and you can't get them to budge from their final unacceptable proposal, one device that sometimes is helpful is to come back with a final proposal in the alternative and offer to the union that it choose which of *your* final proposals it wants. Of course, it may not want either of them, but in many cases the offering of a choice is enough of an enticement to produce movement.

Another tactical point to bear in mind when you reach the final stages of negotiations is to avoid making any significant concessions in the final stages unless the offer is contingent upon reaching a complete agreement.

One way of getting around sticky points is the side letter. There may be items that the union wants and you are willing to agree to but would cause the union political problems if they appeared in the collective bargaining agreement. The way to handle these items is through a side letter of agreement, which does not become part of the labor contract and which, therefore, does not have to be presented to the membership.

Throughout the negotiations, the chief negotiator should have complete control over who says what and who responds to what question. He should be the only person to make concessions and everyone on your side should understand that he is the only person who has the authority to make a move. Moreover, the same person should be in charge; to change chief negotiators from meeting to meeting is sheer folly.

Don't be devious or misleading; you can lose your credibility. Don't call an offer your "final offer" unless you really mean that no future movement will be made and are prepared to stand by that position. Otherwise, if your bluff is called, future statements will be greeted with disbelief.

Prior to negotiating any labor agreement, management negotiators should have a firm philosophy to serve as a guide for the formulatoin of their proposals and for evaluating union proposals. In the private sector, management negotiators have generally relied on the management rights doctrine as their guiding philosophy. Briefly stated, the management rights doctrine is that management retains all those rights which it does not negotiate away. Integral to this doctrine is the concept that it is management's duty to act and it is the union's duty to challenge if the union feels that management's action is contrary to the negotiated agreement. In other words, management acts and the union reacts.

This functional basis for management rights does not allow any room for the union to acquire rights to manage and slide in as a "joint manager" of the district because unions are not functionally managers. But, public employee unions, particularly teacher unions, are increasingly asserting the right to co-determine matters of public policy. *These attempts should be resisted;* management is not required to negotiate matters of inherent managerial policy. Moreover, proposals that management must first obtain the union's agreement before acting in such areas as discipline, scheduling overtime or subcontracting should be avoided. These "mutual agreement" or "veto" clauses are contrary to the management rights doctrine.

Since management's rights come from the duty of management to carry out its designated public policies and to operate efficiently, it is essential that management be considered the "acting" party and the union the "passive" party insofar as the day-to-day relationships of the parties under a collective bargaining agreement are concerned. It is impossible for any school district to be run properly if there are two "acting" parties. Thus, union leaders should never participate in day-to-day decision-making under a labor agreement.

If union representatives aren't to participate in day-to-day decision-making, then what is their function under an agreement? Of course, during the negotiation of a collective bargaining agreement, union representatives must be recognized as having bargaining rights equal to management's, except as to those subjects declared by law to be outside the permissible scope of bargaining. However, once the agreement is executed, the union representatives should assume an entirely different role. That role should be the policing of the agreement to determine whether actions taken by the school district are contrary to the contractual commitments previously agreed upon by the parties. Thus, the union's function under the agreement can best be described as a "watch dog" function — watching the actions of the employer, the "acting" party — to see whether such actions are in compliance with the agreement.

If being the "watch dog" is the union's proper function under the agreement, then the union must have the necessary rights to perform this function. In the private sector, these rights are contained in a properly conceived grievance and arbitration procedure. Approximately 95 percent of the collective bargaining agreements in private industry contain such provisions, and some state laws specifically authorize public school employers and unions to enter into an agreement providing for the arbitration of disputes as to the interpretation or application of the contract. A binding grievance and arbitration procedure is logically consistent with the management rights approach. However, it must be carefully drafted; otherwise, grievance handling and settlement procedures can become a means of eroding management rights during the term of the agreement.

In addition to providing a basic framework within which to negotiate a collective agreement, the management rights doctrine provides a test by which to analyze union contract demands. Thus, to preserve the district's right to carry out its designated public functions and to efficiently manage its operations, one fundamental question should be asked as each union demand is placed on the bargaining table: *Does the proposal prevent the district from taking actions necessary to implement the public policy goals entrusted to it by law in an efficient manner? If it does, the proposal should be resisted.*

In the private sector, this management rights philosophy often is incorporated into the labor contract in the form of a management rights clause. Such a clause usually begins with a provision to this effect:

> It is understood and agreed that the board retains the right to operate the district and that all management rights are reserved to it, but that such rights must be exercised consistently with the other provisions of this contract. These rights include but are not limited to the following. . . .

After this kind of preamble, the basic management rights should be listed. Some of the basic management rights include the right to:

1. Hire, assign, or transfer employees;
2. Determine the mission of the school district;
3. Determine the methods, means, and number of personnel;
4. Introduce new or improved methods or facilities;
5. Change existing methods or facilities;
6. Establish and require observance of reasonable rules and regulations;
7. Discipline and discharge for just cause;
8. Contract-out for goods or services.

Undoubtedly, the union will oppose any attempt to obtain a strong clause, but this should not deter you from attempting to negotiate as strong a clause as possible.

The effectiveness of a management rights clause can be reinforced in other provisions of the contract. For example, a provision might state: "If the employer changes the shift starting hours, it shall notify the union two days in advance of the effective date of the change." This language constitutes contractual recognition that the employer has the right to change the shift hours unilaterally, *i.e.* without prior negotiations with the union or agreement by it. Thus, what appears to be a restriction (that is, the requirement that the employer notify the union in certain circumstances), in fact, enhances management's rights.

Legislation may include a kind of statutory management rights by limiting the scope of representation. Perhaps the most outstanding example is the California statute, which limits the scope of representation to "wages, hours of employment, and other terms and conditions of employment." The statute goes on to define "terms and conditions of employment" as meaning:

> "health and welfare benefits. . ., leave and transfer policies, safety conditions of employment, class size, procedures to be used for the evaluation of employees, organizational security. . ., and procedures for processing grievances. . . ."

The statute further provides that "all matters not specifically enumerated are reserved to the public school employer and may not be a subject of meeting and negotiating." This constitutes a kind of statutory management rights provision because it relieves school management of the obligation to negotiate over matters not specifically listed in the statute.

However, despite this statutory recognition of the right to manage in certain areas, it still is important for public school employers to secure a management rights clause in their labor contracts. There are several reasons for this:

1. Although the union has the statutory right to negotiate over the subjects listed in the statute, it has the legal power to waive these rights during the term of the labor contract, and it is important that you secure such a waiver in the form of a management rights clause covering these subjects to protect you from having to bargain over these subjects during the term of the agreement. Thus, a public school employer has a duty to bargain over class size when negotiating a new contract, but it may seek from the union a provision in the management rights clause that, during the term of the contract, the employer has the right to change class size.

2. A management rights clause constitutes contractual recognition by the union of the school district's basic rights.

3. A management rights clause notifies the union and the employees that the public employer expects to exercise its rights.

4. It reinforces the argument that union activity interfering with the employer's rights is prohibited.

5. It protects the public school employer in the event the present statutory guarantees are modified or eliminated.

Remember that specific clauses of the agreement will limit the exercise of management rights, no matter what the language of the management rights clause states. Accordingly, the draftsman of an agreement must recognize that a management rights clause, standing alone, is only a general charter of reserved rights. Management rights often will be limited, in whole or in part, by the general language or specific terms of the remaining clauses of the agreement. To the extent these other clauses restrict the management right in question, these expressed restrictions will control.

The task of negotiating and drafting labor contracts in public education unquestionably is difficult and challenging. However, the task can be made considerably easier if management negotiators understand the roles of the public employer and of unions both during negotiations and during the term of the agreement.

Moreover, the history of collective bargaining in the private sector during the past 30 years should be studied carefully. Management negotiators in the private sector have learned by trial and error how important it is to carefully draft labor agreements. In this regard, arbitration awards are a rich source of information. They reveal the importance of a sound philosophy for the negotiation and administration of the contract as well as pointing out the practical do's and don'ts.

The outcome of any negotiations, however, depends upon many factors that necessarily vary from district to district. The chances of negotiating sound collective bargaining agreements are substantially increased, however, if the district's negotiators and board understand and vigorously defend the right of the employer to carry out its designated functions in an efficient and orderly manner.

Collective bargaining, in addition to being subject to detailed regulation by the law, differs from other negotiations in that it is a continuous process. Unlike the negotiation for the sale of a house, it does not end with the signing of the contract. The parties to a labor contract continue to have to live together. During the term of the contract, they have to administer it jointly. When the contract expires, they will have to negotiate a new one. The necessity for a continued, close relationship should play a role in all your tactical decisions. If you act through weakness or unnecessarily inflict wounds today through deception or overkill, you'll be paying the price in many future negotiations. But if you deal with the union firmly and honestly now, you'll reap the benefits for years to come.

20. To Succeed at Bargaining, Learn the Language of the Teacher

It's important that you understand the special language of collective bargaining as your teacher union uses it. It's even more important that you make sure your public understands it. Example: When the union cries, "the board is not bargaining in good faith," it really means, "the board isn't giving us what we want." So, as you can see, the difference between what is said and what is meant is crucial.

The basic elements of the special bargaining vocabulary that has been developed by organized teachers can be traced to certain qualities that are common to all teachers. First, teachers are, by nature and training, planners. They form their unions and their bargaining positions as they would form a well-developed lesson plan. "If teachers would devote as much time to their lesson plans as they do to their union activities," one administrator recently complained to me, perhaps in a fit of hyperbole, "Johnny would be able to read."

A second factor in the development of the special bargaining vocabulary of teacher unions: Teachers tend to be verbal and to adapt the basic principles of teaching to fit negotiations. The educational community does not call a child "dumb"; it calls him "exceptional." Until recently, teachers didn't even call their labor organizations "unions"; they called them "associations." When a school board takes a tough position in negotiations, the teachers don't call this posture "hard bargaining"; they call it "bad faith bargaining."

The third characteristic of teacher bargaining terminology, which is basic to all other considerations, is an attitude of self-righteousness. While this is a trait most union people share, it finds quintes-

This chapter was prepared by Anthony P. DiRocco, negotiations specialist with Thealan Associates, Inc., Albany, NY. (It appeared in a slightly different version in *The American School Board Journal,* January, 1977.)

sential refinement in teachers. They are always right. It is this self-righteousness that makes so many teachers contemptuous of school administrators, leads them to flaunt strike prohibitions, and provides them with the zeal to bargain for months, and, in a growing number of cases, for years. This attitude of self-righteousness can make teachers ungracious in success and petulant in failure. It also can make them very difficult to deal with during negotiations.

Perhaps because they are verbally oriented, teacher negotiators have developed a myth — and a flood of jargon to support their version — of a "belief in good labor relations and negotiations." Anyone who has worked with teachers in labor relations for any length of time will see through this. Just as the Bible is one of the most widely circulated but least read books, "good labor relations" is preached more than practiced by teacher unions. To understand the truth in this, all a school board need do is examine the favorite slogans of the teacher unions.

The "good faith" bromide mentioned at the start of this chapter is an instructive example. When a school district disagrees with the union's demands, the board is accused of refusing to bargain in good faith. Indeed, cases exist in which an offer by a school board is viewed as excessively generous by observers, but fails to meet the expectation of the union. Result: The cry of "bargaining in bad faith" rings through the community and appears in newspaper headlines.

"Bring in the board" or "The board is refusing to bargain" are commonly heard union statements when the district is represented at the bargaining table by administrators or professional negotiators. These negotiators are perceived by the union as standing in the way of teacher ambitions and, therefore, must be circumvented — or better yet — removed. The objective of this union position is to exhaust or harass the board into concession. Some teacher union leaders call this effective public relations.

"The contract is going to help the district as well as the teachers" is bait dangled by unions and swallowed by more school boards than some board members and superintendents like to admit. Many school districts have discovered subsequently to taking the bait that the document that has emerged from the bargaining is not the philosophical statement outlining recommended procedures the board thought it was getting, but a ball and chain attached to the administration of the schools. Such a contract is not permissive, it is restrictive. But many school boards find this out too late.

"We don't want a lot, just give us a 'little'" language is another commonly heard union plea. Board after board has listened and given more than a little; they've given a lot. Many school boards incorporated the model contract provided by the National Education Association (NEA) into their local agreements. Later, in arbitration, these boards discovered the real meaning of the language they had adopted. In truth, many teachers did not realize the power of the verbal weapons they had forged in their negotiated contracts until years after the provisions and clauses had been inserted. Class size, maintenance of standards, academic freedom, and teacher evaluation are a few examples of contract provisions that now are being used effectively by the teacher unions in arbitration, and in the courts.

Here are four more examples of teacher union language that need translation:

1. *"The contract isn't for us; it's for the kids."* No teacher negotiator has adequately explained how personal leave days, extra sick leave days, increased health insurance, a reduced work year, a shortened school day, and the elimination of supervision benefit the students. Of course, the teachers claim that, by having these benefits, morale is heightened and that teachers perform better when such fringes are offered. Next year, of course, the teacher union will want even more personal time, more sick leave, more benefits. Even in the face of the previous concessions made by the district, teacher morale is said to be sinking even lower. Often the dissatisfaction increases as more concessions are made.

2. *"We only want a reasonable settlement."* Understand that this is the basis for the arguments that ensue as teachers work toward the half-and-half theory, which is that the teachers expect to get half of what they ask for. They ask for a 25 percent increase in wages, and, based on the split-down-the-middle theory, they expect to get 13 percent. This "let us reason together" tactic also is used to support the union argument that teachers should be involved in the deci-

sion-making processes of the school district. Teachers want to be involved not only in curriculum and program approval (something like the United Auto Workers wanting to have a say in the design of Chevrolet transmissions) but also in the selection of the teaching staff and administrators.

3. *"Bargaining is a process of give and take."* More properly translated, in terms of the teacher union, it is a process in which the district gives and the union takes. Yearly, school boards groan when the teachers present their package of proposals for bargaining. The union representatives demand that the board "bargain in good faith" and theorize about the "give and take" of negotiations as they arrive at the table with 50, 100, 200 or 300 separate new proposals and proposed changes in the contract. Twenty or so imaginary demands are given up by the union in exchange for a number of real concessions on the part of the school district. Then the union says: "Look at what we've given up!" Many professionals, neutrals and advocates alike, including professional union representatives, consider this an overkill of the bargaining process before it ever begins. Optimists hope that as the teacher unions become more comfortable and secure they will be more inclined to make massive withdrawals and get to the real issues.

4. *"The grievance procedure will make things run more smoothly because it will open communications and clear up problems before they become serious."* At the same time the teacher union is propagating this myth, it is urging its membership to file grievances. Grievances, to be sure, can be legitimate, but the number of petty items that are grieved and proceed to arbitration is enormous. Unfortunately, the grievance procedure can create its own problems in the relationship between teachers and the school district that employs them. Problems such as these:

• Unions often use the grievance process not only as a problem solver but also as a means of extracting concessions from the school board during the life of the contract. If the union does not get what it wants at the lower steps of the grievance procedure, it demands arbitration. The theory: "You win some and you lose some."

● A basic tenet of effective labor relations is the early resolution of conflicts. Unfortunately, many teachers and their organizations remain unable to cope with this aspect of the grievance procedure. When an administrator, whether it is a principal or the superintendent, admits an error in administering the contract, the teacher representatives seldom exhibit the good grace or the good sense to be magnanimous. Too often they pounce on the situation and say: "See, we told you he was inept."

● The grievance-arbitration arena is often the breeding ground for future strike issues. For political rather than substantive reasons, the union demands arbitration of an issue that would have been better left alone. But as the union says in its practice of "good" labor relations, a "contract without a lot of grievances isn't worth the paper it's written on."

Too many school districts are blessed or cursed, depending on the point of view, with active grievance committee chairpersons who, like grand inquisitors, attempt constantly to ferret out grievances to keep the administration hopping. In one school district, the grievance chairperson instigated or initiated 35 grievances in one year, 15 of which proceeded to arbitration before the end of the school year. Settlements at the lower levels only resulted in more grievances. The district was in a steady state of turmoil. When the grievance chairperson resigned, the number of grievances dwindled and the district returned to a more even keel.

One short reminder: None of this is to suggest that troubled labor relations are the result solely of rapacious teacher unions and virtuous school districts. Plenty of school districts make their own labor problems. Trouble is sure to erupt in a school district whose administrators are reluctant to accept their role as managers. Labor relations and collective bargaining in the public sector, a phenomenon of modern times, have been imposed on the educational establishment, whose history stems from medieval scholasticism and finds its present roots in the 19th Century. Today's administrators are not taught to manage but to fulfill functions that were established long before the age of contracts, negotiations and labor relations. College and university courses dealing with school administration are still taught mainly by

theoreticians and geared to 10 years ago but are dangerously out-
dated today. So it's to the great credit of school administrators in
the U.S. and Canada that they have done as well as they have in
protecting school districts in the face of the teacher concept of
"good" labor relations.

21. Rhetoric and Reality in Teacher Bargaining

Teacher unions are making it increasingly difficult for school boards to fire incompetent teachers. Teacher union leaders will argue that the union is no more interested in protecting incompetents than is the board. The union's determination is merely to exercise its right and responsibility to ensure due process for its members; that, say the leaders, is why teacher unions bargain so earnestly on questions of teacher evaluation, job security, and grievance procedures. The unions are only trying to make sure that no adverse actions are taken by school boards against teachers without affording those teachers proper due process.

This is a plausible, difficult-to-oppose argument. It also is a myth. Skeptics on this issue might consider the following contract clause proposed to school boards by numerous locals of the California Teachers Association (CTA):

"A teacher who is supervising an instructional aide or voluntary aide shall be empowered to terminate the services of such aide if such teacher alleges that the aide is interfering with the teacher's performance or is not performing his own services satisfactorily."

Just like that — teachers should have the right to fire aides. Teachers need not file charges against the aide, alert the aide to deficiencies, or give the aide time to correct such deficiencies. They need not afford the aide a hearing, give the aide the right to cross-examine the teacher, or supply the aide with a statement of charges. Notice that the teachers aren't proposing merely that they be given the right to exclude unwanted aides from their classrooms. They are proposing a teacher right to fire an aide at any time for any reason. If anyone supposes that teachers really espouse the principle of due process, this proposal — submitted to school boards all over California — should help dispel such naive ideas.

The teacher proposal ignores completely the thought that aides have and may want representation and bargaining rights at least as much as teachers do.

What if a school board were to agree to such a clause in its contract with the teacher union? Probably that board would be guilty of an unfair labor practice. The aides could argue, rightly, that the board had adopted a term or condition of employment without bargaining over it with the exclusive representative of the aides.

Actually, some California boards countered the teacher proposal with the following proposal: "A principal who is supervising a teacher shall be empowered to terminate the services of such teacher if such principal alleges that the teacher is interfering with the principal's performance or is not performing his own services satisfactorily."

The absurdity of this counterproposal is matched only by that of the original union demand concerning teacher aides, but the counterproposal may have served to place the matter in some reasonable perspective.

Indeed, reasonable perspective is essential in assessing union rhetoric. To illustrate, every board member and superintendent has heard repeatedly about professed teacher concern for pupils. Whatever the sincerity of that assertion, the following proposal (actually made to many school boards in California by CTA locals) suggests teacher indifference to the due process rights of students:

"1. The board shall, upon recommendation of the student's teacher, exclude from a class any student who, in the teacher's opinion, has filthy or vicious habits; or suffers from a contagious or infectious disease; or suffers from a physical or mental disability which would cause his attendance to be inimical to the welfare of other students; or acts in such a way that the teacher believes good cause exists for such student's exclusion.

"A. The board shall act upon the teacher's recommendation within five days.

"B. Should the board fail to follow the teacher's recommendation, it shall provide the teacher with its reasons in writing.

"2. A student excluded under paragraph 1 above shall not be entitled to return to any classroom until such time as the board determines that the condition which prompted the exclusion no longer exists and the teacher into whose class the student is to be assigned concurs in such assessment."

Of course, any school board that became party to so blatant a disregard for pupil rights would be in immediate and deep trouble with civil rights and civil liberties agencies. Under the union proposal, a teacher could exclude a pupil from class forever, regardless of the basis for the exclusion. While it may or may not be a good idea to accord teachers more authority over pupils than they currently have, the teacher proposal, with its flagrant disregard for pupil rights to due process, would be an outrageous solution to the problem. Fortunately however, most California school boards seem sensitive to the due process needs of pupils, even if the teacher associations do not.

It is not difficult to find other instances of teacher rhetoric promoting the view that teachers can do no wrong — a status they accord to no other group or individual. In proposing leave policies, for example, teacher groups often urge clauses that enable teachers to be given leave with no requirement that reasons or evidence be forthcoming to demonstrate that the leave was used for its designated purposes. In negotiating hours of employment, teachers frequently demand that any requirements for a minimum number of hours on the job be dropped, and that school boards simply trust the teachers to get their job done. When a board responds to such a proposal by insisting upon safeguards against teacher abuse, the board's posture often is characterized by union rhetoric as an attack upon the integrity or professionalism of the teachers.

The nonsense in such rhetoric sometimes is as clear to the union as it is to the board. Nevertheless, absurd proposals, such as those discussed in the foregoing, are regularly proposed by teacher unions.

The union rationale usually runs about like this: "Our proposals merely represent a bargaining position. We don't expect to win everything we propose, so the extreme nature of the proposal isn't any big deal."

Unfortunately, this rationalization simply isn't good enough. It is one thing to ask for more than you expect to get, and to be prepared to settle for less. It is quite another to submit proposals that you have no moral right to make or to accept in the event that the other party is unwise enough to agree to them. In other words, there is a crucial difference between a proposal that is morally unacceptable to virtually everyone, and one that is practically unacceptable to the employer. To see this more clearly, suppose the teacher association proposed that black teachers be paid less than white teachers. Would the fact that the association really did not expect the board to agree to it constitute any justification whatever for such a demand? One does not propose elimination of due process rights for aides or pupils for any justifiable reason, including that of having a position from which to begin bargaining.

Teacher rhetoric frequently suggests that school boards and administrators are tyrants who demonstrate little or no regard for the rights of teachers. For the sake of argument, assume that every such allegation is true. Nevertheless, the remedy proposed by teachers suggests that the cure would be as harmful as the disease. In short, one alleged tyranny would be replaced by another one.

22. Bargaining Techniques for the Inexperienced

Preparation for collective bargaining — like conditioning for an upcoming athletic event — may make all the difference in the outcome. Negotiators, naturally, hope to plan for the variety of situations that arise during negotiations. The difficulty is that it's impossible to provide a recipe for every situation that arises. The following suggestions are not guaranteed to save time and energy and keep bargaining on a comparatively rational track; they are likely to be helpful, provided that they are recognized as guides and not prescriptions.

1. *Plan ahead for time commitments.* Anyone involved with teacher bargaining quickly learns that it is difficult, if not impossible, to mix bargaining with other time-consuming tasks. Sessions that were to end at noon but break up in the early morning hours, missed travel connections, illness of team members — unexpected developments such as these all are a part of bargaining. Sometimes thorough preparation is wasted because the union walks out of a negotiating session for reasons that are completely unrelated to the bargaining issues. Sometimes a session is canceled or terminated because one side is not prepared and does not want to admit the fact or negotiate with inadequate preparation. Some board negotiators are rather lax in insisting upon adherence to agreed-upon schedules, perhaps because the board negotiator also is pressed for time. In any case, effective time management is an important key to effective negotiations.

2. *Get control of paperwork.* Consider the volume alone: You start with last year's contract to which is added proposals from both sides, records of agreement and disagreement, information on salaries, benefits and costs, school policies, local laws, counterproposals and schedules. All this information is important, but if it isn't available promptly, it can mean lost time and vulnerability. A negotiator can't keep all this information in his head, but it does no good to have the information on paper if it can't be retrieved when it is needed. For this reason, effective negotiators usually have an efficient information system.

3. *Avoid inflexible strategy and tactics.* School negotiators often are tempted to adopt a strategy of "Let's wear them down by stalling before we lay out our final proposal." Or "Let's push hard for a quick settlement so everyone can get back to other business." Make sure that your strategies are flexible enough to quicken the pace of bargaining or to slow things down, whichever tactic is called for. Such flexibility will give you the chance to take advantage of situations as they arise.

4. *Pace the presentation of complicated issues.* Avoid injecting a complicated and controversial issue just as bargaining is about to conclude. If you do, you may create such turmoil that the rest of the contract has to be renegotiated. It is not suggested that you never introduce new proposals in the final stages of bargaining but try to avoid proposals that upset the progress that already has been made. This is not always possible. Sometimes an issue arises and both parties find they are faced with a new, but important disagreement. If teachers resort to a work slowdown as a pressure tactic, for example, the district may be well advised to propose increased contractual protection against future slowdowns. Experienced negotiators on both sides avoid making new demands or forcing the other party to make them, but you don't always face an experienced negotiator.

5. *Don't waste time on items that are rarely, if ever, activated.* Suppose you are negotiating for a small school district employing 20 to 50 teachers. Avoid negotiations over items such as teacher exchange leave, Peace Corps leave, or other leaves that are unlikely to be relevant more than once in a generation in the district. Instead, try to develop language that accommodates all special cases: "Nothing in this agreement shall preclude the district from granting leaves (Peace Corps, Teacher Corps) not specified in this agreement."

6. *Avoid restatements or reiterations unless they serve a purpose.* Contrary to popular practice, bargaining does not require endless reiteration. When repetition sets in, try politely to cut it short. Although bargaining may involve a battle of wits, it is also a contest that requires sufficient physical and mental stamina to stick to a reasonable and defensible position. Many unwise concessions are made under stress of mental and physical fatigue; for this reason,

strong action may be needed to cut through the nonsense and repetition, and save one's energies for the important issues. Physical and mental fatigue are often disastrous when this is not done.

7. *Steer clear of vague compromise solutions.* Experienced negotiators never lose sight of the fact that the district must administer the contract that is negotiated. As most legislators know, it is much easier to develop ambiguous solutions to controversial issues than it is to develop clear, concise legislative solutions. The same temptation applies to collective bargaining. Both sides find it easier to accept an ambiguous solution than to continue negotiating a sensitive issue. If such solutions do get into the contract, however, make sure that the negotiating history will support your view as to what the language really means. If you can't, you may be better off to confront the issue squarely, despite the immediate difficulties of during so.

23.   The Comparison Game

The most important influences on the terms of a bargained contract are the terms of other comparable contracts. The closer other settlements are to a school district, the more they will influence the settlement in that district. Teacher bargaining in St. Paul, for example, is affected more by teacher bargaining in Minneapolis (or vice versa) than by teacher bargaining in New York or San Diego.

In fact, geographical proximity can be more influential than occupational similarity. A cost-of-living increase granted to firefighters in St. Louis will have more influence on teacher bargaining in St. Louis than will a cost-of-living increase won by teachers in Seattle.

Comparisons are especially crucial in public education because school district bargaining is a political as well as an economic process. A school board that pays more than nearby boards for the same supplies and equipment faces criticism for waste and extravagance. Teachers, of course, are not standardized as precisely as chalk or desks or projectors, but it is difficult, nevertheless, to demonstrate meaningful differences in staff effectiveness between school districts. Clearly, the taxpayers rarely distinguish one district staff from another on this basis. For this reason, a school board that pays teachers (or other employes) substantially more than the going rate in the area is risking political retaliation. Minor differences usually are ignored or can be safely explained away; major differences cannot be so easily rationalized and are not likely to be ignored.

The political process is also at work on the teacher side. Obviously, every teacher negotiator would like to win as much as possible from the employer school board. In most cases, however, the concern of the teacher negotiator is not so much with achieving a victory as it is with avoiding a defeat, i.e. a settlement that is visibly inferior to other settlements in the immediate area. Comparisons are thus the keys to the politics of bargaining.

To get as much as possible from the board, the teacher negotiator tries to show how disadvantaged his constituents are. When agreement is reached, however, the negotiator must try to portray it as a victory for his side, which means emphasizing how the teachers have fared better than their counterparts in nearby districts. This is not always easy to do. A good union negotiator frequently has to tell the district negotiating team what a rotten deal they are offering, then walk into the next room to tell his own team what a terrific contract they are getting.

In bargaining, each side emphasizes comparisons that can be expected to strengthen its respective case. If the salary schedule in District A has lower maximums than in District B, the teacher negotiator will stress the injustice done to deserving teachers at the top of the schedule. He'll say nothing, however, about the fewer steps required to achieve the maximum, or the fact that the teachers at maximum in District A received more on their way up the schedule than did their counterparts in District B.

Of course, school board negotiators follow the same strategy. District A's board negotiators are likely to propose increasing the number of steps to reach maximum, on the grounds that this aspect of the schedule is too generous (again, in comparison with nearby districts). The same board negotiators, however, can be expected to de-emphasize the lower maximum, the very point stressed by the teachers.

In the early days of teacher bargaining (the 1960's), teachers often cited data on what doctors, lawyers, and dentists were making. Apparently, some teacher negotiators naively believed a particular school board would or could deviate drastically from its neighbors, or from national patterns, by paying teachers at levels comparable to the fee-taking professions. Fortunately, much of this rhetoric has been abandoned or is recognized for the rhetoric it is.

The search for advantageous comparisons extends beyond individual items to entire settlements and patterns of settlements. Suppose your school district has the third lowest salary schedule in a metropolitan area that includes 20 districts. To raise your standing, you offer a settlement of higher percentage than that of your neighboring districts, and the offer is accepted.

Next time around, though, you find that you can't quite keep up with neighboring districts. As a result, you try to emphasize the fact that you provided the most generous percentage increase last time. This argument normally falls on deaf ears. The teacher negotiator will be stressing the need to maintain your comparative position. "We rank tenth," he'll say, "and your offer will drop us to the lowest quartile in the area. My teachers will never accept such a lousy settlement."

And so it goes — on both sides.

If a school board can maintain a favorable comparative position even with an unfavorable percentage increase, it will stress the after-settlement position; the teachers will stress the unfavorable comparison relating to the percentage of increase. In other words, no matter what a district offers, the teacher negotiator can always find a basis for alleging that the teachers are disadvantaged vis-a-vis their neighbors. If a district pays the lowest salaries, the need to improve its position will be emphasized.

No earthshaking strategic conclusions follow from this, but some suggestions may be helpful. In the first place, most school districts — and most teacher organizations — are necessarily pattern followers, not pattern makers. What would be acceptable to one side for an early settlement is almost invariably unacceptable to the other. Early settlements involve the risk that subsequent settlements elsewhere will make the early settlement look bad. For this reason, the union normally will not settle early, except on terms the district cannot offer. In other words, there is usually no early settlement. In most districts, a lot of time is wasted in trying to get a settlement before the time is ripe, i.e. before a basis for comparison materializes.

In the second place, a district negotiator should pay attention to the basis for comparisons, even though union negotiators will always try to shift the basis next time to justify a better offer. If you settle on the basis of comparative data which are not likely to favor the union in the future, emphasize the comparison in such a way that you can use it advantageously next time. For example: Suppose the teachers want dental insurance in spite of the fact that no district in the area provides it. If you agree to provide individual dental insurance, other districts also will do so, and you soon will have lost your competitive edge. On the other hand, the union will try next time to get family coverage so that you "maintain your leadership." It may be perfectly appropriate for you to move in front on a particular item, but you should exact a price for this, e.g. explicit acceptance on the part of the teachers that you will remain behind on other items. In other words, don't negotiate particular items on which your school district lags behind other districts in isolation from those on which your district looks good (if you are behind on everything, of course, you have a problem).

It seldom is feasible to include in the agreement itself any mechanism for resolving the comparison problem. Some school districts have negotiated clauses that specify that the salary schedule shall be a certain rank in the district's geographical area, but such clauses are of dubious legality and practicality. Aside from the fact that they constitute a delegation of authority to set salaries, they tend to ignore the need to compare settlements as a whole.

As fringe benefits consume an increasingly larger share of settlement costs, there is a growing need for management to compare total packages instead of individual items. If you know how your district's total salary and welfare package compares to those of others, you can be less concerned about comparisons of individual items in the package. The amount devoted to a particular item, such as sabbatical leave, can be considered chiefly in terms of the preferences of your teachers as to how they want funds for their welfare to be allocated. From a management point of view, it need not be of great concern to pay more for insurance benefits if district over-all personnel costs are less. One persistent management problem, however, is the primitive state of comparing total packages.

The importance of comparisons is reflected in regional strategy. The state teacher organization, or any regional organization, tries to bring in the most generous settlement first. On the other hand, management hopes that contracts favorable to management will be negotiated first. The upshot is for the parties to wait — and then to reach agreement en masse as deadlines approach. Inasmuch as interdistrict differences are often negligible, there might as well be regional bargaining in many areas. Such bargaining appeals to teacher organizations, which cannot service a large number of small districts on an individual basis. It also may appeal to management, on the grounds that the costs of district autonomy in bargaining is not worth the minor differences in the agreements reached. Of course, settlements will be made on a regional basis and the comparison game will then be played between regions instead of school districts.

24.   Bargaining
Under Financial Duress

Suppose you are on a lifeboat carrying ten persons. Unfortunately, its capacity is only nine. Furthermore provisions are dwindling and someone has to be thrown overboard — and fast. Who shall it be?

Answer: The other guy.

That appears to be the unanimous answer, judging from California's experience since the enactment of Proposition 13. School revenues there are being reduced 9 to 15 percent below their anticipated 1978-79 levels; not since the Depression has there been such a widespread cutback on government expenditures, including those for schools. A look at school board reactions to Proposition 13 in California provides a good idea of what to expect from school systems that are under the financial ax.

As is common throughout the country, about 80 to 85 percent of school system expenditures in California are for salaries and fringe benefits. In most cases, therefore, districts must consider either a reduction in staff, a lower level of compensation, or some combination of the two.

Theoretically, boards that have to reduce expenditures first evaluate programs and then establish priorities. But the process is inevitably overshadowed by pressure from interest groups that want to shift the sacrifice to somebody else. For example, the most senior employees want a raise and are usually willing to accept layoffs — "by seniority," of course. Ordinarily, this approach would prevail except when it runs counter to affirmative action programs. The most recent hires tend to include a large proportion of minorities and females, and these groups are not reticent about protecting their rights. Their proposals as to who should be cut are to scrap seniority and use a lottery or some other procedure that doesn't emphasize seniority. In addition, personnel in special programs (teachers of the handicapped, gifted, disadvantaged) are appealing to parents to speak up for their children. Translation: Save our jobs; drop somebody else's.

The throw-the-other-fellow-overboard approach to the problem is not edifying, but neither is it unexpected. Most board members or school administrators caught in a similar squeeze probably would behave in the same way.

A key factor in any budget reducing plan is the role of the union. In most cases, it will favor raises even if they require layoffs. Layoffs adversely affect newer and younger employees who don't have much influence in the union. Furthermore, the union's *raison d'etre* is threatened more by a wage freeze than by layoffs. A no-raise situation makes members disenchanted with their union.

Next to salaries, one of the largest cost items in a typical district budget is likely to be welfare benefits, especially health and dental insurance. The escalation of health and dental costs in recent years is stimulating some districts to look for savings in this area. Inevitably, the next few years will bring greater interest in self-insurance for larger districts. There is no question about the potential economies, but any change to self-insurance will require overturning established relationships between carriers and unions. Some of the major carriers pay unions a "service fee" for explaining insurance benefits and options to their constituents. Existence of this relationship between unions and insurance companies will make a change to self-insurance more difficult, but the rising costs of conventional health insurance may force the issue.

Hard times also are creating a trend toward user charges. This movement is a pervasive and growing one. The concept of public education as a right available to everyone will remain, but its application increasingly will be limited to basic education. In the future, items such as summer and evening school, extracurricular activites, books and supplies, and field trips will be subject to fees more than they've ever been in the past.

Finally, any reduction in annual district revenues, whether due to Proposition 13 type legislation or other causes, will greatly increase the time and energy devoted to bargaining for these reasons:

1. When revenues are decreased, multi-year agreements become extremely difficult to get. Employee organizations will not want to lock themselves into multi-year contracts with no economic im-

provements in sight. Most union leaders would perceive such contracts as professional suicide.

2. Generally, it is more difficult to negotiate a distribution of sacrifices than a distribution of benefits. Union leaders are more likely to make an all-out effort to avoid catastrophe than they would to improve a good contract.

3. Unions will go to great lengths to broaden the scope of negotiations to cover layoffs, severance pay, bumping rights, and other items that become crucial in retrenchment situations. When budgets were increasing, there was little need to negotiate on these items. In a retrenchment situation, however, they are crucial.

Whatever the impact on the over-all budget, retrenchment generates increasing pressures to bargain every year—at least over economic issues. Paradoxically, a district with decreased revenues generally devotes more time to bargaining. True, the less money, the fewer options, and the fewer options, the less there is to negotiate. But this situation points up one of the biggest pitfalls in bargaining: the tendency to make concessions on the work rules to compensate for the district's inability to improve economic benefits. This is a road to disaster. The less money, the more imperative it becomes that a district remain able to operate efficiently.

Significantly, the economic necessity of taking certain actions does not relieve districts of the duty to bargain over them. Example: An increase in class size required by declining revenues does not relieve the district of the obligation to negotiate over the impact — on teachers — of increasing class size.

Perhaps the most crucial issue in a retrenchment is the ability of the board to establish rational priorities. Forced to choose among several competing pressure groups, the temptation is to cut all programs a certain percent. This is the easiest solution and has the political advantage of "treating everyone alike." Unfortunately, perhaps not everyone should be treated alike. The board's job, after all, is to make decisions, not to avoid them.

25. Specificity: Key to Preparing for Bargaining

Among lawyers, it is axiomatic that careful preparation of a case is essential to winning it. This axiom is, in many respects, even more important in board-teacher negotiations. The board negotiator's job is not simply to persuade an impartial judge to agree with him; it is to persuade an adversary to accept a settlement on terms acceptable to the board. This calls for careful preparation. The board negotiator may have to understand the teachers' position as well as they do in order to persuade them to modify it. To reject teacher proposals and then show that you don't understand them is an invitation to trouble.

Preparation will vary, depending upon whether a first agreement or the re-negotiation of a current agreement is involved. Because more and more districts have agreements, the following discussion will deal with preparations for a second or subsequent contract. Even so, most of the comments will be appropriate to a first-agreement situation, as well.

A basic point of departure is to review the effectiveness of the existing contract. Have any grievances been initiated under it? If so, what was the outcome? The grievance record should be reviewed carefully. Such review should include careful study of grievances that did not go to arbitration and even those that were not pursued at a formal level.

Frequently, grievances involve clauses that are not clear. If this is the case, the administration should be prepared for teacher proposals on such clauses. At the same time, the management team should prepare proposals that clearly provide what management needs to administer the schools effectively.

The review of the current agreement should not be limited to grievance evaluation. The administration must make sure it is not prohibited by the agreement from taking any actions which are needed for the welfare of the system. The absence of teacher grievances, or even of expressed dissatisfaction with the existing agreement, may be due to administrative acceptance of undesirable policies. It may also be due to the fact that the circumstances that would trigger the application of an undesirable clause have not yet arisen. District salary policy frequently provides increments for additional study — regardless of the courses taken. Although the teachers may lack advanced training in their teaching fields, they may elect to take courses in administration. The school board may rightly feel uneasy about subsidizing training for would-be administrators, especially if the district already has more teachers with administration degrees than it would ever need. Meanwhile, the system may lack teachers who are familiar with important new curricula in their fields.

In this type of situation, routine acceptance of the status quo avoids teacher conflict, but only at the price of reduced educational effectiveness. What if the board no longer wants to pay this price?

Obviously, one of the first things it must do is to ascertain the facts concerning advanced study. It needs to know the practice in other districts, especially nearby ones. It can be extremely helpful to be able to document assertions that district teachers are taking an excessive amount of credit courses unrelated to their teaching fields. The board has to be prepared for arguments that every course can be so related, or who is to judge anyway? It must also be prepared for a "grandfather clause," to overcome the objection that teachers had the right to expect additional compensation for whatever courses they took in the past. The point is that the board has to be prepared for the problems of transition and the apparent inequities in moving to a new position.

Good preparation thus requires knowing more than just one's negotiating objectives. It requires the framing of a strategy to reach those objectives. Management must formulate proposals with some idea of the concessions that can be made without jeopardizing its objectives. This means reviewing teacher proposals to assess what they want that can be conceded, especially if tied to acceptance of management proposals.

In the 1960's, school management simply reacted to teacher proposals. Then, it began to initiate its own proposals, largely for bargaining purposes. Today, effective preparation calls for a more sophisticated approach, *i.e.* what changes are needed to make the schools more effective? This should be management's guide. The objective is not just an agreement, but an agreement that facilitates better education in the district.

Sometimes, the administration team is aware of a weakness in the current agreement but is reluctant, for tactical reasons, to do anything about it. For instance, a few years ago, I was preparing to re-negotiate a contract that provided 183 working days for everyone in the negotiating unit. The unit included department chairmen, who by tradition and practice had devoted five to 10 extra working days to departmental duties that could not be performed within the 183 days. Thus the chairmen were expected to come in during the summer to interview prospective teachers in their departments.

In getting ready to negotiate a new contract, we came to the conclusion that the chairmen probably could no longer be required to perform such extra duty without additional compensation. The chairmen had worked the extra days before the opening of school in the fall, but we were not sure of their intentions regarding work after the regular school year.

Our negotiating dilemma was obvious. If we insisted upon changing the contract to explicitly make the extra work part of the load assignment for chairmen, we might be alerting the chairmen to the probability that they were already entitled to additional compensation. If we merely incorporated the present language in the new agreement, without surfacing the issue of extra days, we would again be vulnerable to a grievance on the issue later on.

In this case, we decided to negotiate the change for several reasons. First, we felt that the agreement should spell out the board's right to the additional time. Secondly, we thought it unwise to assume that the teachers were unaware of their legal rights, or would remain unaware of them. And finally, since the chairmen had already put in the additional time before the opening of the school in the fall, we deemed it best to protect ourselves contractually before the teachers raised the issue in a grievance proceeding.

The point of the example is simple but fundamental: Don't assume that the present contract language is acceptable merely because the teachers have not complained about it. They may be waiting for the "right" moment to do so, or it may take a crisis to jolt them into full awareness of their rights.

The administrative staff, especially at the building level, should be asked to react to the present agreement and to suggest needed and desirable changes in it. The negotiating team should make sure that the administration is not avoiding essential actions because the actions are prohibited by the agreement. In asking the staff to review the agreement, it is important to get their reactions on a school-by-school basis. Frequently, a clause that is completely workable in one school is not in others.

The administration team should review organizationl publications, including state and national ones devoted to negotiations. A common practice is for the state teacher associations to develop model agreements, which are then submitted by local associations with little modification. Some state school board organizations, such as those in Michigan and New Jersey, have prepared analyses of the model agreements which can be very useful, even outside the particular states involved. These analyses raise questions about the teacher proposals which may be overlooked by a negotiating team.

Some of the most important material to be assembled and studied are copies of agreements recently negotiated in the area. The single most important influence upon negotiated agreements are the other agreements negotiated in the area. Admittedly, this isn't very helpful to districts that negotiate first, or before a pattern is clear, but not many districts can be first. At any rate, once a pattern is clear, it is extremely difficult to deviate unfavorably from it without good reason.

Teachers invariably want some items because other districts allegedly have them, *i.e.* you are being "hardnosed" not to concede them. At the same time, the management team will typically reject some proposals, partly on the grounds that no other district in the area has made this particular concession. A teacher proposal should not be accepted merely because it has been accepted elsewhere; management should not always refuse to be the first to make a particular concession. But management should know what has been done elsewhere and not rely upon the oral assurances of teacher negotiators. There is no safe substitute for the actual agreements from other districts.

The best time to review nearby agreements is before they become an issue in your district. What were the important concessions by management in these arguments? By the teachers? Are your circumstances different, thereby requiring a different solution? Sometimes you will see clauses that would be detrimental in your own system; an informal call to a nearby system may reveal facts about the concession that will be very helpful if the issue arises in your situation.

The differentials for guidance counselors in another district, for example, may be much higher than you deem appropriate. An informal call may reveal that their work-day or work-year is much longer than yours, even though the differences are not reflected in the agreement. The negotiator who can say, "I realize there's an hour duty-free lunch period in the Smithville agreement, but that is due solely to the fact that almost all of their students have to eat lunch at home, whereas our students eat in school," is not likely to have much trouble on the item.

Money items should be reviewed carefully. The district team should have its computations available in the all-too-likely event that its cost figures are much higher than the teachers'.

A frequent issue with respect to money is where and how to find any in the budget for negotiating unexpected, last-minute concessions that must or should be made. Obviously, any budget line labeled "reserve for negotiations" would be as good as gone, so the administration has to adopt other means. The most common is to budget, in certain areas, for more then you need, if pressed (but not more than you could sensibly use). This approach is defensible, but don't go to the same well too often. After all, teacher negotiators can analyze school budgets about as well as administrators can. As they say on the basketball court: "Move it around."

Changes in the cost of living, in the consumers' price index, and in other economic indicators should also be reviewed and be available in handy form. At the same time, don't load yourself down with a great mass of paper; it's very disconcerting to search for some document while 10 or 12 persons on both teams are impatiently staring at you.

Some negotiators like to have the teacher proposals in a three-ring binder, with a tab for each proposal. Relevant material can then be inserted next to any item with a minimum of effort. The teacher proposals should be annotated, so that you can make a systematic response to each item. It is also desirable to have counterproposals available, with fall-back positions, if any, clearly outlined for handy reference. A negotiator should not rely upon memory to make sure that he has covered every important aspect of a given proposal. This may call for the development of a checklist. to make sure nothing has been overlooked. All of this, obviously, must be set up well in advance of table negotiations.

In addition to being prepared on the substantive issues, the management team needs to develop its position on several procedural and policy matters. First, it should agree upon the mechanics of its own operations. This covers the designation of a spokesman, if only one is to be used. Also needed: assignment of the recording function; identification of any data needed and the format in which it is to be presented at the negotiating table, and the preparation of looseleaf binders for the negotiating team. The management team should review its position on the time and place for negotiations, negotiations schedules, caucus procedures, the order in which issues will be negotiated and the mechanics for recording tentative agreements. It is also advisable to provide each member of the management team with copies of the pertinent legislation, school board policy books and teacher proposals.

Ordinarily, a single spokesman should be designated. Other members of the team should help to develop the administration's position and be accorded specific duties related to data gathering or observations or both. Some teams use structured work sheets. These work sheets are forms which outline the proposal; summarize the present data and present practice; set forth the proposals of the parties, in order, with appropriate comments; and sum up the final agreement on the proposal. Such worksheets are helpful in future negotiations and may be crucial in grievance proceedings as well.

Perhaps the most important aspect of preparation is to see it in the proper perspective. Adequate preparation is like insurance. You may not need it, but it's far better to have it and not need it than to need it and not have it. Realistically, the outcome of negotiations doesn't always depend upon adequate preparation. After all, if two opposing lawyers are both perfectly prepared, one of them is still going to lose. In negotiations, preparation is more complex, because it requires giving careful thought to possible outcomes where both sides can win, or at least make that claim with some semblance of accuracy. Where there is this kind of preparation, sometimes just on one side, it is often enough to ensure a successful outcome to negotiations.

26. Role Reversal: Teacher Unions as Management

School boards and administrators are often unaware of the fact that unions, acting in the role of management, must negotiate collective bargaining agreements with unions representing the employees of the union. For example, the National Education Association, as an employer (and one that employs more employees than do most school districts), must bargain with two employee unions representing NEA's professional staff.

The NEA Association of Field Service Employees (AFSE) represents about 75 field representatives (organizers and negotiators) in the regional offices, and the NEA Staff Organization (NEASO) Local 2380 of the Communications Workers of America, represents about 400 NEA employees, professional and non-professional, who are assigned to NEA's Washington, D.C., headquarters. The following is based upon the AFSE and NEASO contracts in effect from June 1, 1975 to May 31, 1978.

The contracts NEA has with its union of union organizers and its union of Washington-based staff should be interesting to school board members and superintendents, since they reveal the extent to which NEA practices as management what it preaches as a union. They should also be interesting to local teachers, who, after all, foot the bill for the benefits won by NEA's unionized staff. Chances are, however, that neither school officials nor local teachers ever have seen a NEASO or AFSE contract. NEA has never disseminated to its members the contracts it has negotiated with its own employees, nor are copies of these contracts available to the membership for the asking.

NEA has good reason for not disseminating its own union contracts to either school boards or local teachers. On the one hand, the contracts are generous, to say the least. That could be awkward when, for example, NEA urges teachers in Mississippi, who average $8,338 a year (and some of whom are afforded no sick leave at all),

149

to increase their NEA dues so that NEA's own "Instruction and Professional Development Specialists" can be paid $10,550 to $33,022 in 13 steps for a 37^1/$_2$-hour workweek (plus a lump sum salary payment of up to $1,150 but not less than $750); plus very generous paid leave (administrative, annual, bereavement, jury duty, military, parental, personal, sabbatical and sick); plus liberal medical, dental and life insurance; plus 11 paid holidays treated as working days; plus generous travel allowances; plus a host of other benefits that few if any teachers ever have enjoyed. On the other hand, the contracts show NEA maintaining some important management prerogatives — a fact that could embarrass NEA when telling local teacher unions to demand that school boards give up similar prerogatives to association negotiators.

Furthermore, some items in NEA agreements with its own employees run squarely counter to association bargaining rhetoric at the local level. The AFSE contract, for example, includes a job description, which is more than can be said of most board-union contracts. The AFSE job description is for an "organization specialist." Because this is the "benchmark position" in the union, it is analogous to including a job description for teachers in an agreement — something that school boards could consider. After all, if they specify precisely what teachers are to be paid, why not also specify as precisely as possible what boards ought to receive for their money? Obviously, a local teacher union that is resisting the inclusion of job descriptions could be embarrassed by the fact that its NEA negotiator was employed under a contract which included job descriptions.

The contracts also reveal clearly that NEA does not practice what its local affiliates preach to school boards: Supervisors and management personnel are not included in any NEA bargaining unit and are not covered by any collective contract. In other words, as NEA would have it, supervisors and management personnel should have bargaining rights — only as long as they work for school districts, not for the NEA. This inconsistency can be laid to NEA's realization, as an employer, that it could not function effectively, or *as* effectively, if it agreed to these demands, which NEA's own locals frequently make to school boards.

School boards may also be interested in the manner in which NEA's employee contracts deal with inflation. First, both of NEA's employee union contracts provide regular employees with one-shot lump sum payments in addition to the regular salary schedule. Although mandated by the contract, these payments are not incorporated into the schedule. The lump sum payments are made only to those who were regular employees on the effective date of the agreement; persons employed subsequent to that date are not eligible for the lump sum payments.

In this way, NEA provides a salary increase without incorporating it into the regular schedule — a good idea for school districts (where almost every item of compensation is incorporated into the regular schedule). Example: Inflation may justify a substantial increase, but what will happen if prices stabilize or even decline? If every salary payment is incorporated into the regular schedule, school boards that over-estimated inflation are faced eventually with having to negotiate a salary reduction, an extremely difficult thing to do. A lump sum payment obviates this need and puts the burden on the employee to request inclusion of the payment in the next contract — instead of on management to take it out. For NEA, this technique also has the effect of giving NEA members an erroneously deflated impression of what NEA is paying its own employees.

NEA's contracts with its own employees provided cost-of-living increases (in 1976 and 1977) of 50 percent of the percentage increase shown in the nationally published cost and price indexes, not to exceed 4 percent of the salary schedule each year. Such a formula — not necessarily NEA's, however — can be useful in negotiating multi-year contracts that provide both stability for the employer and reasonable protection from inflation for the employees.

Significantly, neither of NEA's employee agreements includes a preamble. There is not a word about teaching (or union organizing) being a profession, or about the welfare of children (or of the dues-paying membership), or any of the other non-contractual rhetoric that NEA advocates at the local level. And school boards haggling over how much to pay teachers for advanced degrees or graduate credits may be interested to know that advanced training is not used as a basis for salary increments in either of NEA's contracts with its employees. NEA leaders, apparently, are not really convinced of the value of more education.

In spite of these and a few other "pro-management" items, however, NEA's employee contracts over-all provide salaries and fringe benefits that probably would shock most dues-paying teachers, who have absolutely no idea what "their employees" are getting. Needless to say, the concessions to union security are indeed ironclad. The major concession is to the union shop — NEA employees must join the union or lose their jobs (a far cry from the 1960's when the NEA opposed such "union tactics").

Although the work-week is only $37^1/_2$ hours, with several qualifications that undoubtedly reduce the number in practice, all NEA employees are granted time off each year with pay to attend union general membership meetings. NEASO representatives as a group receive a total of 20 hours off with pay every two pay periods (four weeks) to attend union meetings. In addition, the NEA provides a total of 75 hours time off with pay every two pay periods for individuals (designated by the union) to conduct union business. Because each pay period is 75 hours, this clause alone requires the NEA to pay half of a full-time salary for staff union purposes.

The NEA also is obliged to provide its employee union with office space free of charge, and to employ the union's six top officers regardless of their relative seniority, provided that they are qualified to perform in any job category. This tender loving care for the staff union undoubtedly is related to NEA's concern that its local affiliates be securely entrenched — and to the great embarrassment that would result if the NEA provided less organizational security than its affiliates were demanding of local boards. Of course, the over-all result is highly conducive to inefficiency, but obviously teachers at the local level are not going to make this an issue.

The generous level of NEA employee benefits can be illustrated by provisions relating to sabbatical leave. After five years of continuous employment, an employee is eligible for a six-month sabbatical at full salary or a 12-month sabbatical at half salary. All benefits are continued for employees on sabbatical. Employees going on sabbatical need not return to work for the NEA, but if they don't return, they are liable to the NEA for salary paid during the sabbatical. Employees going on sabbatical at half pay can contribute to the NEA retirement plan at half pay, in which case NEA will do likewise. The same option, incidentally, is available to employees who go on leave without pay; they also have the option of buying back time lost during their unpaid leave.

Some sections in the contracts reflect an indifferent NEA attitude to family life. For example: Article 3, Section 1 of the AFSE contract reads as follows: "The NEA and the Union agree that the provisions of this agreement shall be applied without discrimination on the basis of race, color, religion, sex, marital status, *lifestyle, sexual preference,* age, national origin, membership in the Union, or participation in the lawful activities of the Union, provided that nothing contained in this section shall be construed to prevent the NEA from implementing any provision of this agreement which affords preferential treatment to an individual on the basis of one or more of the aforesaid factors." (Italics added.) Curiously enough, the italicized phrases are not included in the NEASO agreement. Apparently, NEA can "discriminate" on the basis of sexual preferences or lifestyle if the employee works at NEA headquarters in Washington, but not if the employee is located elsewhere.

The NEA's indifference to family life also is illustrated by Section 4 (A) of the AFSE agreement, in which the NEA agrees to reimburse an employee for vouchers submitted for travel and subsistence expenses incurred by a "companion" up to $500 for each contract year in which the employee travels on official NEA business and remains overnight in connection therewith for more than 45 nights.

Another illustration is Article 24, Section (B) of the AFSE agreement, which provides that: "A male employee shall be entitled, upon request, to a leave to begin at any time between the birth of a child to his wife *or whom he has fathered* and one year thereafter." (Italics added). In other words, you can get a parental leave at NEA by impregnating someone else's wife. I would not recommend that school boards adopt such a policy; the aggrieved husband may live in the district, too.

This discussion has been confined to a few items in a lengthy contract. Nevertheless, this brief review may prompt school boards and superintendents — and teacher locals, too — to inform themselves as best they can about the kinds of deals that the NEA and the AFT (and their state affiliates) are negotiating with their own employees. School boards won't find a model contract to propose to their own teachers, but they will learn a lot that will be helpful in deflating the teacher union rhetoric at the bargaining table.

Author's Note:

In preparing the foregoing material on the National Education Association's contracts with its own employee unions, I asked the NEA to provide me with its estimate of the value of fringe benefits for NEA employees. My request was rejected. In December, 1978, I asked NEA for copies of its new contracts with unions representing NEA staff. This request was ignored completely. These actions are disturbing to me, an NEA life member for 17 years. If NEA's own members cannot find out from their own officers and staff how those officers and staff members are spending member dues, it would appear as if these leaders have become a law unto themselves. It is clearly cause for concern when the largest national teacher union finds it necessary to treat such information as "staff privileged," as it has for several years. Significantly, NEA — possibly the nation's largest educational publisher — never has published its staff contracts in any membership publication.

The NEA's refusal to provide me the information I requested was based ostensibly upon danger of misrepresentation (apparently by me). To protect NEA from such misrepresentation, I offered to provide NEA with an advance copy of any material I wrote for publication concerning the fringe benefits it provides NEA employees, and to publish an NEA rejoinder next to such material. NEA's refusal suggests that its refusal to provide the information requested because it might be abused is not a good faith refusal. Perhaps the real danger, as NEA sees it, is not that the facts would be misrepresented but that, for the first time, rank-and-file NEA members would know what they are.

I believe, in any case, that any NEA member is entitled to information on how NEA is spending members' dues, and without screening or cross-examination by an NEA officer or staff member — regardless of rank. Perhaps NEA officers and staff who are so zealous in urging school boards to be open and to share information will follow such a policy with their own membership, which is paying the bills just as taxpayers do for teacher contracts. Unless this is done, teachers will be ripped off — not by school boards but by their own union officers and staff.

— Myron Lieberman

27. Time Management in Bargaining

In many districts, the most disturbing aspect of collective bargaining is the enormous amount of time it takes. Few, if any, other aspects of bargaining seem to catch districts as unprepared as the ongoing need to devote substantial board and staff time to the process

Any experienced negotiator can cite several factors that can and do affect the time required for bargaining: the size of the district, the sophistication of the parties, the history of bargaining in the district, the timing of the negotiations, the state aid situation, the economic environment, and so on. Some of these variables are subject to control by school boards (for example, whether the board's chief negotiator is a knowledgeable professional usually is within the scope of board control). Another set of factors, while not subject to unilateral control by the school board, can have considerable effect on the amount of time devoted to bargaining. To illustrate: Ordinarily it would be futile to begin negotiating in November for a contract that won't take effect until the following July or September. Boards and unions alike should realize that there would be no immediate pressure to settle and no patterns to follow. Furthermore, the fact that so much time is available would encourage long laundry lists of demands, many of which would never be made, let alone bargained, if bargaining were confined to a month or less before the current agreement expires.

A third set of factors, such as the general economic environment, is not subject to board control or influence. Controversy may arise over how to interpret or weigh these elements, such as the cost of living, but no way exists for a board to change the circumstances themselves.

In my personal experience, the time required to negotiate an agreement has ranged from a low of one meeting to over 24 months of protracted meetings, including the impasse procedures.

The presence or absence of an existing agreement is, of course, an important consideration that bears upon the amount of time needed for bargaining. The process of reaching a first agreement, in fact, frequently requires considerable time merely for the parties to get to know each other.

Even in re-negotiating current agreements, the course of bargaining can vary enormously. Much depends upon the range and language of the current agreement. If it is comprehensive and loosely worded, and being re-negotiated long before any deadline is in sight, bargaining may drag on indefinitely. If, on the other hand, the existing agreement is tightly drafted and meets the basic needs of both parties, they may not need to re-negotiate anything but the economic package.

Today, especially in states with bargaining laws, teacher bargainers are likely to be full-time field representatives of the union. Like their administrative counterparts, they are not paid by the hour. After negotiating several contracts a year for several years, their main concern becomes how to get the bargaining over with as quickly as possible, consistent with what the teachers will accept without serious dissatisfaction.

Some teacher bargainers are employed on a per-diem or per-session basis. In 1977, the New York State United Teachers (NYSUT) NYSUT employed 80 full-time and 25 part-time negotiators. Full-time representatives typically had responsibility for four contracts; part-time negotiators were paid $35 per session. Part-timers, consequently, may be motivated to drag out the bargaining, as may be board negotiators who are paid on a per-diem or per-hour basis.

If the parties are afraid to settle until the question of state aid is resolved, it usually is futile to begin extensive bargaining on either economic or non-economic items, since the resolution of the former is often tied to resolution of the later.

Probably the best way to conserve time is to use a combination of incentives. This might entail providing released time for bargaining during the school day for a small number of teacher representatives. If the district grants released time, its action should be conditioned upon agreement by the union not to press for bargaining before there is a good chance of success, and also upon significant progress in bargaining during the school day. Frequently, the teacher union negotiator welcomes such an arrangement, since it helps obviate the need to appear in several places during the same evening. In any event, boards should not provide released time until there is pressure on the union to bargain seriously. Negotiating sessions "on school time" without some appropriate concession from the other side is usually a tactical mistake.

A great deal of time at the bargaining table can be saved if the board negotiator insists that the consultation procedure be used during the year. If the parties are in regular communication, surprises (hence delay) can be averted. If teachers weren't concerned sufficiently within the year to raise an issue during consultation, board bargainers should not feel obligated to devote a great deal of time to that issue. Bargainers who are surprised are not prepared, and when they are not prepared, they tend to equivocate and delay. Of course, the same obligation to use the consultation procedure (and, consequently, avoid surprises) applies to the board also.

Board negotiators should avoid devoting excessive time to estimating costs of union proposals that are not offered seriously, or with any genuine expectation that will be taken seriously. When union demands are submitted, board negotiators should request their estimated costs. If teachers haven't developed such estimates, board negotiators are relatively safe in assuming teachers are not especially serious about the demand. When bargaining gets serious, teachers typically have a good idea of what costs how much. In any case, the public relations value of estimating the expense of outrageous demands usually is not worth the effort, at least at the beginning of bargaining. But if, as deadlines approach, teachers are holding our for excessive demands, management can and should be prepared to cite the costs to the public.

Once a demand has been rejected and explained, it is important to avoid listening to the same proposals and arguments. The district negotiator should make it clear that, unless something new has been added, he has stated the district position and is not about to rehash it. Of course, the item must be covered thoroughly, but sheer repetition is to be minimized — it can't be avoided altogether.

If the union is offering a new proposal or a counterproposal, it should be considered carefully to determine whether it satisfies district objections. It is also important to make sure the demands submitted constitute the entire package. If the answer is negative, it may be desirable to stop bargaining until the district has the entire package. This should not be done in a way that encourages the submission of additional demands. Occasionally, it may be advantageous to bargain on a late proposal — as distinguished from a counterproposal — but only if the union understands that an exception is being made. If you've overlooked a demand of your own, this is the time to introduce it. If the union is allowed to introduce additional demands at will, the board will be severely disadvantaged in bringing bargaining to a conclusion.

If there is good communication during the year, agreements should be consummated in four to six weeks (one to three sessions per week) of serious bargaining on both sides, and even more quickly if released time for bargaining is provided during the school day. Long periods between meetings usually are a mistake because considerable time will be needed merely to agree on the status of bargaining when it was suspended. Two consecutive days near the expiration of an agreement are worth 10 to 20 days six months before expiration. Preparation away from the table is extremely important in conserving time at the table — but not if negotiators have to repeat the preparation process because a long period has elapsed between preparation and bargaining.

The central considerations in conserving time are assigning a proper value to time and accurately identifying the factors that waste or conserve it in the bargaining process. Negotiators who do not respect and value their own time do not expect their adversaries to do so. They will conclude, and rightly so, that it isn't worth much.

28. Additional Suggestions and Sources on the Bargaining Process

Collective Bargaining and Contracts, Bureau of National Affairs, Washington, D.C. Although oriented to the private sector, this information service includes practical suggestions on bargaining.

Wollett, Donald H., and Robert H. Chanin: *The Law and Practice of Teacher Negotiations,* Bureau of National Affairs, Washington, D.C., 1974. This manual includes useful material on most of the issues discussed in this text. Although somewhat employee oriented, it provides an excellent discussion of many practical questions faced by boards and board negotiating teams in the bargaining process. It includes a substantial amount of material on legal issues, strategy and tactics, and the substantive issues involved in bargaining.

RECURRING ISSUES AT THE TABLE

29.   Managerial Discretion in Negotiations

Managerial prerogatives or managerial discretion is one of the most troublesome areas in collective negotiations. Even the semantics are troublesome. Some negotiators prefer "managerial discretion" to "managerial prerogatives," mainly because the former tends to be less offensive to teachers. But semantics aside, the issues remain. To what extent should school management accept limitations upon its discretionary power in transfers, assignments, schedules, work day, work year and promotions, to cite some of the more crucial areas of controversy?

It is important to recognize that every collective agreement per se is a limitation on managerial discretion. If you agree to a salary schedule for a specific time, such as one year, you have lost your discretion to change salaries during that time. This may not seem to be of any importance, but it has had important practical application in some unusual situations. For example, districts that have lost tax levies or revenues could not reduce teacher salaries during the year as they could have done, legally at least, in the absence of a collective agreement. And there have been cases where districts have negotiated salary schedules so low that the districts were not able to hire any new teachers. In such cases, the districts had to get acceptance from the teacher organization to raise salaries.

Most administrators need not worry about such unusual emergencies. These situations, however, do illustrate one important caveat. In negotiating on work rules, the adverse consequences of giving up discretion over a decision made only once in several years may be much more important than the adverse consequences of relinquishing control over decisions made every day. It may be far more harmful to lose discretion over the appointment of the high school principal than to lose it over how teachers will be pre-empted to cover classes in the absence of substitutes.

Administrative discretion is involved in questions such as these: Should we agree to promote the most senior of all qualified candidates? Should summer school or extra-curricular assignments with extra compensation be based upon seniority or upon qualifications? Or should such opportunities be rotated among those qualified, again limiting administrative discretion? And so on.

Ideally, the basis of agreement at the bargaining table should be balanced by two considerations. One is whether discretion on the issue is essential to effective management. The other is the importance of the issue to the employees. For example, discretion in assigning classes to individual teachers is important to management in order to maximize full utilization of personnel. Without such discretion, management might be forced to employ additional teachers whenever it reached its contractual limits with existing staff. Obviously, school management would be in a weak position with the taxpayers if additional teachers had to be employed even though the present staff was not assigned a full load. Suppose, for example, that teachers cannot be assigned more then five classes and preparations. Teacher X has four classes and three preparations. No other class requiring the same preparation needs to be covered. What then?

It seems to me there is merit in limiting the number of preparations. A limitation of three is fairly common; less than three would unduly restrict management in many systems. Thus the issue is not simply management's prerogative to assign; there can be discretion within limits that should enable management to function effectively. This does not mean, for example, that circumstances never arise in which it might be desirable to have a teacher assigned four preparations. It means instead that an agreement to limit managerial discretion to three preparations may be a reasonable price — for there are or may be real costs involved — for employee security on this issue. Note that there are other ways to resolve the problem; for example, teachers could be paid an additional amount for added preparations. In other words, there would be no limit on the number of preparations that could be required, but the teachers would still have some protection on the issue.

Administrators from the pre-bargaining era tend to scoff at the need for such clauses and lament the "union" attitude of teachers. Yet a little reflection suggests that limitations on discretion have always been part of our political philosophy. All of our public officials, from the President on down, have to work within a set of legal constraints on their discretionary powers. No doubt some of these constraints are unwise; on the other hand, perhaps there are areas in which constraints should, but do not, exist.

At any level, the problem has to be resolved on the merits of the specific claims for or against specific areas of managerial discretion. Merely lamenting a general trend toward the erosion of administrative discretion is really irrelevant to concrete bargaining. Furthermore, careful thought must be given to what will replace administrative discretion. Sometimes the most honest posture is not that administrative discretion is good, but that it is better than any proposed alternative, such as seniority or rotation. If a decision is discretionary, mistakes can be corrected. In any case, if you give up discretion that subsequent experience shows you need, insist upon it in the next contract. Do not buy the argument, which is demonstrably false, that management can never regain what it has once lost. It's difficult, but such "give-aways" can be recovered.

Many difficult problems arise because of favoritism dressed up as needed discretion. Favoritism is frequently not perceived as such by an administrator, especially one who has never had to defend his decisions at the bargaining table. He may believe that teacher A is really better able to teach advanced students every year, but the teachers left to struggle year in and year out with slow classes may have quite a different view. It is often salutary for administrators to be required to defend such decisions in negotiations, provided that you do not end up negotiating a specific grievance. Granted, such defenses may mean calling attention to embarrassing individual cases, but that is less harmful than never requiring an administrator to account for the use of his discretion.

One common problem of negotiations involves the distinction between "qualified" and "most qualified." Suppose the issue is extra-curricular assignments for compensation. Suppose also that the extra-curricular positions are represented by the union. The union may propose that those appointments be based upon seniority from among those "qualified." The administration will probably argue that it wants the freedom to choose not just any "qualified" person but the "most qualified." This can be a troublesome issue, especially if the staff is upset because teachers with much less seniority were recently promoted ahead of veteran teachers. The teachers' attitude tends to be that if a senior teacher can do the job, the teacher should be promoted regardless of fine distinctions among those qualified.

Here again, solutions have to be *ad hoc*. Suppose there is an opening for head football coach. You may not want to appoint the assistant coach, who has applied for the position, but you don't want to assert that he is unqualified in order to keep him from getting the position. This is the kind of problem that may not arise often, but when it does, contractual protection for managerial discretion is absolutely essential.

On the other hand, what about the teacher who has had an extracurricular assignment for several years? Should there come a time when he can count upon his reappointment in this capacity as long as he performs adequately? Some stability and assurance of continued employment seem reasonable here as well as in regular assignments. One solution is to permit a teacher to keep such an assignment after he has had it two or three years without any negative evaluations and as long as he performs competently.

The larger the system, the more pressure there is for automatic rules, such as rotation or seniority, to replace administrative discretion. Many informed organization leaders do not see anything wrong in this, apart from the pressure they inevitably feel from teachers unhappy about the exercise of administrative discretion. In fact, many administrators are finding out that things function about as well, or even better in some cases, when a measure of seniority or rotation is introduced. The skies simply do not fall in all cases.

Some administrative personnel even prefer automatic solutions to discretionary ones. As with merit rating, administrators often feel they must support "managerial discretion" publicly, while they are relieved privately, because they do not have to separate the sheep from the goats — or the qualified from the most qualified.

30. Statutory Benefits and Teacher Contracts

Collective bargaining establishes a dual system of employee benefits: contractual and legislative. In most states, the legislatures unfortunately ignored this duality when they enacted public employee bargaining laws.

Every state has some legislation dealing with teacher welfare. State retirement systems are probably the most important example, but minimum salaries, tenure, sick leave and duty-free lunch periods are also common subjects of state legislation. A few states have even enacted statutory grievance procedures. Board negotiators should carefully consider the relationships between statutory benefits and the negotiating process.

Teacher welfare statutes frequently pose difficult problems at the bargaining table. For example, suppose your state law mandates that teachers receive at least a 30-minute, duty-free lunch period a day. At the bargaining table, the teachers ask for a 60-minute, duty-free lunch period. If you decide you cannot provide more than the statutory benefit, you are likely to be asked to include the statutory benefit in the contract. "After all, you are only giving us what we legally have anyway." This will be the argument of the teacher representatives. They will often urge that statutory benefits be included in the contract to make the contract more attractive to teachers, presumably without any substantive concession by management. What should be management's reaction to such apparently harmless requests?

First, the board negotiator should be absolutely clear on a central issue. Incorporating a statutory benefit into a collective bargaining agreement is not just a meaningless gesture. Such incorporation may constitute an extremely important concession to teachers. To see why, one must compare the benefits of a contractual, as distinguished from a statutory, right.

Hopefully, you will always accord teachers a duty-free lunch period, whether they are entitled to it by statute or by contract. Suppose, however, a controversy arises as to whether a teacher's right to a duty-free lunch period was in fact violated. If the right is only a statutory one, the teacher is not likely to pursue an alleged violation of it by the administration. The reason is that the teacher would have to bring a lawsuit against the school district. Most teachers would be unwilling to initiate such a lawsuit. Furthermore, the statutes seldom prescribe or even authorize any remedy for the teacher; even if they did, the remedies in many situations would not compensate for the time and expense of a lawsuit.

By contrast, consider the case of teachers who have the duty-free lunch period pursuant to a collective agreement. In most cases, such teachers will have recourse to a grievance procedure, terminating in binding arbitration by an impartial third party, to remedy any alleged violation of their contractual rights. In the early years of collective bargaining, teachers were reluctant to utilize such grievance procedures, but this reluctance is rapidly disappearing. Contractual grievance procedures are far less costly and less time consuming than lawsuits. Furthermore, the bargaining organization can often process a grievance in ways that it could not process a lawsuit. For instance, courts are not likely to permit the teacher organization to file a lawsuit alleging that John Smith did not get a duty-free lunch period on September 15, 1970. Smith would ordinarily be required to file such a lawsuit himself. True, Smith's organization could provide the necessary funds in either case. However, a teacher organization, like individual teachers, is much less likely to initiate a lawsuit than a grievance to remedy an alleged violation of teacher rights.

In short, the board negotiator who agrees to include statutory benefits in a collective agreement can be making a very significant concession to teachers. This does not mean such a concession should never be made, but the board negotiator should not delude himself into thinking he didn't give the teachers anything they didn't have anyway. He has given them a contractual remedy that may be crucial in specific situations. Teachers initiate and process many grievances that would be ignored if the teachers' only recourse was a lawsuit.

Suppose the teacher negotiator does not pretend that no concession is involved but tries to negotiate for the concession on its merits. His argument might sound like this: "Look, it's true we would be getting additional procedural rights if you include these statutory benefits in the contract. However, what's wrong with that? The reason we have a grievance procedure in the first place is to facilitate speedy resolution of grievances.If you really believe in this principle, why not apply it to statutory benefits? Why force a teacher to file a lawsuit if the teacher sincerely believes he's not getting a duty-free lunch period or some other statutory benefit?"

This argument has some merit. It overlooks, however, some cogent considerations. In the first place, there is always the possibility of abuse of a grievance procedure. The more costly the grievance procedure is to teachers, the less likely it will be used for harassment of the administration or for organizational propaganda. If you reduce the risk to the teachers in initiating grievances, you are increasing the likelihood that teachers will initiate invalid as well as valid grievances. A board negotiator should think carefully before making a concession that has this effect.

Actually, teachers still do not always appreciate the advantages of contractual rights and remedies over statutory ones. In part, this slow awakening is due to a pre-negotiations ideology, when teachers put most of their efforts to improve teacher welfare into state legislation. Today, as teachers become more sophisticated about their ability to enforce their rights, there is much greater emphasis upon embodying them in collective contracts with boards of education. A statutory right seems more secure, but contractual rights are usually much easier to enforce.

The preceding comments should not be construed as suggesting that it is always undesirable for board negotiators to include statutory benefits in a contract. Consider however, the *quid pro quo* in these cases as well as the particular circumstances in the district. Often, the board itself will want certain statutory provisions in the contract, e.g. the statutes may prescribe certain penalties for teachers who jump their contracts. It can be to the board's advantage to have such statutory obligations of teachers included in the contract. Therefore, if you want explicit inclusion of statutory teacher obligations in the contract, you can sometimes reach agreement on the basis that either both parties get inclusion of the statutory provisions desired by each, or neither does.

If a statute provides that teachers have to renew their contracts by a certain date, incorporation of the statutory requirement in the contract would have at least two specific advantages to the board. First, it would be a valuable means of publicizing the obligation among teachers. Second, and more important, inclusion would effectively eliminate a likely teacher defense in case of a dispute. Suppose a teacher does not submit a renewal of his contract before the deadline, and the board does not re-employ the teacher. Subsequently, the teacher may claim his job, alleging that the collective agreement takes precedence over the statute in governing the relationships between the parties. This is virtually certain to happen if the collective agreement can be interpreted in the teacher's favor on the point at issue. Obviously, if the collective agreement itself includes the statutory obligation of timely renewal, the teachers cannot rely upon the argument that the agreement takes precedence over the statute.

Board negotiators should be very careful about deciding what is an item of teacher welfare. A state law that requires schools to be in session 180 days a year does not constitute the legal work year for teachers. One could keep schools open for 180 days a year without having any particular teacher work more than 90 days. Of course the number of days required by state law for state aid or accreditation or whatever is often the crucial factor in how many days teachers are asked to work, but the items should not be confused. Another example relates to the length of the school day. A state law might require that schools be in session at least five hours to count a particular day toward state aid. Such a requirement would not mean that state law required teachers to work at least five hours a day. Obviously, schools could be kept open five hours a day by employing a large number of teachers who worked less than five hours a day. Unless board negotiators are very careful in this area, they may end up relying upon non-existent statutory conditions of employment.

There is merit in the view that the collective agreement should govern the relationships between the parties. But if the teachers make this argument, they should be required to accept the consequences of it. Among other things, this requires that teachers give up their statutory remedies for contractual rights. If, for example, you include a statutory duty-free lunch period or sick leave in the contract, the teachers should agree to waive any statutory remedies they have for alleged violations of these statutory rights. After all, the school administration should not have to contest an alleged violation both in a grievance proceeding and a court room. Statutory remedies for statutory rights, and contractual remedies for contractual rights — this should be the general approach of board negotiators. Avoid agreements that provide both statutory and contractual remedies for the same administrative act. The best way to do this is to avoid including statutory benefits in the collective agreement.

31.   Due Process and Arbitration Problems

Many public employers are under union pressure to include in their labor agreements "seniority" and "grievance and arbitration" provisions modeled upon those commonly found in private sector union contracts. The wide acceptance of such provisions in the private sector makes it hard to resist such demands. Indeed, it appears that increasing numbers of public employers are inserting seniority and/or grievance and arbitration provisions in their collective bargaining agreements. Use of private sector contract models in the public employment sphere, however, ultimately may prove to be a costly mistake.

The "due process" provisions of the U.S. Constitution's fifth and fourteenth amendments continue to generate court rulings against public employers whose decisions to discharge, discipline, or otherwise alter the status of their employees are considered by the courts to invade those employee's constitutionally protected "liberty" or "property" rights. Meanwhile, identical actions taken by private non-governmental employers continue to be practically immune from such judicial scrutiny. As a result of the "due process" constraints which already affect them, public employers which "merely" transport into their public sector labor agreements such well-established private sector principles as seniority clauses and grievance and arbitration provisions may be granting to their employees far greater rights, at far greater cost, than their private sector counterparts.

A public employee's possession of a "liberty" right does not depend upon tenure rights, contractual provisions, or length of service, but rather upon the seriousness of a public accusation upon the employee's standing in the community. Although the events giving

The material in this chapter was prepared by James Baird of Seyfarth, Shaw, Fairweather and Geraldson, Chicago, and Matthew R. McArthur of Pope, Ballard, Shepard & Fowle, Chicago.

This article originally appeared in the April 1976 edition of the *Journal of Law and Education*. Authority supporting the legal propositions referred to herein are set forth in the Journal's edition.

rise to a public employee's claim that his liberty has been unlawfully violated frequently arise in the employment context, the duties of the public employer in such a case are tested by standards unrelated to the structure and substance of the employment relationship itself, and therefore the liberty right concept will not be further discussed here.

Constitutional "due process" requirements also protect the "property" rights of public employees. Public employees do not possess protected property rights to their job merely by virtue of their employment relationship. However, a constitutionally protected "property" right to one or more attributes of public employment can arise from the structure and substance of the employment relationship. Property rights may arise, for example, from statutes such as those granting tenure or civil service protections; they may arise from individual agreement between the employing governmental unit and the employee involved; and they may arise without any formal agreement at all, if, in view of all of the surrounding circumstances, a court can be convinced that there was, in fact, an understanding that the employee would be accorded continued employment in his job. The breadth of the judicial decisions in this area strongly supports the conclusion that, when squarely confronted with the question, the courts will hold that a collective bargaining agreement between a public employer and a union representing that employer's public employees is sufficient to vest in those employees a constitutionally protected property interest in the employment conditions it establishes.

The Constitutional due process requirements which public employers must meet when dealing with the property rights of public employees can create special problems for the public employer which must negotiate contractual seniority rights and grievance arbitration provisions with a union representing its employees. On the one hand, the employer is faced with union demands for contract clauses such as "seniority" provisions, which are likely to expand still further the "property" rights of employees protected by the Constitution's due process requirements. On the other, the employer is also faced with demands for traditional grievance and arbitration provisions, which not only fail to resolve, but may actually aggravate the due process problems the employer must overcome. Obviously, a solution must be found.

Two possible solutions are immediately apparent. In the course of negotiations with the union the public employer can either seek to eliminate entirely the grievance and arbitration provisions from the collective bargaining agreement, or the employer may seek to alter its established grievance and arbitration procedures so that they will incorporate all the necessary due process requirements. While these solutions most certainly have some surface appeal, we believe that, upon analysis, they must both ultimately be rejected.

The exclusion of grievance and arbitration provisions from a labor agreement has a number of serious drawbacks. First, of course, it is virtually certain to meet with vigorous union opposition because such provisions are normally "must" items on the union's negotiating agenda. A complete rejection of such provisions during negotiations may easily frustrate agreement on other issues and perhaps even precipitate a work stoppage. Second, even if the employer has successfully excluded such provisions from the contract, it may find that it has only succeeded in moving from the proverbial "frying pan into the fire."

Undoubtedly, disputes will frequently arise concerning the contract's meaning and the parties' rights thereunder. With no sound contractual mechanism for resolving such disputes available, the frequent use of economic force by the union or the employees becomes a strong possibility. Obviously, the weighty nature of the two practical considerations will, in most cases, lead to the conclusion that an outright refusal to incorporate a grievance arbitration provision in a contract is undesirable.

Similarly, it is undesirable in our opinion to incorporate all the necessary due process requirements into a contractual grievance procedure. In the first place, because of the rapidly evolving state of the law in the due process area, any such attempt is likely to produce a document which is out-dated soon after it is negotiated. Second, a grievance and arbitration procedure containing "only" those due process requirements which some courts already require would be so cumbersome and unwieldy that it would cease to be an effective mechanism for resolving contractual disputes.[1]

A more realistic solution to the public employer's due process problem is the promulgation of a formal expedited hearing procedure for use in those cases where employee "property" interests are involved.[2] The expedited procedure should be written and published, but it should be separate and apart from the labor agreement so that it may be revised as frequently as necessary to meet the current judicial requirements. It should set forth in detail the manner in which the due process requirements are going to be met.[3] But most important, the procedure should be carefully designed so that at all times it retains its character as an expedited procedure. Such a procedure is of little use to management if it is not able to produce decisions within a reasonably short period ot time; hopefully within forty-eight hours of management's initial decision. While it is undoubtedly important to preserve constitutional rights, it is also important for the employer to be able to make and rely upon important decisions with a minimum of delay. Although any employee adversely affected should be allowed to retain counsel to represent him during the expedited hearing procedure, it should be made clear that the retention of counsel will not be permitted to delay the proceedings.

Adoption of a non-contractual expedited hearing procedure is likely to resolve many of a public employer's due process problems, but at least one remains. In the private sector, union contract grievance and arbitration provisions function effectively as a substitute for court litigation. When such provisions exist, the courts will not normally permit an employee to sue his employer over an alleged contract violation without first exhausting his rights under the grievance procedure. If, in the course of the grievance procedure, the employee's union settles the grievance, that settlement will be binding on him. And if the case has gone to arbitration, the arbitrator's award will be dispositive of the claim. Thus, as a practical matter, the chance that an alleged contract violation will end up in the courts is remote indeed.

It is questionable whether the presence of a grievance and arbitration procedure in a public sector union contract will have a similarly salutory effect. On the contrary, it must be remembered that although the origin of a public employee's right may be contractual, once established it becomes constitutionally protected. The treatment accorded the contractually protected rights of private sector employees by the courts, therefore, cannot safely be relied upon to forecast the treatment they will accord the constitutionally protected rights of public employees.

In a case arising out of the federal civil rights laws, the U.S. Supreme Court ruled that an employee who arbitrated a discrimination claim, and lost, could nonetheless get a complete new hearing in the courts because the employee was not seeking a "review" of the arbitrator's decision, but "[r]ather.... asserting a statutory right independent of the arbitration process."[4]

If the presence of statutory protection warrants imposing on an employer the burden of trying the same issue twice, what, then, is likely to be the result when the right in question is protected not merely by statute but by the Constitution itself? It may indeed be that a public employer, having created by a contract a number of constitutionally protected property rights, will be forced not only to arbitrate disputes concerning them, but to litigate the same matters in the courts even after it has prevailed in an arbitration proceeding.

To avoid the problem of repititious litigation, still further alternatives must be explored.

One alternative is the adoption of a grievance procedure without arbitration as the terminal step "where constitutionally protected property rights are arguably involved."Although this possibility is likely to be less objectionable to a union than complete elimination of a grievance procedure, it must still be recognized that its suggestion will generate a heated and hostile response. This possibility has the decided advantage of providing arbitration for certain contractual claims while at the same time further limiting the employer's exposure to repeated litigation of the same claim. It also, however, has serious drawbacks.

If the employer asserts that the subject of a grievance involves a constitutionally protected property right and is therefore excluded from arbitration, due process litigation in the courts may well be assured. Further, such an assertion may possibly prejudice the employer's position when that litigation does commence. Moreover, the employee's failure to assert that a property right is involved is probably not sufficient to stop a court, in a subsequent proceeding, from finding that such a right did exist and that due process litigation is proper in spite of the prior arbitration award.

A second alternative would be the addition of a new step in the grievance procedure between the normal last step prior to arbitration and the arbitration step itself. In this new, additional arbitration step, a joint employer-union committee could be formed to meet and consider whether or not the grievance involved rights which were, "arguably constitutionally protected property rights." Perhaps modeled after the joint committee concept common to many International Brotherhood of Teamster contracts through the country, this joint committee might provide the advantage of ferreting out from the arbitration procedure those claims involving obvious constitutionally protected rights while at the same time providing a release of employee and union frustrations over managerial decisions adversely affecting the institutional interests of the union. There are, of course, many of the same defects in this approach which were mentioned previously. However, unlike the prior suggestion this approach may be more palatable to the union for it does enhance the union's role in, and control over, the grievance procedure and those grievances filed by its members.

A third possible solution involves the concept of indemnification. It could be proposed during negotiations that, as a condition of the employer agreeing to a clause which subjects constitutionally protected rights to the grievance and arbitration procedure, the union specifically agree to indemnify the employer for any and all additional fees or costs incurred by the employer should a dissatisfied employee losing before the arbitrator disregard the arbitrator's award and file a lawsuit alleging deprivation of his constitutionally protected due process property rights.

Obviously, numerous enforcement problems will be created by such an indemnification procedure. Additionally, unions can be expected to oppose such arrangements as they would be most reluctant to subject their union treasuries to the whims of dissident bargaining unit employees seeking to take advantage of such a situation. However, from the employer's standpoint such a proposal has a great deal of negotiation appeal and merit. It certainly does put the union to the test of determining exactly how important the union considers the grievance and arbitration procedure to be.

A fourth possibility would involve the use of a specific waiver of the right to sue signed by the individual employee whose rights are the subject of the grievance. Thus, a contractually agreed upon grievance procedure could incorporate a requirement that, as a condition of proceeding to arbitration, the grievant (and perhaps all other employees similarly situated) sign a specific individual waiver of their right to pursue subsequent due process court litigation over matters involved in the arbitration proceeding. The terms of such a waiver could be stated in the contract and, additionally, be repeated on a grievance form signed by the employee prior to the convening of an arbitration hearing. Only after such signatures had been obtained would the arbitration step in the contract be activated.

A possible disadvantage to the express waiver alternative is that it conceivably could be used by a dissident employee to block grievances the union leadership or a majority of union employees believed should be taken to arbitration. To ensure against this eventuality a modification of the same concept — and one which in the authors' opinion may prove to be the most "workable" of the alternatives explored here — could be adopted, which permits grievances to proceed to arbitration in the normal manner, but which limits any remedy awarded by the arbitrator to those employees signing the release.[5] Thus, the grievance procedure would be available, insofar as a remedy is concerned, only to those employees who first sign the release of suit. Little benefit would be gained by exploring further alternatives, though obviously others do exist.

One point should be clear. Public employer bargaining representatives on both sides of the negotiating table must accord recognition during negotiations to the fact that, in the public sector, union seniority proposals which may create constitutionally protected property rights, and union grievance and arbitration proposals which may well create additional due process problems and liabilities, have a practical and legal impact far different than they do in the private sector.

Whether a public employer seeks to modify an existing grievance and arbitration clause or to respond to an initial union proposal in the grievance or seniority area, the public sector negotiator must educate his principal to achieve a greater appreciation of the problems and possible disadvantages associated with such proposals. These problems and disadvantages must thereafter be vigorously asserted across the bargaining table, to obtain for the employer more in return for the grant of contractual seniority benefits or grievance and arbitration procedures than has heretofore been the case. In these two areas, private sector comparisons fail. Unless public employers obtain more in return for agreeing to these benefits than do their private sector counterparts, they have not, quite simply, received fair value from their bargain.

---

[1] For example, in order to be reasonably certain of meeting existing due process requirements, a contractual procedure would have to: prohibit the union from resolving grievances short of arbitration; allow sufficient time to transpire before any action was taken to provide notice to all employees who might arguably have property rights which might be adversely affected; management actions would have to be deferred further until the arbitration process had been completed; formal rules of evidence would have to be applied; the right to counsel (with the inevitable delays and extensions that occasions) would have to be assured; the right to examine and cross-examine witnesses would have to be allowed; a formal transcript would have to be provided; a written decision would have to be rendered; and, perhaps, some further form of court review would have to be insured.

[2] Many public employers have already instituted such procedures, though a number have been of an informal nature.

[3] For example, such a procedure might provide for a prompt informal hearing before an individual or body separate and apart from the one which made the initial decision. Affected persons would be notified of the reasons for the action to be taken as soon as possible and of the expedited hearing procedure available to challenge that action. Employees would be allowed to retain their own counsel, call witnesses and confront accusers during the proceeding. The proceedings at the hearing would be recorded, and the decision of the body hearing the matter would be issued along with a brief summary of the reasons in support of the decision. Thereafter, if desired, a more detailed opinion may be issued. Any individual involved would receive a written explanation of the decision. For further safety the procedure would provide for some review mechanism for the decision beyond this expedited hearing procedure.

[4] *Alexander* v. *Gardner-Denver Co.,* 415 U.S. 36, 54 (1973).

[5] Most arbitration clauses already contain a provision restricting the arbitrator's authority to add to, detract from, or modify in any way the provisions of the labor agreement. To this might be added, for example, language such as: "nor shall the arbitrator award back pay or any other form of retroactive relief to any employee who has failed to execute a waiver agreement which is incorporated in the record of the arbitration proceedings."

32. Bargaining With Non-Teaching Employees

In recent years, the fastest growing union in the American labor movement has been the American Federation of State, County, and Municipal Employees (AFSCME). At a time when union membership in much of the private sector has leveled off, or even declined, unions of state and local public employees have grown dramatically in recent years.

This development highlights an increasingly important reality in contemporary school administration. While most attention has focused on teacher negotiations, administrators have become more and more involved in bargaining with other employee groups. Clearly, this trend will continue. As a matter of fact, in many school districts, negotiations with non-teaching employees preceded teacher negotiations, sometimes by decades. Negotiating with non-teaching employees will be — if it is not already — as pervasive a phenomenon as teacher negotiations.

Negotiating with non-teaching employees has most of the pitfalls of negotiating with teachers. It also poses some additional problems that can be extremely troublesome.

In some states, only teachers have negotiating rights by statute. Nevertheless, the administration may be faced with a request for negotiations from non-teaching employees. What should they do?

All such requests should be referred, immediately, to a person knowledgeable in labor relations, either on the staff or outside of it. In general, this individual should first satisfy himself that the organization seeking representation rights does, in fact, represent a majority of all the employees in an appropriate unit. Once this is done, it is normally advisable to negotiate with this organization, even if there is no legal obligation to do so.

The lack of any legal obligation to negotiate may be useful in avoiding negotiations with an irresponsible employee organization. But it is not wise to avoid negotiations by reliance upon the absence of a statutory mandate to do so. The employees will use the administration's refusal to negotiate to build resentment against the administration and to increase the strength of the employee organization. More often than many administrators realize, militant employee organizations are built by the administration, as much as by the organization leadership. It's good policy to avoid giving employee organizations a target.

Nevertheless, even a school district willing or forced by statute to negotiate has knotty problems of procedure. Suppose the school secretaries want to negotiate a contract. If a separate contract is negotiated for secretaries, a host of other groups, such as bus drivers, custodians, and cafeteria workers, may also ask to negotiate a separate contract.

On the other hand, the employees, or some of them, may object to representation in a negotiating unit that includes widely disparate kinds of personnel. Secretaries may feel that they lack a community of interest with bus drivers, and vice versa. Cafeteria workers may feel that they should not be in the same negotiating unit with custodians, and so on.

Let's suppose, however, that most of the bus drivers and custodians want to negotiate a written contract, but the secretaries do not. Situations like this sometimes arise when one group of employees becomes dissatisfied and seeks a written contract while another group remains satisfied with a non-contractual approach to employment relations.

If the administration agrees to negotiate separately with every category of employee, it could find itself negotiating with an excessive number of employee unions. Therefore, in the example given, the administration may be tempted to say to the bus drivers or custodians: "We are willing to negotiate but not with every separate category of employees. If an organization represennts a majority of all non-teaching employees, then we will negotiate with it."

The administrator who adopts this position could be taking a gamble. By insisting that the negotiating unit include the secretaries, the administration may be able to avoid negotiations altogether. The reason is that an organization that can command majority support from bus drivers and custodians may not be able to command majority support if the negotiating unit is broadened to include secretaries or other groups that do not support negotiations with management.

On the other hand, if the secretaries are included in the negotiating unit, and the union is still able to develop majority support, the administration then has to negotiate the working conditions for secretaries. This would not have been necessary if the administration had not broadened the negotiating unit to include the secretaries.

This example is oversimplified, but it serves to illustrate the issue. Actually, most school districts, as is the case with most employers generally, find it advantageous in the long run to negotiate with as few unions as possible. This has several advantages that usually (but not always) outweigh the advantages of negotiating separately with several different unions. First, the fewer the unions, the less danger that the administration will be whipsawed by competing groups. Second, negotiating with one union saves time, since there is only one process of negotiations, even though it is more complicated than negotiations conducted separately with a number of unions. Third, there will be better coordination than if there were different sets of negotiations. Perhaps most important, if fewer unions are involved, the employees themselves must play a more responsible role in the negotiations process.

The last reason bears elaboration. If there are several separate negotiating units, each represented by a different union, there will be intense competition among them to get the best possible agreement, regardless of the effects on the other employees. But if one union represents several different kinds of employees, the union must work with the administration to adjust the claims of the competing groups. The bus drivers can't say: 'We want more regardless of the effects on the other employees." The other employees will not vote to ratify the contract if one group, such as the bus drivers, received an excessive settlement at the expense of the others. In other words, as more diverse kinds of employees are included in the same negotiating unit, more pressure is put on the union negotiators to allocate resources equitably.

Of course, the larger the school system, the more likely it is that there will be different employee groups wanting separate organizational rights. Fifteen custodians may not want a separate union; 1500 are likely to want it.

In small school districts in some states, the teacher organization represents the non-teaching employees as well as teachers. After all, if there are only 40 teachers and 8 non-teaching employees, a single negotiating unit may be more satisfactory to all concerned than separate units for teaching and non-teaching employees. In districts of 500 to 1,000 non-teaching employees, it is not unusual to have a blue collar and a white collar unit; in fact, there may be three to five units, especially if supervisory employees are accorded negotiating rights in separate units. The most crucial factors are the legislative criteria for unit determination.

If the secretaries seek negotiating rights, either as a separate group or with other employees, the administration should be careful to exclude secretaries serving management personnel who are active in negotiations. Clearly, it would not be appropriate to have the secretary for the superintendent included in a negotiating unit. The confidential aspects of her position would leave both her and the superintendent in an untenable position. The superintendent could hardly entrust the dictation or typing of confidential memoranda on strategy or on the board's bedrock position to a secretary who was one of the employees affected by the memoranda. Similarly, the secretary would be in an embarrassing position if she were represented by a union but failed to give it information available to her during negotiations.

The best practical solution is to exclude personnel from the negotiating unit if they hold sensitive positions of this sort. The administration should be very careful of its terminology in negotiating with representatives of the district's non-teaching employees.

It is not advisable to apply the term "non-professional" to the non-teaching employees. This term suggests invidious comparisons which may be resented by the non-teaching employees. Many non-teaching employees like to consider themselves "professional," whether or not they are certified. In some states, the fact that secretaries, bus drivers, and other categories of non-teaching personal are certified has strengthened their professional image, at least in their own eyes. In fact, the administration should avoid anything that smacks of second-class citizenship in negotiating with non-teaching employees.

The administration must also always visualize how its teacher contract will affect the attitudes and aspirations of other employees. For example, will the percentage of raise given to teachers be available to the others? If not, why not? It is undesirable to provide the same percentage of increase to all groups of employees every year; however, differences should be justified. Comparative data may reveal significant differences in how different groups of employees rank in the area. Factors such as these may be valid reasons for differential treatment during negotiations.

If more than one contract is to be negotiated, it is better to complete the one that will provide the least relative improvement first. Reason: It is extremely difficult for subsequent negotiators to accept a less favorable package than their predecessors. Remember that negotiators must answer to their constituents, who are not likely to ratify a contract they regard as less favorable than the teachers' contract. Not that custodians expect as much as teachers. But the pattern of settlements is crucial.

Furthermore, on some items, the administration will find it difficult to treat non-teachers less generously than teachers. For example, it would be difficult to allow teachers more religious leave than is allowed other kinds of employees. Such a difference would be embarrassing to support, either at the bargaining table or in the forum of public opinion. Hence, in negotiating with teachers, the administration must consider the implications of a concession for other employees.

Sometimes, the same benefit will have a much different impact from one negotiating unit to another. Consider the experience of a district which gave three days of religious leave to teachers. Many were Jewish and took the full three days. When the non-teaching employees negotiated their contract, they also asked for three religious days. The administration felt it could not refuse, but did not expect the concession to be very costly, because a much lower proportion of non-teaching employees were Jewish. However, adherents of other religions in the non-teaching unit did begin to take religious leave on days that previously had not been characterized by such leave. The point is that the benefits accorded one group are likely to be reflected, one way or another, in negotiations with other groups. Give the teachers leave for personal business without having to give reasons and you can be certain that other employees will be asking for the same concession.

A sensible policy would be to review every concession made to any group from the standpoint of its potential effects on other employees in the system. Needless to add, such review ought to be made before, not after, the concession is made.

It is desirable to have the same person responsible for negotiations with all groups. This may not be feasible where the line administrator for non-teaching personnel is a different person from the line administrator responsible for teaching personnel. All non-teaching employees may be administered through the office of the business manager, for example; whereas the assistant superintendent for personnel may be responsible for teacher bargaining.

However, even if each negotiating team has a different chief negotiator, there should be common representation on all management negotiating teams. At the minimum, there must be good communication between management personnel responsible for negotiating with different groups. Otherwise, items negotiated in one contract may create unanticipated difficulties in another.

In the long run, negotiating with non-teachers turns out to be very similar to teacher negotiations. The non-teaching employees call in their AFSCME or SEIU representative to negotiate for them, just as NEA or AFT locals call in their field representatives, where they do not have a full-time local organization leader. Fortunately, the non-teaching employees are not so pressured by rival organizations as are the teachers, and their negotiations tend to be more down-to-earth than the "everything-is-negotiable" school of teacher negotiators.

But what is true in general may not be true of your school district. Regardless, the best policy is to be as well-prepared for negotiations with non-teaching employees as you are for teachers.

33. Additional Issues, Suggestions and Sources

Chanin, Robert H.: *The United States Constitution and Collective Bargaining in the Public Sector,* National Education Association, Washington, D.C., May, 1971.

Chanin, Robert H., and Elise T. Snyder: *The Bugaboo of Federal Preemption: An Analysis of the Relationship Between a Federal Collective Bargaining Statute for Employees of State and Local Government and State Statutes Affecting Such Employees,* National Education Association, Washington, D.C., March, 1975. This reference may be regarded as the NEA's position on the matter, inasmuch as the senior author is NEA's Deputy Executive Secretary and General Counsel.

Hanslowe, Kurt L., and Walter E. Oberer: "Determining the Scope of Negotiations Under Public Employment Statutes," *Industrial and Labor Relations Review,* Vol. 24, April, 1971, pp. 432-41. This is a discussion of the important but much neglected relationship between state public employee bargaining laws and state laws on terms and conditions of public employment.

Lieberman, Myron: "The Impact of Proposed Federal Public Employee Bargaining Legislation on State Legislation on Mandatory Subjects of Bargaining," *Journal of Collective Negotiations in the Public Sector,* Vol. 4 (2), pp. 133-35. This article, which is a summary of a study funded by the National Institute of Education, analyzes the potential impact of federal legislation on the state legislation dealing with teachers salaries, tenure, retirement and other terms and conditions of employment.

TERMS AND CONDITIONS
OF EMPLOYMENT

34. Tenure and Collective Bargaining

Teacher tenure has always been a controversial matter, but collective bargaining has intensified the controversies over it. In the pre-negotiations era, the question of whether tenure decisions should be subject to grievance arbitration was not even asked. Even during the 1960's, the issue was seldom raised in negotiations. Nevertheless, making tenure decisions subject to the grievance procedure is a major negotiating objective of teachers at the present time.

Decisions affecting probationary teachers should be distinguished from decisions affecting teachers already on tenure. Paradoxically, some reasons for making tenure decisions affecting probationary teachers subject to the grievance procedure do not apply to decisions for teachers who already have tenure. Similarly, some reasons for making the discharge of tenured teachers subject to the grievance procedure do not apply to decisions concerning probationary teachers. And some reasons for not making either kind of tenure decisions subject to grievance arbitration apply to both probationary and tenured teachers. This sounds confusing, and perhaps it is, but the issues are complicated.

Let us first consider making the discharge of tenured teachers subject to grievance arbitration. If you negotiate for the administration, your first reaction to this proposal in some states will be that tenure is a statutory matter. For example, some states provide that boards shall have an unlimited right to discharge during the probationary period, which is usually three years. After the probationary period, boards can fire teachers only by following a statutory procedure.

At least in some states, the statutory procedure makes it all but impossible to terminate tenured teachers. In some cases, however, administrators simply have not really documented the alleged incompetence of tenured teachers. The incompetence may be there but the administrators may not have done their job adequately.

Be that as it may, however, there is probably no legal barrier to negotiating a contractual procedure covering discharge of tenured teachers. That is, even if a state provides a statutory procedure concerning teachers who have allegedly violated their tenure status, the district could negotiate a contractual procedure that was more favorable to teachers, e.g. by making the probationary period two instead of three years. The district could also negotiate a less favorable procedure, but teachers obviously are not going to propose that.

What you can do legally and what you should do practically are two different things. Districts should have serious reservations about providing a contractual procedure concerning tenure in addition to the statutory one. There is usually no valid reason for two remedies for what is essentially the same grievance.

Teacher negotiators will argue that they cannot take away any statutory rights of teachers in the collective agreement. This is probably true, although there is some question as to what the statutory rights of teachers are in some situations. Suppose, however, that the teacher organization agrees to waive the statutory protection for members of the bargaining unit in exchange for contractual protections. Or suppose that the union agrees that if a teacher uses the contractual remedy, he thereby waives the statutory one. Such proposals can be drafted as tight as would be desirable from management's view.

Even in these situations it makes sense to oppose grievance arbitration of tenure, partly because the objection is to the option as well as to the existence of dual remedies. Nevertheless, at this point, teacher negotiators have a much stronger argument than a proposal simply to provide contractual procedures in addition to statutory ones. "Let's settle discharge cases at the lowest level possible," they might argue, "instead of escalating them into lawsuits. Forcing you to resort to the courts to fire an incompetent teacher is costly to us as well as to you. Furthermore, it is likely to result in damaging publicity, which may be unjustified. Let's utilize all the advantages of grievance arbitration over lawsuits to settle these problems." Clearly, there is some merit to these arguments even to an administration determined to retain the most unlimited rights possible to discharge tenured teachers.

In private employment, unions often bargain for more protection for regular employees in exchange for management's unlimited right to terminate probationary employees within a specified period, such as 90 days. This is a perfectly routine *quid pro quo* in the industrial setting: more protection for regular employees in exchange for less protection or none for probationary ones. School board negotiators may see no reason to accept any such proposal, since state laws usually give boards the right to terminate usually within three years, without having to hold a hearing.

It is entirely possible, however, that these state laws may be declared unconstitutional. Some Supreme Court decisions indicate that although no one has a constitutional right to public employment, public employers must provide due process in termination of probationary employees. This may mean that probationary employees have the right to a hearing, to a statement of the reasons for termination, and to an opportunity to rebut the reasons. Such decisions put an altogether different light on grievance arbitration of decisions applying to probationary employees.

To see why, suppose that probationary employees have a constitutional right to due process in termination cases, regardless of the tenure laws that state that boards need not give reasons or hold hearings on their terminations. In this case, the question of how to provide due process will be important to both employee organizations and administrators. Boards may conclude that grievance arbitration provides all the elements of due process that are constitutionally required for probationary teachers. Should this happen, making a tenure decision applying to probationary teachers subject to the grievance procedure would seem much more feasible to board negotiators. Not that they will jump for joy at the prospect, but they may see it as a solution to a difficult problem.

Actually, personnel administration in education is moving toward the industrial patterns previously mentioned. School management will continue to have a virtually unlimited right to discharge but within a much shorter probationary period (one to two years). Meanwhile termination after this period is likely to become subject to grievance arbitration. (Of course, boards will not have the right to refuse employment or terminate employment for clearly unconstitutional reasons, such as religion or race.) Such an approach would make good sense if the tenure statutes are repealed, a course of action that has more appeal to teacher organizations than is generally realized. For one thing, repeal of the tenure statutes would obviously enhance the power of teacher organizations. It would be clear to teachers that their protection lay with the organization, not with the statutes. This would be conducive to membership, since teachers would feel, rightly or otherwise, that they had better pay dues to ensure organizational interest if they ever need help. Also, the idea that three to five years are needed for tenure decisions is being widely questioned. Granted, the more time the administration has to make a tenure judgment, the more informed the judgment is likely to be.

Contrary considerations, however, have merit. One is that management would be more careful in recruitment, and would evaluate better and faster, if the probationary period were shortened. Another consideration is that equity to the employees requires earlier decisions on tenure. Finally, there is always the question of what negotiating concession you can get for making tenure grievable.

Many administrators complain about the difficulty of discharging tenured teachers. How will they respond to teacher proposals that would not only shorten the probationary period to one or two years at most, but would also replace statutory procedures with binding arbitration of decisions to discharge a tenured teacher? Management could hardly complain about the administrative difficulty of discharging incompetent teachers if such proposals were accepted and implemented.

If management complaints about the difficulty of firing tenured teachers are justified, management as well as teacher negotiators ought to be seeking a more expeditious way of resolving disputes. It will be interesting to see how this issue is resolved as teacher organizations emphasize job security in the immediate future.

The practical issue may come down to whether administrators are willing to shorten the probationary period and provide some elements of due process in refusing tenure to probationary teachers, in exchange for the provision of a simpler way of terminating the employment of tenure teachers. Whether this trade is worthwhile may vary from district to district.

35. Negotiated Teacher Evaluation Procedures

Teacher evaluation is one of the most troublesome issues in collective bargaining. Understandably, teacher organizations are constantly seeking to expand contractual protections for teachers. At the same time, administrators and supervisors are becoming more concerned about their eroding authority to discipline or discharge teachers, and such authority is often related to teacher evaluation. If teacher evaluations do not meet all of the contractual obligations of the administration, the administration's authority to take action against a teacher may be successfully challenged.

A Michigan arbitration case dramatically illustrates these points. The case involved a probationary teacher who was not rehired after three negative evaluations. The collective agreement in effect at the time included the following clauses:

"Prior to March 15 of each year, the principal shall submit a recommendation to the superintendent regarding the employment of all teachers. Should this recommendation include dismissal or additional probationary status it shall state fully and completely the reasons therefor and a copy shall be sent to the teacher. The teacher may submit a counter report in writing to the superintendent within five days if he chooses to do so." (Article XV, Section E.)

"No teacher shall be disciplined, reprimanded, reduced in basic salary schedule or deprived of any professional advantage without just cause. Any such discipline, reprimand, or adverse evaluation of teacher performance asserted by the board or any representative thereof resulting in reduction in rank and/or compensation, shall be subject to the grievance procedure hereinafter set forth.... All information forming the basis for the disciplinary action will be made available to the teacher." (Article XVI, Section E.)

The teacher, whom we shall designate Miss B, was first evaluated in November and then in January by her principal. The evaluations, although negative, were specific and included recommendations for improvement. The third evaluation was conducted on March 10 and was followed by a conference on March 12 between Miss B and the principal. During the conference, Miss B learned that the principal would not recommend her re-employment. She did not receive a written copy of the evaluation until the afternoon of that day and did not sign it.

On the same day, March 12, the principal sent the superintendent a long detailed memorandum explaining his recommendation that Miss B not be rehired. On March 25, ten days after the date required by the contract, Miss B received a letter from the board, informing her that the board had voted unanimously not to offer her a contract for the upcoming school year. The letter quoted the principal's memorandum verbatim to explain the reasons for this decision. In other words, Miss B saw the principal's evaluation and his adverse recommendation prior to March 15 but did not see the board's detailed memorandum justifying her non-renewal until March 25. This memorandum included some points covered by the three evaluations prior to March 15 and others not discussed or implicit in the principal's evaluations.

It should also be noted that Miss B prepared a report on March 17, attempting to rebut each of the three evaluation reports prior to March 15. Miss B also stated at this time, "I must receive a list of specified reasons for the recommendation that I no longer be employed.... When this list is forthcoming, I shall submit a rebuttal of those specific reasons."

To summarize, Miss B did not receive a copy of the board's reasons until after the board had acted upon the principal's recommendations. The teacher did have an opportunity to respond to the principal's evaluations, but the principal's recommendations to the board included some items and inferences which were not on the evaluation forms. Since these recommendations were relied upon by the board, and the board acted upon them prior to deciding against renewing the contract, the teacher filed a grievance.

In its argument, the board contended that a refusal to re-employ a probationary teacher should not be construed as a disciplinary action or deprivation of professional advantage. The arbitrator cited a number of cases to show that this issue had divided courts and arbitrators, but as a matter of law and policy, he supported the view that refusal to rehire constituted a deprivation of "professional advantage." In other words, a district can't refuse to rehire a probationary teacher and then claim the teacher hasn't lost any professional advantage. Since Article XVI, Section E, specified that the board could not deprive a teacher of any "professional advantage without just cause," the board had to show just cause.

The gut issue in the case, therefore, was whether the board had complied with the contractual requirements concerning notice to the teacher. The arbitrator ruled that this had not been done. True, the teacher knew about the negative evaluations by the principal, but these did not meet the contractual requirements. The teacher was entitled to know the board's reasons *prior* to the time the board took action on them. Otherwise, the teacher would be denied her contractual rights to rebut the reasons while the matter was still open. The arbitrator gave little weight to the possibility that the teacher would have a fair opportunity to rebut the reasons after the board had refused to rehire; at this stage, the board would have developed a vested interest in upholding its prior negative judgment, hence its objectivity was suspect. For this reason, the arbitrator ordered re-employment of Miss B with back pay as a result of the board's refusal to re-employ her.

This case is significant in several ways. One is that the arbitrator did not challenge the competence of the principal's evaluations. The problem was due to the fact that the board's reasons, which must be distinguished from the principal's, were not communicated to the teacher by the contractual deadline. Although based upon the principal's memorandum to the superintendent, the board's reasons differed in some important respects from the reasons communicated to the teacher by the principal prior to March 15.

What if the principal's recommendation to the superintendent about Miss B had relied upon precisely the same points he had made to Miss B prior to March 15? In other words, suppose the board had given as its reasons the evaluation report made available to Miss B prior to March 15, instead of a separate memorandum which Miss B did not see until after March 15. The arbitrator would probably have upheld the grievance, although it would have been a closer case. Unless and until the board adopts a set of reasons recommended by a subordinate, the reasons remain those of the subordinate, not the board. Realistically, a teacher might adopt a very different approach with the board than with the subordinate of the board, even though both are citing the same reasons. For example, an effort to discredit a reason cited by the board might involve data concerning the principal which would be omitted from efforts to discredit the same evaluation at the principal's level.

The practical implications of the case under discussion seem to be clear: (1) Administrators must make sure that the substance of their observations and evaluations will support the recommendations they make; (2) they must scrupulously observe the procedural requirements spelled out in the collective agreement before taking action adverse to teachers; (3) boards must recognize that the reasons for a personnel action recommended by a subordinate are not those of the board unless and until the board officially adopts them. Such adoption, however, cannot be used to deprive teachers of their rights to know the board's reasons by a specified date. (Of course, the board might have avoided the problem altogether by different contract language, but any language on the issue is likely to be interpreted very rigorously by arbitrators.)

In the instant case, the failure to fulfill the procedural requirement was the fatal weakness in the administration's position. To avoid such setbacks, administrators should systematically review teacher evaluations with the principals and supervisors. Such review should aim at ensuring that evaluations are comprehensive and are completed in time to fulfill all contractual deadlines. Fulfilling both the substantive and procedural requirements pertaining to teacher evaluation is an essential ingredient of effective contract administration.

36. Should Teachers Evaluate Other Teachers?

Management negotiators frequently are confronted by teacher proposals for "peer evaluation." The teacher negotiators typically assert that principals, supervisors and chairmen have done a poor job of evaluation. "Let's have experienced classroom teachers help probationary teachers," the teacher negotiator may assert. "Teachers are more receptive to suggestions from other teachers than from management personnel. Since the purpose of evaluation is to improve teaching, it would be better for everyone involved to have experienced teachers conduct the evaluation."

Such proposals often include the procedures for selecting the teacher evaluators. For example, in some contracts the teacher organization selects two "teaching coaches" from a list submitted by the administration. The evaluations are placed in the file of the teacher being evaluated, along with those made by the administration.

In general, peer evaluations are undesirable in theory and practice. If teacher organizations propose peer evaluation, management ought to reject it. At least, peer evaluation ought to be rejected as part of the process by which the administration decides whether to retain a teacher.

To see why, suppose an experienced teacher evaluates a probationary teacher. Suppose further that the probationary teacher feels that the evaluation is unfair or incompetent. In such case, whom does the organization represent — the teacher evaluated or the evaluator? Since both teachers are in the bargaining unit, the organization must either neglect the probationary teacher, or adopt an adversary stance vis-a-vis the experienced teacher. In the nature of the case, the experienced teacher is likely to have more organizational influence than the probationary teacher. The latter, who is more likely to need effective representation under this system, turns out to be the one least likely to get it.

Teachers as well as administrators sometimes forget that a basic purpose of the teacher organization is to protect teachers from unfair or incompetent evaluation. If other members of the bargaining unit conduct the evaluations, the organization is likely to support the teacher with the most organizational influence. The organization is not likely to provide effective representation for new teachers if new teachers are pitted against experienced teachers.

Teacher negotiators tend to dismiss this possibility. They will assert, for example, that if peer evaluation results in a difference of opinion, the organization (or its grievance committee) can decide which position is right. This view is naive at best. A lawyer is not so likely to defend a client vigorously if the lawyer is also serving as the judge in the case. If the teacher organization tries to serve as judge as well as advocate, it will inevitably weaken its role as teacher advocate.

At first glance, peer evaluation seems attractive to administrators. It seems especially attractive if the organization has been vigorously contesting management evaluations and personnel actions based thereon. The prospect of having the teacher organization, and/or teachers, assist management in the unpleasant task of evaluation has obvious appeal to beleaguered management.

Nevertheless, the practice should be avoided. The teacher evaluators will come under severe organizational pressure "to take it easy" in evaluation. Many will do so, since most teachers were not employed to evaluate and don't relish the prospect. Since it is not one of their major functions, they may not be well-prepared for the task, technically or psychologically.

Furthermore, suppose teacher and management evaluations differ significantly. If the peer evaluation is favorable, management is more likely to hesitate in making negative evaluations; the difference will be cited as evidence that management is biased or incompetent. If the teacher evaluation is unfavorable and the management evaluation is favorable, management will be accused of recommending incompetent teachers for tenure. Either way, the peer evaluation is likely to have undesirable effects. If peer and management evaluations coincide, there is no need for both.

Teacher evaluation of other teachers is really a holdover from the pre-bargaining era. In those days, *who* conducted the evaluation was perceived to be the all-important issue. Neither teachers nor administrators pressed the crucial issue: Is evaluation right because of who makes it, or is it right because whoever made it followed appropriate criteria and procedures? Presumably the latter. For this reason, collective agreements should spell out the criteria for evaluation.

Nevertheless, it is management's job to interpret and apply these criteria for evaluation. If management fails to do so, the remedy should be through the grievance procedure. In other words, teacher protection should flow from managerial adherence to a collective agreement, not to the substitution of teachers for management personnel in the evaluation process.

The dangers of peer evaluation are particularly evident in higher education. In one campus after another, one encounters professors who believe, often meritoriously, that they have not received due process at the hands of their colleagues in the bargaining unit.

At one leading university, peer evaluation is conducted through personnel and budget committees in each department. By university statute, the deliberations of these committees, which pass upon tenure and promotions, are to be kept confidential. At the same time, the collective agreement in force at this institution entitles faculty members to read administrative evaluations of their performance and to append their objections or reservations for inclusion in their personnel files. In other words, the faculty members who are entitled to due process from the administration are nevertheless subject to secret evaluations by their peers.

Such practices dramatically raise the issue: Is evaluation sound because of who does it, or are there independent criteria for evaluation, regardless of who does it? Emphasis upon *who* evaluates instead of the criteria and procedures will lead both teachers and administrators into a hopeless morass.

Peer evaluation might be acceptable where it is not used in personnel administration. If teacher A observes teacher B, provides teacher B with suggestions and criticisms, and that is all, peer evaluation might be acceptable. The question is whether the benefits are worth the costs. Is it worthwhile to pay for the released time of teachers, to conduct evaluations or observations which will not be used in personnel administration? Ordinarily, this would be doubtful. In any case, peer evaluation should not be accepted where the evaluations are included in the files of the teachers being evaluated. Evaluation should be management's responsibility. When management abdicates this function, the outcomes are likely to be bad for everyone.

37.   Negotiating Fringe Benefits

Fringe benefits have outgrown their label. When districts pay $3,000 a year per teacher just for insurance (as some systems do) and then add leave time, vacation time, sick days, and so on, fringe benefits amount to a substantial percentage of salary — often much more than the public or even the school board realizes.

This development is similar to private sector experience. In the early years of private sector bargaining, fringe benefits were just that. They rarely amounted to as much as five percent of wages. Over the years, however, various factors led to increasing benefits. While the federal government occasionally has opposed inflationary wage increases, it has not equally opposed improvements of fringe benefits. Also, as tax rates increase, so does the attractiveness of fringe benefits which are usually tax-free. If the cost of insurance coverage were paid directly to employees, it would be taxable income; employees also would lose the benefits of group purchasing power if forced to purchase health insurance individually.

Perhaps the leading cause of the increased costs of fringe benefits is medical insurance, which has gone up much more rapidly than have salaries and the cost of living generally. This means that once districts began providing any health insurance at all, their costs escalated rapidly even if they did not provide increases in benefits to employees.

Because of all these factors, fringe benefits in the private sector now average more than 20 percent of direct salary payments. Although comprehensive data is not available for the public sector, the same factors apply and the results are substantially similar. Theoretically, the number of insurance benefits (from dental to accidental death to legal) and their cost could constitute an alternative way of spending similar dollar amounts. A district and its teacher union might agree to devote more money to insurance benefits and less to the salary schedule. The result could be a lower salary schedule but greater insurance benefits in comparison to neighboring districts, where the parties chose to allocate more to the salary schedule and less to insurance benefits. In such cases, there obviously is no over-all inequity between the districts — only a difference in how each system allocates the same dollar amounts.

At the bargaining table, however, the parties don't always see it this way. The salary schedule is the most visible part of the package so it tends to dominate. When pay schedules are compared, districts may not get full credit for their liberal fringe benefits. This is especially true of fringe benefits on which it is difficult to place a dollar value. For example: A system may have a generous leave policy, for which it pays heavily in terms of higher substitute costs and increased allocations of management time to recruit and orient the substitutes. This system's substitute budget, however, may lump together *all* substitute costs, making it impossible for the system or the union to ascertain (and compare) the costs of specific leave policies.

Because their costs are not always visible, fringe benefits can be attractive to both parties when direct wage boosts face legal or political obstacles. The improvements in benefits can be used to conceal increases in compensation that neither board nor union wants to be highly visible. But board members should remember that sometimes a fringe benefit that is inexpensive when first established later can become a financial burden. A one-week increase in vacation allowance for employees with 10 years of service may seem like an inexpensive way of getting support from a few key senior employees. Five or ten years later, however, with an older work force, the same concession will be much more costly.

Another thing to watch for — and minimize or avoid altogether if possible — is an agreement by which substantial benefits go only to a few employees. Example: Giving a preparation period to high school teachers generates a similar demand by junior high school teachers. And once the junior high teachers have it, the elementary teachers demand one also as a matter of "equity." What may have begun as a concession to high school English teachers who had too many essays to read ends up as a systemwide benefit.

It can be as difficult to cut back on fringe benefits as on salaries. In certain fringe benefits, such as retirement contributions, it is legally impossible to make cutbacks. In general, once a fringe benefit is established, it tends to remain in existence, and its cost, like all others, tends to increase. Technically, it should not matter whether the district increases salaries or fringe benefits as far as its bargaining position is concerned; practically as a result of the greater public awareness of salary schedules, the district may be better off allocating funds to it instead of fringe benefits.

In addition to financial considerations, fringe benefits have important implications for policy matters. In the private sector, fringe benefits are interpreted primarily as cost items, *i.e.* as a method of allocating resources. In education, as in public employment generally, the issues are more complex. Whether teachers must be paid for evening meetings is not simply a compensation issue. It is also a school-community relations issue because of the necessity that teachers be available to parents who cannot meet during the regular school day. The tendency to broaden the fringe benefits package can weaken board discretion; the more it costs to implement a policy, the greater the danger that the policy will not be implemented. This factor should be considered in deciding whether or not to add new forms of compensation.

38.   The Use and Abuse
of Joint Committees

The "joint study committee" is one of the most common scenarios at the negotiating table:

The teacher negotiators want something very badly or, at least, they say they do. For various reasons, board negotiators reject the demand. Finally, as time is running out and the board negotiators are as eager as teacher representatives to wrap things up, the teacher negotiators say: "If you can't agree to do something now, at least agree to establish a joint committee to look into the problem. If you do that, we can show we tried to achieve something and you aren't committing yourself to anything."

This kind of talk can sound very attractive to a board negotiating team, especially in the final stages of negotiations. And sometimes, a proposal for a joint committee does make sense for both sides. On the other hand, many boards are finding out they have opened up a Pandora's box by agreeing to a joint committee.

When do joint study committees make sense? And when don't they? As a general rule, don't establish a joint committee when you know that nothing can be done about the substantive problem involved. The sense of relief over temporarily resolving an issue with a committee will eventually be replaced by teacher feelings of outrage ("The administration agreed to a joint committee as a subterfuge!"). It won't help to point out that you told the teacher negotiators that nothing could be done. They sincerely may regard the joint committee as just a device to bypass a sticky issue and get an agreement. However, they are not likely to put the matter this way to the teachers. To do so would destroy the value of the joint committee from their point of view. Teacher negotiators — even if they privately believe that the administration will do absolutely nothing about a problem — aren't going to say that to the teachers, at least before the teachers ratify the agreement. Instead, they will hold out the joint committee as a possibility of achieving something when the committee reports. In other words, regardless of the private thoughts of the teacher negotiators, joint committees have a logic of their own.

Sometimes the parties in negotiations don't fully realize that "No" or "We can't make any concession on that proposal" can be as legitimate as "Yes" or "Maybe" or "Something can be done." Refusal to accept a negative reality leads to a joint committee. Instead of getting closure on negotiations, the parties may find themselves in endless negotiations under the guise of "joint committees."

Implementation of a joint committee can be a more troublesome problem with a small or medium-sized teacher organization than with a large one. Quite often, the small or medium-sized organizations try to achieve clauses found in the larger districts. However, the smaller ones simply may not have the manpower to staff joint committees as effectively as a large teacher organization. Thus, they tend to appoint whomever they can get as teacher representatives — and they may not be able to get very much. Furthermore, once a joint committee is appointed, the teacher representatives will want released time for committee work and meetings. This can be a drain in a smaller system.

Joint committees should not negotiate. Sometimes, during the course of negotiations, it is helpful to refer particular issues to subcommittees of the negotiating teams. Remember, however, that the binding agreements are made between the board and the teacher organization, not their constituent sub-groups. In any case, referring a problem to a joint committee *during* negotiations is different from having a problem referred to such a group after an agreement is reached. Unless the task of the joint committee is clearly defined, the administration may discover that it is embroiled in continuous negotiations.

Most problems that are referred to joint committees for study are the subject of negotiations in the next contract. You can expect the teachers to use the report of a joint committee as a point of departure, at least if there is anything in such committee reports favorable to teachers. If there has been a report by a joint committee, especially on a matter subject to negotiations, members of the administration team should know what was said about the issue. Ignorance of the committee report would encourage teacher belief in the bad faith of the administration. By the same token, if you can show that the *teachers* are unaware of the contents of such a report, you can avoid a lot of Mickey Mouse committee work.

District negotiators should avoid having joint committees do work that should have been done prior to negotiations. If the facts were available but the teachers did not collect and present them, insist that they be better prepared at the next contract talks if they want progress on the item. *The point is to avoid encouraging poor preparation by agreeing to study something when the teachers have had a year or more to consider the problem.*

On the other hand, new issues may arise or there may be new proposals or questions from either side that legitimately require data — the "facts" of the matter — not available during negotiations. Put the burden on the teacher organization to make its case; avoid, if you can, the idea that you have an initial burden to show cause. If, however, there is honest disagreement over the facts themselves, it may make sense to have a smaller group mutually ascertain the facts and report back.

Having joint committees explore a problem *before* negotiations begin can facilitate a joint set of facts and eliminate a great deal of unproductive controversy. However, it is a mistake to believe that agreement on the facts means that the parties will easily get agreement on the issues involved. As Richard H. Tawney, the famous English historian once pointed out, the conflicts that really matter in life are not those which result from misunderstanding the other fellow, but those that result from understanding him too well.

39.   Job Security:
Not Just Another Issue

During the past few years, teacher organizations have frequently negotiated clauses governing teacher layoffs. Such clauses were rarely negotiated in the 1960's. At that time, school districts were usually concerned about recruiting more teachers, not with identifying the teachers to be laid off or the criteria to be used in carrying out staff reductions.

Several factors have converged recently to change the outlook concerning supply and demand. In many districts, enrollments not only have stopped increasing, but have been decreasing. Voter resistance to school taxes has increased dramatically, so that many districts are being forced to reduce staff even with an increase in enrollment. Another factor is that, because of the softer job market, fewer teachers are leaving the profession. This means that staff reductions cannot be implemented through attrition quite so often. If there is need for a five percent reduction in staff, while 10 percent are resigning anyway for various reasons, the administration may not have to lay off any particular teacher. On the other hand, the expanding teacher surplus has influenced many teachers to continue in positions from which they would have resigned in the days when teaching positions were available just about anywhere. In short, layoffs or the possibility of layoffs are a problem in a growing number of school districts.

Management negotiators should not initiate negotiations over staff reductions. Insofar as possible, the criteria to be followed in implementing staff reductions should be maintained as board policy outside the contract.However, the likelihood is that the teacher organization will initiate a proposal relating to layoffs. If its proposal is simply the addition of boilerplate (language taken verbatim from another contract) and is there only for the sake of appearances, management should be able to exclude the item from the agreement. On the other hand, if a real teacher concern underlies the proposal, the contract is likely to reflect this.

After all, if a teacher negotiator knows that his constituents are really concerned about being laid off, he will find it essential to include some sort of protection in the contract. If the concern is real, there may or may not be great difficulty reaching agreement on the criteria to be followed in reducing staff. This may depend upon the extent to which both sides prefer some form of seniority in the matter. The teacher organization prefers it because the senior teachers tend to have more influence in the teacher organization than the less senior ones. Furthermore, seniority is easily administered, or can be if drafted properly. This means clarifying such issues as whether seniority is based on employment in the district or in a particular school; whether it relates to the date of first employment or the date of employment in the position currently held, and the rights of teachers being laid off to re-employment.

Management is most likely to push for some discretion in making staff reductions. It can be disheartening to be forced to release an outstanding teacher who has less seniority than an average one. Nevertheless, school management may find that bypassing seniority can be quite embarrassing, even in the absence of a collective agreement. Very often, the community as well as the teachers will oppose the discharge of senior teachers when newer ones are retained. Unless a teacher has really performed poorly and management can document its case conclusively, it is very difficult to dismiss an experienced teacher in favor of someone with less seniority. Thus, while it may be advisable to get some organizational concessions for agreement on seniority, management should not necessarily resist a seniority provision to the bitter end.

Seniority should be districtwide, but limited to those qualified. An English teacher should not be retained over a physics teacher who has less seniority, for a position requiring a physics teacher. This seems to be simple enough, but complications can arise. Suppose a teacher is qualified to teach two subjects. If a reduction eliminates a position he has actually taught, but not one he is legally qualified to fill, what then? Generally, the teacher organization will want seniority based upon legal qualifications, not upon what teachers have actually taught. If you want seniority based on what teachers have actually taught, it's advisable to make this clear in the contract.

To the teachers, few things matter as much as a teacher's right to keep his job. Partly for this reason, the teacher organization is likely to insist upon a resolution of the issue which will provide the most protection for experienced teachers. Therefore management negotiators should ordinarily be able to gain some important concessions in return for layoff security. There are recent contracts in which teachers have made important concessions in exchange for job security. Sometimes, the job security was in the form of assurances that tenured teachers would be retained regardless of budget cuts; in other cases, teachers were guaranteed severance pay, depending on their length of service in the district.

Despite the preceding comments, agreements that cover job security often contradict some of the principles that are supposed to govern the economics of collective bargaining. It is not unusual to find salary raises coexisting with widespread unemployment in a particular field. The teacher negotiator, like employee negotiators, generally will be dominated by the need to satisfy the most experienced employees. Such employees are likely to put their own job security ahead of other considerations. They may even give higher priority to their own job security and salary increases than to jobs for new teachers. In other words, the bargaining agent may stress benefits for those already employed, or those who have been employed for a substantial period of time, over benefits for those not employed or employed in the bargaining unit for only a short period of time. In extreme cases, the benefits for the in's may mean unemployment for the out's, or for those at the bottom of the seniority lists. Teachers who are not already employed may desperately wish for a share-the-work attitude among their colleagues who already have jobs, but those out of work may have little influence at the bargaining table. Of course, if unemployed teachers are members of the negotiating organization, they will be able to vote on ratification of the proposed contract, and their potential influence at this point may effect the teacher negotiators.

Generally, however, negotiations are conducted for the benefit of the in's, not the out's. As a matter of fact, school management may find itself more favorably disposed to spreading the work — at the cost of some benefits to senior members of the bargaining unit — than are the teacher negotiators. This is especially likely where management does not want to lose some excellent teachers who would be laid off as a result of policies that overemphasize benefits and protection for teachers with the most seniority. As with so many other issues, a careful analysis of the employment history of the teachers in the bargaining unit may provide management with essential clues to organizational strategy and objectives at the bargaining table. In the last analysis, however, management must decide how it should implement needed staff reductions and bargain hard for its position during negotiations.

40.   The Value of Reducing Class Size

It is very difficult to believe that changes in class size within the range commonly experienced in U.S. schools have any measurable impact on over-all pupil achievement. This skepticism is due to the following:

1. Relatively few studies even concluded that class size was significantly related to pupil achievement.

2. The relatively limited types of situations where class size did seem to make a difference were somewhat inconsistent from one study to another.

3. The nature of statistical analysis is such that one must expect to get some false indications of significance out of a number of studies.

4. Those studies that assessed the relative contributions of pupil ability and school expenditures to pupil achievement consistently indicated that most variation in pupil achievement could be explained without reference to school inputs.

Evidence against linking class size to pupil achievement does not prove that class size is not linked to other desired outcomes of schooling. However, it certainly doesn't support such linking either. Further, we have been decreasing class size nationally over the years, while crime rates, as an example, have risen considerably. It is doubtful that this would happen if reducing class size was a major socializing force. The major conclusion of this review is also reinforced by the fact that during the last ten or so years, while class sizes have been reduced, student achievement from about the 5th grade onward has steadily declined. This would not likely happen either if reducing class size had anywhere near the academic impact required to justify it financially.

This chapter was prepared by Richard L. Harris, superintendent, and Loyd E. Eskildson, chief deputy, Maricopa County, Phoenix, AZ.

It can be argued that reductions in class size have a very serious non-academic effect. The primary rationale offered for class size reduction is to allow more individualized attention to the pupils. It seems logical to assume that such would encourage greater dependency by the pupils, "teach" them to expect the world to take care of them, and dull their abilities to develop personal initiative. If so, our reductions in class size over the years would therefore be partly to blame for the claimed decline in the motivation and discipline of our young workers.

Despite the mass of contrary evidence, it is difficult for many to accept the fact that class size is not an important input to the learning equation. It seems so logical that it would. However, it also seems logical that the world is flat. Progress in educational outcomes will be seriously hampered unless we stop trying to defy the facts and instead use them judiciously to our advantage. When ships sink and airplanes crash, good naval and aeronautical engineers do not simply call for more of the same techniques and approaches. Educational engineers must do likewise. Furthermore, education can hardly impart a thirst for truth to pupils if its decision-makers are allowed to act oblivious to it.

Several reasonable explanations exist as to why class size is not an important factor in pupil achievement. One is that the answer to the question, "Which is more important — initial ability or environment?" is heavily slanted to the initial ability side in most situations. This also implies that there are severe limits to what any additional schooling resources can accomplish. A second explanation is that the main limiting factor in learning is the maturation rate of the pupil's brain. This implies that one doesn't learn multiplication tables or U.S. history any faster with Albert Einstein or Arnold Toynbee as private tutors than in a class of 35 taught by a reasonably alert high school graduate. A third explanation would, of course, be some combination of the preceding two. Considerable research evidence exists to support the conclusions of all three explanations.

How can the continuing concern for class size by most educators be explained? Again, several explanations exist, including the following:

1. Teaching a small class is less demanding of the teachers.

2. Smaller classes result in larger staffs and greater administrator prestige and salary.

3. Smaller classes result in more teachers and greater teacher union revenue and power.

4. Colleges of education historically have turned out by far the least well-prepared graduates, as measured by standardized verbal and mathematical achievement tests. Because research studies are relatively difficult to integrate, this results in their being seriously deficient in the ability to use research results.

5. Public schools suffer very little pressure for financial astuteness because of the pervasive erroneous linking in the public's mind of education quality and education expenditures, fostered, of course, by the educators themselves.

6. Public schools enjoy almost total freedom from accountability because of their very limited, mostly secret, and mostly non-comparable pupil testing programs.

7. It is easier and safer to focus on alleged deficiencies in resources than to contend with achieving results.

In summary, the research evidence from across the U.S. and around the world strongly indicates that at least for most children class size and pupil-teacher ratios within a very broad range have little, if any, impact on academic achievement. The direct logical implication of this is that most money spent on reducing class size or pupil-teacher ratios and/or keeping them at relatively low levels is wasted.

41.   Additional Conditions and Sources

Allen, Donna: *Fringe Benefits: Wages or Social Obligation?* School of Industrial and Labor Relations, Cornell University, Ithaca, N.Y., 1969. This is an excellent treatment of the increase in fringe benefits. Although devoted to the private sector, the analysis will be useful to anyone with substantial negotiating responsibilities in the public sector.

Ferguson, Robert H.: *Cost of Living Adjustments in Union-Management Agreements,* School of Industrial and Labor Relations, Cornell University, Ithaca, N.Y., 1976. Proposals for cost-of-living adjustments are being made more frequently than ever as inflation continues; the complexity of cost-of-living adjustments is evident from the analysis.

Fogel, Walter, and David Lewin: "Wage Determination in the Public Sector," *Industrial and Labor Relations Review,* Vol. 27, April, 1974, pp. 410-31. This article argues that terms and conditions of public sector employment tend to exceed those in the private sector. Although an analytical and conceptual study instead of a "how-to" treatment, the reference is helpful in thinking about salary schedules.

Harris, Richard L., and Loyd E. Eskildson: *Research Evidence Regarding the Impact of Class Size on Pupil Academic Achievement,* Office of the Maricopa County Superintendent, Phoenix, Ariz., 1977. A comprehensive bibliography on class size is included in the study.

Weisberger, June: *Job Security and Public Employees* School of Industrial and Labor Relations, Cornell University, Ithaca, N.Y., 1973.

Wollett, Donald H., and Robert H. Chanin: *The Law and Practice of Teacher Negotiations,* Bureau of National Affairs, Washington, D.C., 1974. This is one of the most comprehensive treatments of bargaining issues in the literature. The authors are experienced labor attorneys with extensive negotiating experience.

STRIKES AND IMPASSE PROCEDURES

42. Coping With Mediation

Sooner or later, most boards are involved in mediation. In states that have just enacted bargaining laws, such involvement is likely to be sooner, especially if the board must negotiate with more than one employee union. Because mediation is so frequent and can be used so effectively in certain circumstances, every board should have some understanding of the process.

Mediation, sometimes called "conciliation," is an attempt by an impartial third party to help move the bargaining forward or to settle an employment dispute by means of suggestion, advice, or other ways of stimulating agreement short of dictating an ultimate solution.

Fact-Finding means just what its name implies — the investigation, assemblage, and reporting of facts concerning a labor dispute. Fact-finding can be with or without recommendations for settlement. To the extent that it includes recommendations for settlement, it can be considered a form of advisory arbitration.

Arbitration is a procedure in which an impartial third party actually renders a decision — which can be binding or nonbinding — in a labor dispute. Arbitration is now the most common procedure for resolving disputes over the meaning or interpretation of collective bargaining agreements. Arbitration is seldom used, however, to resolve disputes over what the *terms* of the agreement should be. While interest is growing in use of arbitration as a means to reach agreement on terms, mediation remains the more common method to achieve this objective.

Let us now take a closer look at the mediation process. First, who are the mediators? They usually are either full-time employees of a state labor relations agency or individuals employed by them on a per-diem basis. Those who work for state agencies may come from the ranks of management, or they may be former union officers or union staff members (perhaps their side has recently lost a union election). Per-diem mediators are often moonlighting college professors. Regardless, prior employment is usually irrelevant, at least from the standpoint of ensuring impartiality.

Just as judges don't start out as judges but as advocates, so do mediators get their start as negotiators for labor or management. They can indeed be biased or incompetent, but their professional origins seldom have much to do with this.

The mediator's lot is not always an easy one, as illustrated by a recent controversy in New York. There, the state Public Employment Relations Board (PERB) asked 150 per-diem neutrals to work one day for nothing because of a fiscal crisis affecting the agency. When the neutrals agreed to do so, the president of the state teacher organization alleged that the PERB chairman and the neutrals had compromised their impartiality. Working a day for no pay because of an alleged fiscal crisis was deemed by the union to be an action that would compromise any neutral faced with the same issue in teacher negotiations. Admittedly, the notion that you can't be impartial if you've worked a day for nothing may be difficult for a school board to accept, but it illustrates the problems of being impartial.

How does a mediator get involved? Usually state law prescribes or authorizes the conditions under which mediators become involved in bargaining between boards and unions. Some states trigger mediation any time the parties (board and teachers) have not reached agreement by a certain time (30 days before the adoption of the final budget for the ensuing year, for example). Other states prescribe mediation when the parties have reached impasse, usually defined as a state of affairs in which continued bargaining on *any* item is futile. Some state laws give the state labor agency discretion to send in a mediator, or they stipulate that mediation is invoked automatically under certain conditions.

Whatever the trigger, Mr.* Impartial appears on the scene in your school system. Frequently, his first move is to call the parties together to find out what the issues are. Having done this, he then meets separately with the negotiators for the school board and the union to ascertain whether movement toward agreement is possible on various issues.

This is no easy task for the mediator. He must win and keep the respect and confidence of the board and the union while never taking sides, at least too openly, in their dispute. Ultimately, if and when an agreement is in sight, the mediator may come down hard on one or both parties to modify their positions. Were he to do so immediately, though, he would risk loss of confidence by the leaned-upon party. Consequently, the mediator is likely to phrase his suggestions not in terms of their merits but in terms of their psychological impact:

Mediator (to board negotiator): "You know, if you could shorten the teachers' work day a little, I might be able to get the union to soften its stand on the number of work days."

Board negotiator (aghast): "What! They already have the shortest work day in the county. Why are you defending this outrageous demand?"

Mediator (sympathetically): "I'm not defending their position. I'm only telling you how they look at it. They claim the nervous strain of teaching the kinds of kids in this district justifies a much shorter day. I'm not agreeing with their argument but merely suggesting what might work in this difficult situation."

A few minutes later, the scenario could be:

Mediator (to union negotiator): "You know, if you dropped your demand for a shorter school day, I might be able to get the board to move on the calendar."

Teacher union negotiator (aghast): "Drop our demands for a shorter school day? Not as long as we have the largest class size in the county — not a chance. How can you ask us to drop such a clearly meritorious demand?"

Mediator (sympathetically): "I wasn't questioning the merits of your proposal. My purpose was only to let you know what could happen if you modified it."

In other words, the mediator's role is to avoid taking sides on the merits of any given issue until he has won the confidence of the parties and has reason to believe his initiatives will be successful. Frequently, the mediator states his suggestions in terms of contingencies: "If I can get the union to agree to X, will the board agree to

Y?" When the parties agree on the contingencies, the mediator in effect has achieved agreement. This technique illustrates an advantage of mediation over direct bargaining. A mediator can float ideas without indicating their sources. If a proposed idea is rejected, neither a loss of confidence nor an escalation of conflict is likely to ensue, as might be the case were the proposal to be made by one of the parties at the bargaining table. The fact that a mediator can test proposals without confrontation tends to loosen up the parties, and to encourage them to suggest solutions they might not be willing to propose directly.

The contingency approach is a good mediation technique, but it can pose serious problems for a school board, which may measure success by criteria vastly different from those applied by a mediator. To a mediator, the test of success is whether he can get the board and teachers to agree. Whether the agreement reached is good or bad for the school system (or for education) is of secondary concern to the mediator, if indeed it is relevant at all. A mediator who has achieved 10 agreements in 10 disputes is regarded as more successful than one who has achieved agreements in five out of 10 disputes — even though all 15 agreements are damaging in terms of their substantive educational consequences.

Certainly, this would not be the case if mediation were based solely upon rational policy considerations. The fact is, however, that if a mediator concludes that one side can be pressured into agreement, pressure almost certainly will be applied to that side without a great deal of regard for ultimate consequences. It is not that mediators view the merits of disputes as irrelevant. However, they frequently are unable to assess the merits accurately. Under such circumstances, it's easy to understand why tactical rather than policy considerations dominate their outlook.

Needless to say, boards ought to be cautious in evaluating a potential mediator. The fact that the mediator leans on management doesn't mean necessarily that he's biased for teachers; he may be leaning even harder on the union. Bias, though it can be real, usually prompts fewer problems than does the question of how much to tell your mediator. If both parties refuse to make any concessions (assuming there are some to be made), the mediator will be rendered helpless. The difficulty is that if one party confides a willingness to make concessions, and the other side does not, the confiding party is placing itself at a disadvantage.

Whether such conflict characterizes a particular situation will depend to an important extent upon the experience and judgment of the mediator. An experienced and effective mediator is not likely to reward unjustified intransigeance on either side. One reliable way to assess the potential effectiveness of a mediator is to examine the track record he has established elsewhere — with leaders of other school systems where the mediator has worked. Their perceptions of his skill and judgment can be useful although they won't be entirely free from a bias of their own.

When should a mediator be called upon or made available? Theoretically, this should happen only after the board and union have bargained in good faith to impasse. A good test of whether this has been the case is to ask this question: Has a substantial number of tentative agreements been reached before a need for a mediator arises? If the answer is "No," the .state agency may prohibit mediation, on grounds that the board and union have not tried hard enough to reach agreement on their own.

What happens if no agreements have been reached because the other side (not yours) has been intransigeant and unyielding from the beginning? The position of the state labor relations agency may be that the school board should file unfair labor practice charges in such a case. In effect, the state's rationale would be as follows: "We aren't going to provide mediation services where the parties haven't fulfilled their obligation to bargain. Furthermore, it isn't up to us (the state) to decide who is responsible for the lack of progress. Charge the other party with refusing to negotiate in good faith if you really believe that's what underlies your lack of progress."

This rationale makes sense, but to take advantage of it, boards need adequate records of the bargaining history. Then if the union alleges that the board is responsible for the lack of progress, the board has available a record to refute the charges.

219

Sometimes politics dictates the need for a mediator. To illustrate, the union leaders, having made a continuing public display of their alleged militancy, may fear they'll look weak to their membership if they reach agreement with the board without third-party intervention. Similarly, school board members who may be fearful of public condemnation should they agree to a union demand also may welcome a mediator who can take them off the hook by making the recommendations. In both cases the combatants seemingly are displaying sweet reason by agreeing to a compromise suggested by a third party rather than by knuckling under to each other.

How much are mediators paid and who pays them? Mediators who are provided by the state usually are paid by the state, and their services are not charged to the school board or union seeking mediation. Mediators who work on a per-diem basis usually are paid $150 to $250 a day plus expenses (with rates currently escalating in many areas).

Whatever the method of payment, the major costs of mediation are not represented by mediator fees but by the time devoted to mediation. The fact is that when the mediator is meeting with one side, the other is waiting in a nearby room. It is not possible to predict the amount of time a mediator will need to devise workable suggestions; consequently, both sides find themselves devoting large blocks of expensive time to mediation.

How effective is mediation? Sometimes it is extremely effective; in other cases, a dismal failure. To an important degree, the difference depends on what is to follow mediation. If mediation is used as a final stage in efforts to reach agreement, it is far more likely to be successful than if both parties expect mediation to be followed by fact-finding. When the board and union both are aware that a bargaining stage beyond mediation is available to them, both are likely to withhold "final" offers to protect their positions in fact-finding.

Yes, indeed, some very effective mediators are women; the masculine is used here for linguistic ease.

43   Public Sector Strikes:
The Need for
a Comprehensive Approach

In the wake of the tremendous upsurge in the unionization of public employees in the past 20 years, there has been a substantially greater increase in the number of strikes by government employees. Whereas in 1958 there were just 15 public employee strikes resulting in 7,510 lost days of work, in 1976 there were 378 public employee strikes resulting in 1,690,700 lost days of work.[1] This startling increase in the number of public employee strikes and the resulting inconvenience which they have caused countless communities has focused attention on the ways in which public sector labor disputes can be resolved without reliance on the strike weapon. To date, however, much of the public debate has revolved around such ritualistic assertions as, "There can be no true collective bargaining without the right to strike," or "Public employees do not have any right to strike." These polar positions seldom result in grappling with the very hard issues involved, let alone leading to any viable solutions.

An important part of any solution to the question of strikes by government employees is the recognition of the complexities of labor relations in the public sector. Thus, it is necessary to recognize that the structure and setting in which collective bargaining takes place in the public sector can and does have an impact on the incidence of public employee strikes. It is also necessary to realize that there are many different kinds of public employee strikes and that the solution for each of these varieties of strikes is not necessarily the same. Only an over-all inquiry into the multifaceted problems that give rise to public employee strikes can hope to yield workable solutions which will ultimately reduce the number of such strikes. It is to such an inquiry that I now turn.

This chapter was prepared by R. Theodore Clark, Jr., partner, Seyfarth, Shaw, Fairweather & Geraldson, Chicago. (Copyright 1979 by R. Theodore Clark, Jr.)

One of the major problems resulting from the advent of widespread public sector bargaining has been the crazy-quilt pattern of representation. In many states and localities, bargaining units have been established without any thought being given to the effect that such bargaining units will have on collective negotiations. In New York City, for example, at one time there were over 200 bargaining units, ranging in size from 2 to 28,000 employees. The existence of such a multiplicity of bargaining units has undoubtedly been a contributing factor in the unusually large incidence of strikes and strike threats in New York City. By way of contrast, Philadelphia, which has been bargaining collectively with its employees for approximately the same period of time as New York City, has only three bargaining units (police, fire and all other employees) and, to date, has experienced only one strike by its employees. While it would be naive to say that Philadelphia's enviable record is attributable solely to the existence of broad bargaining units, the importance of this factor should not be discounted. Where there is excessive fragmentation of bargaining units, such as in New York City, unnecessary rivalries between competing unions are created. In such a situation, the competing unions typically try to outdo each other at the bargaining table. That this enhances the possibility of strikes is obvious.

Excessive fragmentation also encumbers the collective bargaining process since many of the items discussed during negotiations with one bargaining unit will have an impact on employees in other bargaining units. Many benefits, such as pensions, sick leave, vacations, and holidays have traditionally been uniform for all the public employees in a given jurisdiction. Where there is a multiplicity of bargaining units, changes negotiated in any of these benefits with one union will necessarily have an impact on negotiations with the other unions with which the public employer must likewise bargain.

These problems can be minimized by establishing broad collective bargaining units to facilitate the negotiation process and to prevent whipsawing which can, in many situations, lead to both strike threats and strikes. Accordingly, the standard for the establishment of bargaining units in the public sector should be the broadest unit practicable in which employees have an identifiable community of interest in order to insure that representation of public employees is not fragmented.

One other structural problem deserves mention. While the term of most collective bargaining agreements in the private sector is three years, the term of a significant number of agreements in the public sector is one year. In fact, some of the statutes enacted in the various states require this, providing that the term of the agreement "shall not exceed one (1) year."[2] Such short-term agreements mean, in many instances, that the parties are constantly in negotiations and that they are constantly faced with contract termination dates, a situation which increases the possibility of strikes. Serious consideration should be given to providing, as does the Postal Reorganization Act, that "collective bargaining agreements...shall be effective for not less than two years."[3] At the minimum, statutory provisions that prohibit the parties from agreeing to contracts for a term in excess of one year should be repealed.

STRIKE OVER RECOGNITION

Over the past twenty years, a significant portion of all public employee strikes have been over recognition. The 1968 strike by garbage collectors in Memphis, TN, that culminated in the assassination of Dr. Martin Luther King was over recognition. During the past twenty years, the frequency of strikes for recognition in the public sector has been approximately double the frequency of such strikes in the private sector. While this may, in part, be attributed to the growing pains of a nascent union movement — recognition strikes were quite common in the private sector in the 1930's — still, strikes for recognition in the private sector have been minimized because of the existence of established statutory procedures that provide for the peaceable resolution of questions concerning representation. Thus, a union that desires to obtain recognition as the bargaining agent for a given group of employees can file a petition with the NLRB, requesting that a secret ballot election be held to determine whether a majority of the employees desire representation. Acceptance of these statutory procedures by employers and unions alike in the private sector has to a large extent eliminated the necessity for strikes for recognition.

In about 20 states, however, there is presently no statutory procedure for peaceably resolving questions concerning representation. Moreover, in the absence of applicable legislation, the courts have uniformly held that, while public employees have a constitutional right to join and form unions, there is no corresponding obligation on public employers to bargain collectively.[4] In most of these states, public employers have the discretionary authority to decide to either recognize or refuse to recognize a union for the purposes of collective bargaining.[5] It is perhaps, then, not too surprising that employees have felt the necessity from time to time to engage in strike activity in order to gain recognition from an unwilling public employer. The experience in the private sector suggests that strikes for recognition can be largely eliminated by legislation that recognizes the rights of public employees to bargain collectively and establishes procedures to resolve peaceably questions concerning representation through secret ballot elections.

JURISDICTIONAL STRIKES

Historically, jurisdictional disputes between unions over the assignment of work have been an important cause of strikes in the private sector and recent experience suggests that the public sector is likewise not immune from such disputes. Accordingly, there is a need to provide some mechanism for the peaceful resolution of jurisdictional disputes.

In the private sector, the National Labor Relations Act provides that it is an unfair labor practice for a union to force or require

> "... any employer to assign particular work to employees in a particular labor organization or in a particular trade, craft, or class rather than to employees in another labor organization or in another trade, craft, or class unless such employer is failing to conform to an order or certification of the Board determining the bargaining representative for employees performing such work."[6]

After a charge is filed, the National Labor Relations Board is empowered to seek a temporary injunction against a jurisdictional strike if it has reasonable cause to believe that the striking union is committing an unfair labor practice. Section 10(k) of the Act then provides that

> "...the Board is empowered and directed to hear and determine the dispute out of which such unfair labor practice shall have arisen, unless, within 10 days after notice that such charge has been filed, the parties to such dispute submit to the Board satisfactory evidence that they have adjusted, or agreed upon the method for the voluntary adjustment of, the dispute...."[7]

A review of existing public sector legislation reveals that only four states — Iowa, Minnesota, Pennsylvania, and Vermont — have legislation that makes efforts by one union to force or require a public employer to assign work to its members rather than to another group of employees illegal, and even these states do not make provision for the resolution of the underlying dispute. Since jurisdictional disputes have historically been a frequent cause of unrest and strikes, especially among the various building trades unions, public sector labor relations legislation should, at the minimum, include provisions similar to those set forth in the National Labor Relations Act.

STRIKES DURING TERM OF AGREEMENT

The Supreme Court has noted that

> "...the basic policy of national labor legislation [is] to promote the arbitration process as a substitute for economic warfare."[8]

Thus, the Supreme Court has held that there is an implied no-strike clause in a collective bargaining agreement where the parties have provided for final and binding arbitration of disputes concerning the interpretation of the collective bargaining agreement.[9] As the Supreme Court observed,

> "...the very purpose of arbitration procedure is to provide a mechanism for the expeditious settlement of industrial disputes without resort to strikes, lockouts, or other self-help measures."[10]

Because of the need to provide for continued, uninterrupted service, this policy is even more important in the public sector. Accordingly, the parties in public sector negotiations should be encouraged and specifically authorized to include in their collective bargaining agreements grievance and arbitration provisions to resolve any disputes that arise during the term of the agreement concerning the interpretation and application of the agreement.

STRIKES OVER WAGES AND WORKING CONDITIONS

At the outset of any discussion of impasse procedures for disputes over the negotiation of a collective bargaining agreement in the public sector, it is necessary to discuss whether all or some public employees should be allowed to strike. In the past several years, an increasing number of commentators and study commissions have recommended that at least some categories of public employees be granted the right to strike. At present, seven states — Alaska, Hawaii, Minnesota, Oregon, Pennsylvania, Vermont, and Wisconsin — have enacted legislation that grants some categories of public employees the right to strike. Court decisions in two additional states — Montana and Idaho — have upheld the right of some public employees to strike. In this author's opinion, however, those who have advocated allowing public employees the right to strike have not adequately considered the fundamental differences between strikes in the private sector and strikes in the public sector.

In the private sector, employers sell a product for which there are generally alternative sources of supply.[11] The purpose of a private sector strike is to bring economic pressure on the employer by depriving the employer to sales and profits. On the other hand, in the public sector the employer provides a service, which is often free of charge, and for which there is generally no immediately available alternate source of supply. Because the service is paid for by tax revenues, a public sector strike generally does not affect the receipt of revenue.[12] Rather than bringing economic pressure on the employer, the purpose of a strike in the public sector is to bring political pressure on the public employer, the pressure being generated by the recipients of the public service which is halted by the strike.

In this regard, it is necessary to consider the essential nature of the work performed by most public employees and the resulting impact of strikes by these public employees upon the public. That a strike of even a few hours duration can have drastic consequences is indicated by the short strike in 1969 by the Montreal police and firemen. *The Chicago Tribune,* under the heading "Crime Grips City in Cop, Fire Strikes," carried the following report on the strike:

> "The Canadian army was called into Montreal last night after a wage strike by municipal police and firemen left Canada's largest city prey to holdup men and rioting taxi drivers.

> "In a day of crime and violence 10 banks were robbed, 3 persons were slain, 12 wounded in a taxi driver riot, and fires blazed downtown with nobody to fight them."[13]

In fact, it is somewhat ironic that so much attention is being given to the proposition that at least some categories of public employees should be allowed to strike when the continued usefulness of strikes in the private sector is increasingly being questioned. The following comments of George Meany, president of the AFL-CIO, in an interview with six labor reporters in August 1970, are particularly revealing:

> "Naturally, we don't want to give it [the right to strike] up as a weapon but I can say to you quite frankly that more and more people in the trade union movement — I mean at the highest level — are thinking of other ways to advance without the use of the strike method.

> "Actually, what it adds up to is that, while strikes have had their part and all that, and we certainly have advocated for years that you have got to have the right to strike, we find more and more that strikes really don't settle a thing. Where you have a well-established industry and a well-established union, you are getting more and more to the point where a strike doesn't make sense."[14]

In this same interview, Mr. Meany stated that some unions, including the United Steelworkers of America, were seriously considering the possibility of submitting bargaining disputes to voluntary arbitration and that the AFL-CIO had agreed to establish a committee to explore the idea with representatives of the American Arbitration Association.[15] Several years later the steelworkers and the major steel companies agreed to an Experimental Negotiating Agreement that provided for voluntary binding arbitration as the terminal step in the negotiating process.

Merely prohibiting strikes by all public employees, however, will not lead to any long-range solution to the increasing number of strikes that do in fact occur. Concomitant with any prohibition of strikes by public employees is the need to establish meaningful procedures to equitably resolve disputes over wages and working conditions. The basic tenet of any such procedures should be to encourage to the fullest extent possible the voluntary settlement of collective bargaining disputes by the parties themselves without recourse to third-party intervention. As Harry Wellington and Ralph Winter have observed:

> "The major hope for avoiding strikes in the public sector is not the post-impasse procedure, but the bargaining process; not the resolution of impasses, but their avoidance."[16]

But even if this objective is largely achieved, it is nevertheless necessary to provide some means to resolve those remaining disputes where the parties are unable to reach agreement.

STRIKE ALTERNATIVES

Initially, the parties should be permitted the fullest freedom to establish their own impasse resolution machinery. As the Illinois Study Commission observed,

> "...the parties should be encouraged to develop machinery most suitable to their own situation."[17]

Such a procedure has the advantage of being consented to in advance by the parties, rather than being imposed by legislation, thus minimizing problems of acceptability. Any statutory impasse procedures should only be applicable when the parties have not mutually agreed to their own impasse machinery.

Mediation

Assuming the parties themselves are unable or unwilling to establish their own impasse machinery, the question is raised as to what impasse machinery should be established by legislation. In line with the underlying premise of encouraging voluntary agreement by the parties whenever possible, the legislation should first establish and adequately fund a career-oriented mediation staff similar in expertise and function to the Federal Mediation and Conciliation Service. The need to make trained and skilled mediators available to the parties is particularly important in the public sector in view of the large degree of inexperience on both sides of the bargaining table. Often, skilled mediators are able to act as a catalyst in bringing about an agreement in such a situation where the parties appear to be hopelessly deadlocked.

The proper function of a mediator is to keep the parties talking and to suggest possible solutions to those issues where the parties remain apart. Thus, the mediation function does not detract from the goal of encouraging the parties to reach their own agreement, but enhances it, since a mediator's efforts are directed to assisting the parties to reach their own agreement. Mediation does not involve an attempt by the mediator to dictate to the parties what the agreement should contain.

Fact-Finding

Despite the existence of skilled mediators, there will nevertheless be occasions when the parties are still unable to reach agreement. In this situation the experience to date indicates that fact-finding with recommendations is an effective way of resolving collective bargaining disputes in the public sector.[18] In a study of the experience in Wisconsin with fact-finding over a three-year period, Prof. James Stern found that approximately 89 percent of the cases where petitions for fact-finding were filed resulted in agreement.[19] Professor Stern observed:

> "The high degree of acceptance of awards suggests that political pressures may offer an effective substitute for the conventional economic pressures in securing acceptance of positions arrived at by collective bargaining procedures."[20]

Professor Stern concluded that fact-finding with recommendations "has made a substantial contribution to the improvement of collective bargaining among public employees in Wisconsin."[21]

In providing for fact-finding with recommendations, however, care should be taken to provide that it is not automatically available to either or both of the parties upon request. The public employee relations board or other body established to administer the legislation should retain the discretionary authority, once a petition requesting fact-finding has been filed by either or both of the parties, to determine whether the circumstances warrant the appointment of a fact-finder. The approach of the Wisconsin Employment Relations Commission in this regard is salutary and should be adopted in other jurisdictions:

> "We will not permit an automatic route to fact-finding. Such a procedure would defeat its own purpose because the recommendations of the fact-finder, in our view, are intended to assist the parties in reaching a settlement of their dispute through collective negotiations. If the fact-finding procedure is regarded as an end in itself it will detour collective bargaining and discourage the possibility of acceptance of the fact-finder's recommendations for a settlement."[22]

To further encourage the parties to reach their own agreement, the applicable legislation should provide that the parties will share the cost of the fact-finding proceedings. The potential cost of a fact-finding proceeding and the requirements that the parties split the cost would deter automatic recourse to such a procedure.

THE TERMINAL STEP: LEGISLATIVE HEARING, STRIKE, OR COMPULSORY ARBITRATION?

Following the issuance of the recommendations of the fact-finder, it is still possible that one or both of the parties will not accept some or all of the recommendations of the fact-finder as the basis for settlement. While the experience with fact-finding suggests that this occurs relatively infrequently, it is nevertheless necessary to decide how the impasse will be resolved if fact-finding does not result in an agreement. My own preference would be to have the legislative body hold a hearing and then make a final decision on all unresolved issues. This is the approach that was embodied in the New York Taylor Law in 1967 and followed in the Florida law that was adopted in 1974.

The ultimate authority for establishing the terms and conditions of public employees should rest with the legislative body which holds the purse strings and is responsible for establishing that body's fiscal priorities. As Justice Powell noted in his concurring opinion in *Abood v. Detroit Board of Education:*[23] "Under our democratic system of government, decisions on these issues of public policy [*i.e.* wages, hours and terms and conditions of employment] have been entrusted to elected officials who ultimately are responsible to the voters."

In recent years, however, the various state legislatures have in many instances considered only two alternatives — either grant public employees the legal right to strike or provide some form of compulsory arbitration. While I have consistently opposed granting public employees the right to strike for a variety of reasons, if I were faced with the task of selecting one of these alternatives, I would favor granting public employees the right to strike rather than mandating compulsory arbitration. My reasons are several in number.

First, the public interest is best served by voluntary agreements reached by the parties rather than mandated settlements imposed by an outside third party. "Compulsory arbitration," in the words of the California Advisory Council chaired by Benjamin Aaron, "is a negation of the principle of voluntarism."[24] Parenthetically, it should be noted that I am not opposed to voluntary binding arbitration.[25] To the contrary, statutes such as the New Jersey Employer-Employee Relations Act which provide that unresolved collective bargaining disputes "may, by agreement of the parties, be submitted to arbitration" are salutary.[26] Voluntary interest arbitration has the distinct advantage of being consented to in advance by the parties rather than being imposed by statute, thus minimizing the problems of acceptability. On this point, my views coincide with those of organized labor.[27] Moreover, the existence of voluntary interest arbitration would give the parties sufficient flexibility to use arbitration for political reasons if this were felt to be necessary.

Voluntary binding arbitration can also be very useful on an *ad hoc* basis to resolve one or two issues on which the parties are deadlocked.

Second, in my experience the existence of compulsory arbitration does have a chilling effect on the collective bargaining process. I am aware of the research and statistical data developed by Professor Rehmus[28] and others which, in their considered judgment, show that arbitration is not being over-utilized and that it is apparently not overly harmful to the collective bargaining process. Most of this data, however, covers the early 1970's, *i.e.* from 1971 to 1973. While I have no hard statistical data to support this, I think that the incidence of arbitration during this three-year period was significantly affected by the existence of wage-price controls.[29]

Moreover, while the statistical data developed by Professor Rehmus and others tend to support their assertion that compulsory arbitration is not unduly undermining the collective bargaining process in a strict *quantitative* sense, I do not think there has been sufficient research into the *qualitative* aspects. It has been my experience that in states with compulsory arbitration statutes there tends to be a higher incidence of arbitration requests among the major public jurisdictions and a considerably lower incidence among the smaller jurisdictions. In many instances a pattern is established by a major jurisdiction within a given geographical area, often through the use of arbitration where it is available, and the other jurisdictions then tend to follow the pattern established thereby. It is thus difficult to compare equally a request by the police for arbitration in Milwaukee, for example, with a similar request in Rhinelander, Wisconsin. When this fact is taken into account, the 15 percent request rate for arbitration in Michigan and Wisconsin assumes considerably greater significance.

Although I would rather grant public employees the right to strike than legislate compulsory arbitration if the choice is limited to these two alternatives, I recognize that there are certain categories of employees, such as firefighters and police in major urban cities, which cannot realistically be granted the right to strike. To assure these employees equitable treatment, there should be some type of terminal impasse procedure, assuming, contrary to my preference, a legislative hearing by the appropriate legislative body is not considered adequate. The basic tenet of any such procedure should be to encourage, to the fullest extent possible, the voluntary settlement of collective bargaining disputes by the parties themselves without recourse to third-party intervention.

While effective mediation assistance and fact-finding will result in many agreements, there may be some disputes where mediation and fact-finding will not end the deadlock. In these situations, if the public employer determines that the health and welfare of the public would be adversely affected if the employees in question were permitted to strike, I would favor compulsory final offer arbitration on a package basis, but only with respect to economic issues. By economic issues I mean specifically wages, overtime and premium payments, holidays, vacations, group hospitalization and insurance, and pensions where not otherwise already provided for by applicable state law or city charter. Since most public sector impasse situations primarily involve unresolved economic issues, by providing a method for resolving in a final and binding fashion such disputes, over-all agreement should be reached in most situations.

Although mediation and fact-finding may not resolve all noneconomic issues, I would nevertheless not favor submitting such issues to compulsory arbitration. It is in the noneconomic area where policy issues are most likely to arise — issues that compulsory arbitration, regardless of the form, is not well suited to resolve. In the final analysis, the contract language which the parties must live under should be written by the parties themselves and not by some outside third party.

In line with the goal of encouraging voluntary agreement wherever possible, the applicable statute should specifically provide that the parties may by mutual agreement amend or modify the award of the arbitration panel on the economic issues.

In considering the economic package offers submitted by the parties, the arbitration panel should be governed by specific criteria which should include appropriate comparisons with employees in comparable communities performing similar services, the over-all compensation received by the employees involved in the arbitration proceeding, the continuity and stability of employment, the effect on other employees of the public employer, and the financial ability of the public employer to meet the cost of any award. This latter criterion, sometimes referred to as the employer's ability to pay, is an important factor and should not simply be glossed over by the arbitration panel. To accomplish this, where the employer affirmatively alleges an inability to meet the cost of the union's economic proposal, the statute should require the arbitration panel to specifically set forth its reason if it rejects the employer's contention.

The problems raised by the steadily increasing number of public employee strikes cannot be resolved by recourse to any simple formula which will be applicable in all situations and in all jurisdictions. What is needed is comprehensive legislation that takes into account not only the various types and kinds of public employee strikes but also the setting and context in which collective bargaining takes place in the public sector.

My conclusion with respect to impasse procedures for resolving disputes over wages and working conditions in the public sector are fourfold. *First,* the overriding goal and objective should be to encourage wherever possible the parties to reach their own voluntary agreement. *Second,* mediators who are professionally trained and career oriented should be available to the parties to assist in resolving collective bargaining disputes. *Third,* despite the surface attractions and the hope of avoiding strikes, the panacea of compulsory arbitration should be firmly resisted. If it comes down to the alternative of either granting public employees the right to strike or providing for compulsory arbitration, I would favor granting public employees the right to strike. *Fourth,* where the public employer determines that certain categories of public employees, such as firefighters or police in major urban settings, must be prohibited from striking, the legislated impasse procedure should provide for final offer arbitration on a package basis with respect to the economic issues.

If the laudable goal of free collective bargaining is to be encouraged, as I believe it should, then compulsory arbitration should be avoided wherever possible. Rather than expending our time erecting elaborate impasse procedures which involve resort to outside third parties, we should devote more time and attention to establishing a framework in which voluntary agreement can be reached.

FOOTNOTES

1 Bureau of Labor Statistics, *Work Stoppages in Government, 1976,* Report No. 532 (1978).

2 *See,* for example, R. I. Gen. Laws, Sections 28-9.1-12 (Re-enactment 1968); Laws of Wyoming, Ch. 197, L. 1965, Sections 27-268.

3 Postal Reorganization Act of 1970, 39 U.S.C.A. Sec. 1 (Supp. 1971).

4 *See, e.g., Indianapolis Education Assn. v. Lewallen,* Civ. No. IP69-C-252 (7th Cir. 1969), 60 LC ¶ 10,198.

5 *See, e.g., State Board of Regents v. Packing House Workers Local 1258,* 175 N.W.2d 110 (1970); *Chicago Division of the Illinois Education Association v. Board of Education of the City of Chicago,* 76 Ill. App. 2d 456, 222 N.E.2d 243 (1966).

6 29 U.S.C. Sec. 158 (b) (4) (D) (1964).

7 29 U.S.C. Sec. 160 (k) (1964).

8 *Teamsters Local 174 v. Lucas Flour Co.,* 369 U.S. 95, 105 (1962).

9 *Ibid.*

10 *Boys Market, Inc. v. Retail Clerk's Union, Local 770,* 398 U.S. 235, 249 (1970).

11 Indeed, the right to strike is limited in the private sector under the provisions of the Taft-Hartley Act, Sec. 206 *et. seq.,* which provides for an 80-day cooling-off period for strikes which threaten to "imperil the national health or safety."

12 This is generally true for the vast majority of public services, such as police and fire protection, but is not so for such services as a public transit system.

13 *Chicago Tribune,* October 8, 1969, p. 1.

14 *New York Times,* August 31, 1970, p. 43.

15 *Ibid.*

16 Wellington and Winter, "Structuring Collective Bargaining in Public Employment," *79 Yale L. Rev.* 805, 828 (1970).

17 Illinois Governor's Advisory Commission on Labor-Management Policy for Public Employees, *Report and Recommendations,* pp. 31-32 (March, 1967).

18 *See* Yaffe and Goldblatt, *Factfinding in Public Employment Disputes in New York State: More Promise Than Illusion* (1971); Stern, "The Wisconsin Public Employee Fact-Finding Procedure," 20 *Ind. & Lab. Rel. Rev.* 3 (1966).

[19] Stern, cited at footnote 18.

[20] *Ibid.*

[21] *Ibid.*

[22] *City of Racine and Racine Fire Fighters Local No. 321, AFL-CIO,* Decision No. 6242-A (1963).

[23] 97 S. Ct. 1782, 1811 (1977).

[24] *Final Report of the [California] Assembly Advisory Council on Public Employee Relations,* 221 (March 15, 1973).

[25] See generally Cushman, "Voluntary Arbitration of New Contract Terms — A Forum in Search of a Dispute," 16 *Lab. L.J.* 765 (1965); Staudohar, "Voluntary Binding Arbitration in Public Employment," 25 *Arb. J.* (n.s.) 30 (1970); Taylor, "The Voluntary Arbitration of Labor Disputes," 49 *Mich. L. Rev.* 787 (1951).

[26] Ch. 303, Laws of 1968, ¶ 34:13A-7.

[27] *See, e.g.,* the June 1972 *Boilermaker-Blacksmiths Reporter* containing the following statement: "The AFL-CIO is opposed to any form of compulsory arbitration. . . . On the other hand organized labor whole-heartedly supports the concept of voluntary arbitration where the parties agree to accept an umpire's decision as final and binding." *Id.* at 8.

[28] Rehmus, "Legislated Interest Arbitration," in *Proceedings of IRRA 27th Annual Meeting* (1974).

[29] It is interesting to note that requests for arbitration under the Pennsylvania Police-Fire Arbitration Act occurred in approximately 30 percent of the available situations prior to the imposition of controls, and that the rate dropped to about 15 percent after the imposition of controls. Undoubtedly, part of the drop can be attributed to the parties' greater experience and sophistication, as Professor Rehmus suggests, but I would submit that the existence of wage controls was probably a significant factor also. This is an area for further research.

44. The Case for Legalizing Teacher Strikes

The amount of time devoted to school district bargaining is frequently excessive. In many school systems, bargaining goes on virtually *ad infinitum,* draining time, energy and resources from both sides of the table, and working especially against management's interests. To change this situation, school officials may have to start thinking the unthinkable — *Legalize teacher strikes.*

This step might actually reduce the amount of time allowed for reaching an agreement on management's terms.

As is frequently noted employees in privately owned utilities or businesses or recreational enterprises can strike legally; their counterparts in the public sector cannot. Similarly, teachers in private schools can strike, whereas those in public schools cannot. Teacher unions have protested this state of affairs, contending that the illegality of public employee strikes constitutes discrimination against them. Whether it is or not, perhaps school boards and administrators should agree to legalize teacher strikes, although not for the reasons advanced by teachers.

Most school board members seem unaware of the legal and practical difficulties of enforcing penalties for illegal teacher strikes. The reason teacher strikes occur with high frequency — in spite of their illegality — is not primarily arrogant or insensitive management. It is because teachers are increasingly aware of how difficult it is to enforce legal restrictions against teacher strikes.

Consequently, teachers come out winners on both counts: While strikes are technically illegal, teachers usually are safe in calling one, owing to the legal and pragmatic difficulties involved in enforcing anti-strike laws (particularly when it comes to applying penalties to individual strikers). In many states, teacher strikes are illegal not because of any state law but because of a judicial decision to this effect. In such states there are no statutory penalties for striking. The penalties, if they exist, are a result of teacher refusal to obey a temporary restraining order against the strike obtained by the district. Getting such an order can be a time-consuming expensive process which can be very difficult for other reasons as well. Many districts simply are unwilling to make the effort to get or to enforce a temporary restraining order of this type. Furthermore, teachers ordinarily gain legislative and public sympathy for the alleged inequity to which they are subjected — the legal prohibitions against teacher strikes.

Significantly, the strike is not an economic weapon for teachers. Indeed, if it works to anyone's economic benefit, it is to management's. The loss, if it can be called that, of production during a teacher strike is scarcely noticeable in the aggregate; who can measure — years or even a couple of months after the fact — the difference in the over-all quality of education resulting from the loss of a few days of schooling? In reality, teacher strikes are *political,* not economic, weapons. And the absence of a legal right to strike strengthens *political* support for teachers while simultaneously depriving management of an economic weapon. Legislatures are typically sympathetic to the contention that something needs to be done to protect the interests of teachers who cannot strike legally. To prevent school boards from bargaining in a high-handed manner, teacher bargaining legislation usually prescribes considerable time for bargaining and impasse procedures. This is supposed to ensure that teacher proposals will get a fair hearing during the negotiation process.

Unfortunately, the typical upshot of these extended procedures is protracted bargaining and impasse procedures. This often results in management's making more concessions than it would in a simple, short-term strike settlement. The reason is that the longer management is at the table, the more it gives away in the end. Even where this axiom does not hold true, the fact remains that the process of extended bargaining consumes enormous amounts of management time, energy, and other resources. To avoid prolonged bargaining and impasse procedures, management often concedes more than it would to avoid a strike.

State legislatures and local school systems alike should be concerned about the fact that too much, rather than too little, time is spent on bargaining with public employees. Instead of stipulating a minimum amount of time for bargaining, legislatures should *prescribe a maximum* — with a definite cut-off. Teacher unions still could be protected adequately from management that does not bargain in good faith during the allotted time; they could have recourse under laws governing unfair labor practices.

Another compelling but often neglected reason can be cited why so-called "adequate" time for bargaining and impasse procedures has been harmful. The more time available, the more teachers persist with unreasonable demands. If the alternative to disagreement is a strike, the parties are more likely to be realistic about the issues remaining on the table. A teacher union that strikes (and thereby exposes its members to loss of income) would find it more difficult to maintain unreasonable demands than if the alternative were a long period of mediation and fact-finding.

The mediation and fact-finding option (instead of a strike) shelters teachers from reality and consequently encourages them to persist in unrealistic demands. Furthermore, the very existence of the impasse option frequently strengthens teacher determination to concede as little as possible prior to impasse, lest they weaken their tactical position in the impasse procedure.

A great deal of management opposition to legalizing teacher strikes might disappear if legalization involved the same risks to striking employees as it does in the private sector. The private sector employer who has bargained in good faith to impasse can replace economic strikers. Having this option (which would, of course, constitute the "equity" sought by teachers) would require repealing, or at least suspending, the tenure laws. These laws were never meant to protect striking teachers anyway. Were this to happen, tenured teachers who went on strike could not only lose their jobs but also their opportunities to increase substantially their retirement benefits. These risks would be a strong deterrent to strikes, at least in small districts. Of course, the legalization of teacher strikes must include realistic limitations on the availability of impasse procedures. Such limitations should prohibit mediation or fact-finding or both from being imposed upon an unwilling employer, as they cannot be in the private sector. Unfortunately, the legislative tendency is in the opposite direction, *i.e.* it is to legalize strikes only after the parties have been subjected to complex and prolonged impasse procedures.

Mediation and fact-finding (especially fact-finding) should be available only for a limited period of time and to parties who have narrowed their differences substantially. To allow parties that cannot agree on most items after protracted bargaining to use mediation and fact-finding at public expense is to encourage unrealistic and irresponsible negotiations.

School board members and administrators need to reassess the relationship between the current illegality of teacher strikes and the excessive time given over to unrealistic bargaining. To get rid of the latter, they also may have to get rid of the former.

45.   Operating Schools During a Teacher Strike

If you don't already know what your school board will do if the local teacher union strikes, you should. Will you attempt to keep schools open? Will you staff them with substitutes? In the 16,000-student Federal Way School District in suburban Seattle, our answer to both questions was a carefully considered "Yes."

When the teachers struck, the school board and administration were ready. As superintendent, I was given complete authority by the board to make operational decisions and to utilize the physical and human resources of the district.

With approximately 600 substitutes and a specially prepared curriculum, we were able to keep schools open and education going throughout the six-day strike. On the first day of the strike, student attendance was at 47 percent. Each day, attendance increased over the previous day, even though regular bus drivers honored teacher picket lines. On the last day of the strike, 60 percent of students were in classes, a statistic that certainly didn't please union strategists whose goal all along had been to keep schools closed and kids at home.

How were we able to curtail the effectiveness of the strike? Careful planning. Faced with the possibility of a strike, we asked ourselves a series of questions. Together, the queries can help any school board answer for itself the basic question, "What are we going to do if the teachers strike?" Here are 14 questions to consider:

1. Will you be able to employ enough substitute teachers during the strike?
First, try to determine how many will be needed. Next, compile lists extensive enough to include replacements for the faint of heart who refuse to brave picket lines more than a day or two.

This chapter was prepared by George C. Cochran, former superintendent, Federal Way School District in suburban Seattle, and currently an administrative consultant to the school board. (It appeared in a slightly different version in *The American School Board Journal,* November, 1975.)

2. Is the board willing and able to raise the pay of substitutes to attract those you'll need from distant communities?
To woo enough substitutes, some (but by no means all) school boards have had to pay as much as double the regular substitute salary.

3. How will students be transported if and when the bus drivers union decides to honor the picket lines of the striking teachers?
If you aren't able to hire enough substitute bus drivers, perhaps parents will transport their children and others in their neighborhoods. Perhaps students will walk.

4. Will secretarial employees stay on the job?
In a strike operation, much will depend on the loyalty and resourcefulness of secretaries.

5. Will maintenance and operations personnel remain on duty?
If not, what provisions can be made to keep the schools maintained safely?

6. Is the superintendent personally committed to keeping the schools open and children learning during the strike?
Whether the operation is successful will depend in large measure on the superintendent's resourcefulness in planning and day-to-day decision-making during the strike. If the superintendent is torn between professional ties to teacher groups and allegiance to the board, this uncertainty inevitably will be reflected in the effort of the staff.

7. Can principals be relied upon during the strike to operate their schools each day in spite of intense opposition?
Long and successful professional relationships between teachers and principals can be severely strained by a strike. Ensuring that principals are important members of your school district's management team should be a continuous effort on the part of board and superintendent.

8. Will the local police or the sheriff's department enforce applicable laws and court orders on request?
Will you ask the courts to require teachers to return to work? Or to limit picketing and harassment? Police officers sometimes are re-

luctant to interfere with the union activities of another governmental employee group even when those activities are illegal. Be prepared to employ your own security force to protect school property and escort substitutes across militant picket lines.

9. Will the board be willing to authorize necessary extra legal expenses?

Competent legal counsel should be available to advise board and superintendent at all times during the strike.

10. Do the board and administrative staff understand typical tactics of radical political action?

Board members who are emotionally unprepared to cope with threats and harassment may find the intensity of the conflict too much to handle. The it-can't-happen-here attitude has no place before or during a strike.

11. Is the school board willing to hire a professional negotiator?

Union demands for around-the-clock negotiations are a familiar tactic. The board will be under extreme pressure from the teachers and the public to reach a settlement. Around-the-clock negotiations may sound like a reasonable solution, but board members who submit to this tactic sometimes don't hold their own under the pressure. Having an experienced negotiator representing the board reduces the chances of settlement because of exhaustion or press of personal business.

12. Is the board prepared to hire temporary professional public relations assistance?

Union statements and media accounts frequently distort board positions during strikes. Professionally prepared releases help communicate accurately the board's stand to the public.

13. Is program and curriculum planning adequate for a strike operation?

Curriculum plans should be designed specifically for use by substitutes who will have little or no time for preparation. Offering a poor instructional program will surely result in increased public pressure on the board to settle with the union regardless of settlement terms.

14. What would be the financial impact of a strike operation?
Check state law to determine state aid during the strike. Will keeping schools open be a financial boon or burden?

Author's Note: Boards actually faced with the prospect of a strike should also get one or more of the various strike manuals listed at the end of this section.

46. Media Relations During Strikes or Strike Build-Ups

As school districts plunge into the world of collective bargaining and contracts, what used to be a relatively small and exclusive group — school administrators who have survived a teacher strike — is expanding rapidly. They know that communication plays the single most vital role in the complexities and emotions of an employee strike against a school district. Good communication can neutralize the efforts of the employee union to influence public opinion — and to influence staff during strike build-ups. It brings order out of chaos during a strike, and can be the glue with which you put the pieces back together after a strike is ended.

Strikes and strike build-ups are won or lost in the arena of public opinion — in the ability of one side or the other to convince the community its position is right. Public opinion is formed by situation reports in or on the media, and through open lines of communication between a school district's board of education and administration and the community. Good, quick communications mean good, quick decisions and the mechanism to keep things together during the strike or strike build-up. Poor, tardy communications mean confusion, possible chaos, and a diminished position of the board and administration in the eyes of the media, the community, students, and employees, especially those who are still on the job (classified, certificated and administrative).

How do you communicate? You stick to the facts — nothing more. You realize that once a strike, or even a strike build-up, starts, it is an organizational stand. You are not dealing with the local teacher association you have known and are familiar with. The plays are

---

This chapter was prepared by Ann H. Barkelew, public information officer for the Office of the Los Angeles County Superintendent of Schools and president of the National School Public Relations Association. (Portions were published previously in *Thrust*, March, 1977.)

being called by professional strike units sent in by state and national employee unions. The strategies and plans are backed up with dollars, how-to manuals, and pre-printed bulletins.

The pros will try in every way to split the board, undermine confidence in the board members and administration, discredit your credibility, and question your integrity. Their primary ploy is to have you react to their stories and tactics. If they can get you on the defensive, they can set the tone for a victory for the union.

With a planned program of communications that can be set into motion the instant a strike build-up begins, you can neutralize the union's manpower and massive efforts to control what appears in the newspapers and on radio and television. If you have a school public relations person on your staff, you can relax a bit before it ever begins. If you have such a person and if you keep that person totally informed and involved, your chances of having to take a strike are greatly diminished.

If you don't have such a professional on your staff, be sure that someone is designated to carry this responsibility during a strike. Here's a short course in what's involved:

- Letters must be prepared and ready to be sent to staff, to parents, to high school seniors, to community leaders, and the community-at-large to clarify the issues. Report accurately the district's position, and tell how the district will handle a strike.

- A district information center must be set up in the district office. It will be the information source for all electronic and print media people, all interested parents and citizens, all student editors and reporters, all community leaders, other districts, and board members.

  The center must have at least two direct telephone lines — preferably two telephones — and necessary directories, at least one other telephone that goes through the PBX to permit "inside" calls, and a special telephone number and line for usa as an "INFORMATION LINE" for the general public; in addition, the usual supplies should be on hand, plus secretarial help.

- A media contact sheet must be prepared, listing all media who cover the district and for each, the contact person, telephone number, and deadline time.

- The information-gathering and dissemination process must be rehearsed so you're ready with the mechanism to collect data from school sites. Each day you'll need to know how many teachers were in their classrooms, how many were out, how many students were in school, how many replacement teachers were in classrooms, how many support staff and parent volunteers were there, what kinds of questions and concerns are being telephoned in to each school, any incidents of vandalism or violence. Each day everyone will want to know all of these things and more. Are all schools open? Are they on regular schedules? Are buses running? Are lunches being served? Is it safe to send children to school? Are teaching and learning really happening? Will students be penalized if they stay home? What is the district doing to bring the situation to an end?

- A district spokesperson must be identified well in advance.

- Have a quick way to reach all parents via a direct mailing.

- Be ready to do a direct mailing to each employee's home address.

- Plan time for daily reinforcement of management and confidential staff.

- Be prepared to support staff members who have stayed on the job.

- Realize you will be operating with a skeletal central office staff, as many district administrators will be filling in in classrooms.

- Make contact and stay in touch with city, county and state officials, and community leaders. Keep them up to date and confident that you are in charge and in control of the situation.

- Don't agree to news blackouts or joint news conferences. You'll honor it; they won't.

- Be sure all board members and management and confidential staff understand the negotiations process completely. Be sure they are aware of all the items being negotiated throughout the year.

- Set some goals for your board's team — goals that are in the best interests of your schools, the children in your schools, and the public you represent.

- Be sure you have a credible employee newsletter. Use it.

- Know how many teachers have been involved, and in what ways, in study and development committees. Communicate that information regularly.

- Be sure budget information summaries are disseminated to all employees monthly or quarterly.

- The following information must be gathered, checked, re-checked, and ready to use:

   1. About each school — number of students enrolled, number of teachers assigned (not FTE's), number of other certificated staff members, number of classified staff members, normal daily absenteeism (percentage) for each category, schedule of classes with number of students in each, when the school was built, and the kind and cost of recent improvements.

   2. About the district — number of students enrolled (a five-year profile), number of employees by categories, salary and fringe benefit information (current and comparative for past 5 years) for all employees, average class size/staffing ratio, ratio of administrators to teachers (current and past), map of district showing the location of each school, map showing how to get to the district and the district office (and where to park), instances and numbers of teachers involved in study committees affecting decision-making over past two to three years, how the district compares with comparable districts in average salary, fringe benefits, average class size, administrator ratios, percentage of salary improvement, size of central office staff, a 25-word explanation of how the district negotiates with its employees, a salary schedule showing number of employees at each step, examples of financial cutbacks the district has made in the past couple of years, (especially those related to administration and support services), pertinent budget information by percentages (teachers salaries, administration, instructional supplies, etc.), and countywide rankings.

- Keep building administrators fully involved and regularly informed. Be sure they get summaries, progress reports or confidential minutes after each negotiations session. They can assist in person-to-person efforts to continuously clarify board posture.

- Review all employee organization proposals with the media people who cover your district. If you have a good negotiations report vehicle, send it "FYI" to the major media, city officials, and your legislators.

- Alert the press on probable confrontation. Let them know when and how to reach the district's spokesperson.

Once the strike or strike build-up begins:

- Continue and use all of the foregoing.

- Stay cohesive and present a unified stand. Keep your differences behind closed doors. And — no leaks, please.

- Don't react. Suppress that desire to fight back via the media. It's hard not to fire back, to expose the tactics, but management simply cannot react or respond in a retaliatory manner. Stay with the facts. The only firing back you can do is to correct bad information the other side is trying to use correcting it calmly and rationally.

- Report the facts at every opportunity — the day's attendance, the number of staff on the job, the kind of instructional programs and cocurricular activities happening, the status of negotiations, the issues already agreed to, the issues keeping you apart, how parents can get more information, plans for the next day (schools all still open, buses running, lunches being served), a reminder that students belong in school, that the negotiations are not taking place on the picket lines.

- Prepare question-and-answer fact sheets. Disseminate them to everyone and don't forget those on the picket lines. These should be done at least every other day for the first week and then at least a couple of times a week. Have a supply of extras on hand for anyone who comes in.

- Stay in contact with all media people covering the strike. Be sure they have your home telephone number, too. Don't wait for them to call you; keep in touch with them.

- Meet whenever and wherever with community groups to answer questions and give the facts.

- Meet daily with student leaders.

- Visit schools and classrooms. Communicate what's going on.

- Telephone homes of students who are absent. Reassure parents and encourage them to send their youngsters to school.

- Ward off interference from other agencies; stay in control.

- Be prepared for harassment in the form of phone calls, letters to you, community newsletters about you, pickets at your home and your business — none of which will be complimentary.

- Remember the purpose of news conferences prior to and during a strike: that negotiations cannot be conducted through the public media and that the news conference is held only to publicly disclose the status of negotiations, particularly as they relate to the board's goals.

Some of the new strategies being used by employee unions include:

- Telephone trees to parents.

- Threats to new teachers.

- Use of kids and use of parents.

- Concentrated picketing of board members' businesses and homes.

- Parades and rallies giving the organization pitch — complete with refreshments.

- More specific talk of budget money — by more than the union's finance experts.

- More criticism of management people.

- Intensive discrediting of "substitutes," questioning the quality of substitutes.

- Attacks on tax dollars being paid for professional negotiators ("Kids are being cheated").

- Parades through the district office.

- Sit-ins at the district office.

- Sympathy signs in local businesses.

- Emphasis on the civil rights of employees.

With a little awareness and some planned communications activities, each strategy can be handled.

No matter how well-prepared, no matter how credible the issues, you'll be criticized and outnumbered in terms of manpower and union support. Even with that handicap, it is possible to neutralize their best efforts by calmly and rationally persuading others of the position of the board.

Remember, the basic issue that underlies most teacher/board confrontations everywhere in the country is "Who controls the schools?" These confrontations call for men and women in management who make the education and welfare of students their number one priority. They require management staff that is willing to make hard decisions and stand by them, willing to take an occasional risk, and willing to be part of a team.

When a district has management people of this ilk, the likelihood of strikes diminishes; the guarantee of strike survival is sure.

47. More on Strikes and Impasse Procedures

Aaron, Lester: *The Case for Fair and Final Offer Arbitration,* New Jersey School Boards Association, Trenton, N.J., 1975. This is a good statement of the case for final offer arbitration. In this procedure, an arbitrator is allowed to choose either the school board or union final offer as a package. The author is an experienced labor relations attorney and negotiator.

Clark, Jr., R. Theodore: *Coping with Mediation, Fact-Finding, and Forms of Arbitration,* International Personnel Management Association, Chicago, Ill., 1974. This is an excellent manual on how to present the management case in the impasse procedures.

"Public Employee Strikes: Some Proposed Solutions," *Labor Law Journal,* February, 1972, pp. 111-120.

Contingency Planning for Teacher Strikes, Educational Research Service, Inc., Arlington, Va., 1976. Districts facing or likely to face strikes need a comprehensive plan to deal with same. This manual helps to ensure that every aspect of a viable plan has been considered.

Kershen, Harry, editor: *Impasse and Grievance Resolution,* Baywood Publishing Company, Inc., Farmingdale, N.Y., 1977.

Labor-Management Services Administration, U.S. Department of Labor: *Understanding, Factfinding and Arbitration in the Public Sector,* Superintendent of Documents, Washington, D.C., 1974.

Mulcahy, Charles C., and Marion Cartwright Smith: *Last Best Offer, How to Win and Lose,* Labor-Management Relations Service, Washington, D.C., 1976. This analysis shows the need to analyze teacher strikes carefully.

Public Sector Bargaining and Strikes, Public Service Research Council, Vienna, Va., 1976. This summary includes much useful data on teacher strikes. Its conclusions and policy recommendations have been intensively criticized by public employee unions as reflecting the ideological bias of the sponsoring organization.

Shaw, Lee C. and R. Theodore Clark, Jr.: "Public Sector Strikes: An Empirical Analysis," *Journal of Law and Education,* Vol. 2, April, 1973, pp. 217-234.

The Strike Manual, Negotiation Support Service, Association of California School Administrators, Burlingame, Calif., 1973. Although geared to California law, this is a useful manual for any school district.

Work Stoppage Strategies, American Association of School Administrators, Arlington, Va., 1974.

CONTRACT ADMINISTRATION

48. Administering District Contracts

In thinking about collective bargaining, most school administrators are chiefly concerned about the negotiating process and the collective agreement itself. This is only natural. The process is still relatively new, and the administrator's stake in it is very high. His ability to administer his district depends partly on his effectiveness as a negotiator. Indeed, his very job may depend upon how effectively he manages negotiations and on the kind of contract he negotiates.

These considerations should not obscure the importance of contract administration. Bargaining is an adversary process, but the adversaries have to live together after they reach agreement. During negotiations, the adversaries are defining their continuing relationships for a considerable period of time. They also are setting the stage for future negotiations. These facts affect the substance of the contract. They also suggest that the contractual *relationships* between the parties must be viewed as an integral part of the negotiating process itself.

Suppose the district and its teachers have finally reached agreement after long and difficult negotiations. Such negotiations are likely to have exacerbated teacher-board relationships. The parties probably said things during negotiations that tend to jeopardize their relationships after an agreement is reached.

Usually, it is desirable to defuse the atmosphere as quickly as possible after contract agreement has been reached. This can be done by a press conference or some other use of media to announce the agreement. Management should state how happy it is to have the agreement. It should say whatever good things it can about the teacher negotiators — how tough they were, how vigorously they fought for teachers, and so on. It is usually good practice to do this, regardless of how many times the parties have negotiated a contract. The teacher negotiators can always profit from such statements from management, and this works to management's advantage.

Another important first step is to distribute copies of the contract to all supervisory and administrative personnel. This should be done as soon as possible, without waiting for copies made by a printer. Don't forget that although principals, chairmen, and supervisors must administer the contract, only a few of them were on the negotiating team. Thus, no matter how good are internal communications, most of the administrative and supervisory staff will need clarification of the contract as it finally emerges.

Ideally, such clarification should be the responsibility of the board's chief negotiator. This person should be able to explain, clearly, the implications of the contract at the individual school building level. He should anticipate teacher reactions and possible challenges to management's interpretation of the agreement.

Regardless of whether the chief negotiator is assigned the task, the important thing is to *centralize over-all administrative responsibility for contract interpretation and administration.* In other words, there should be one person, at the central office level, to whom other central office personnel, as well as principals and supervisors, can turn for assistance and direction in these matters. This person should also be responsible for maintaining a continual record of facts and figures bearing upon the impact of the contract. For instance, he should try to assess use of sick leave or personal business leave, to ascertain the actual costs to the administration and the extent, if any, of any teacher abuse of such benefits. In this way, the administration will be better prepared to negotiate on the next contract.

It may be useful to consider how the unions police the contract, *i.e.* make sure the district adheres to it.

Generally, a union representative is assigned to each school. Sometimes the representative can take teacher complaints straight to the school principal. Other times, he must obtain permission from a districtwide grievance committee before involving school management.

Grievance representatives are the union's operatives in the schools. They keep union officials advised of teacher attitudes and teachers informed of union programs. They meet with new teachers, explain provisions of the contract, and emphasize that union assistance is available when needed.

Because the processing of grievances is the main function of these representatives, they typically are thoroughly familiar with the language and interpretations of the contract. In many teacher unions, the individual school grievance representatives hold regular meetings to pool information on management practices, decide how to handle questionable complaints, and determine the nature of contract changes to be sought during the next round of bargaining.

Indeed, when bargaining is not under way, policing the contract through the grievance procedure is the union's most important task. Continued employment of union staff members may well depend on how effectively they process grievances. Clearly, school district management cannot afford to take contract administration any less seriously.

Prompt analysis of the new contract with the administrative staff can minimize problems. Some time ago, for example, I negotiated an agreement that provided a duty-free lunch period for teachers. Immediately after the agreement was reached, the teacher negotiators announced that they interpreted a "duty-free lunch period" to mean that teachers could not be assigned to lunch duty. This interpretation had been specifically discussed and rejected by the management team during negotiations. We had told the teacher negotiators: "We will provide teachers with a duty-free lunch period. We cannot guarantee the time of day involved or that teachers will be relieved of all lunch duty. If a teacher aide does not show up at the last minute, the administration may have to utilize a teacher to cover lunch duty. However, even when this happens, the teacher will get a duty-free lunch period later in the day."

This position had been very explicit during negotiations. Naturally, the different interpretation announced by the teacher negotiators caused considerable consternation among those principals who could not relieve all teachers of some lunch duty. Therefore, at our first staff meeting after the contract was reached, we explained very carefully that the agreement was not reasonably open to the interpretation claimed by the teachers. Furthermore, we tried to ensure that every principal was prepared to handle a grievance on this issue if the teachers pursued the matter.

Contract administration involves difficult issues relating to administrative structure and policy. At the school level, principals and chairmen are under immediate pressures to accept teacher interpretations of the contract. Confronted by unexpected interpretations of the contract, principals may not have time to review the contract in depth before making a decision. On the other hand, the administration wants to avoid contract interpretations that may be erroneous and damaging as precedents. Thus, there are pressures in the school to allow the principals to act and pressures in the central office to limit discretion at the school level, in order to ensure consistent interpretations reflecting management's views.

The way out of this dilemma is careful study of the agreement by principals and constant communication on all grievances between principals and central office personnel responsible for systemwide contract administration. It is very important that principals be alert to teacher complaints that are *not* filed as grievances or are not processed to arbitration. Such complaints frequently suggest changes which should be made in subsequent contracts. To cite an actual example: a clause limited teacher assignments to three preparations a day (as distinct from the number of classes teachers could be required to handle). In negotiating a subsequent contract, some teachers asserted informally that the administration was violating the contract. The basis of their assertion was that the administration did not treat classes of different ability levels in the same grade and subject as different preparations. Under the informal teacher interpretation, the administration would have been violating the contract.

The informal teacher interpretation would have severely limited the administration in scheduling teachers. For this reason, its negotiating team insisted upon contractual language that stated clearly that classes of different ability levels were not to be considered separate preparations. Educationally, the teacher interpretation had some merit; administratively, it could not be conceded. It was deemed better to confront the issue in the contract, rather than leave it open to interpretation and possibly an adverse decision by an arbitrator.

The point is that district insistence was based upon reports of informal comments by teachers. Had no principal ever reported the teacher interpretations, the negotiating team would not have insisted upon the change in contract language. Had the district not made the change in the contract, the system might have experienced severe disruption if a teacher grievance had been initiated and pursued to binding arbitration under the language of the old contract.

In many school districts, a contract that is very favorably received in one school or grade level may not be at another. This can be true of the administration as well as the teachers. As a result, there is sometimes pressure for side agreements. These will not necessarily be written agreements. They may simply be practices accepted at the school level. For example, the teachers may have failed to achieve a coffee break in the contract. Nevertheless, particular principals may be allowing teachers to keep an eye on each other's classes in order to permit a coffee break.

Such practices can be troublesome if "grievance" is not defined carefully. For instance, if "grievance" is defined to cover administrative actions contrary to established policy *or practice* affecting the welfare of teachers, failure to provide the coffee break might be grievable. Effective contract administration, as well as effective negotiations, requires both an intimate knowledge of the contract and of school operations.

In some situations, a principal may be tempted to make a supplemental agreement, or to waive a clause in the existing one. Although some flexibility is desirable, such actions should be cleared with the central office person with over-all responsibility for contract administration. Principals often complain that they are inadequately consulted during negotiations, but many principals are guilty of the same failure during the administration of the contract. Many negotiators are familiar with situations in which a principal decided not to insist upon strict observance of the time limits for the grievance procedure. As a result, grievances went to arbitration and the teachers won a significant concession. On the other hand, the grievance would have been dropped at the school level if the principal had not waived the time limits.

In the case just cited, the principal reasoned that, since the grievance was a continuing one, it would be just as well to get the matter settled one way or the other. While this attitude is commendable, it should not be the prerogative of individual principals to waive important clauses in the agreement. The agreement is made between the bargaining agent and the school district; permitting individual administrators to modify or waive it can have disastrous consequences. Such action should be approved only by the person in charge of contract administration. In fact, it is to the mutual interest of both the administration and the teacher organization to specify in the agreement that it can be modified only by the parties themselves.

Perhaps the most crucial aspect of contract administration is a clear understanding of the fact that the administration is initially responsible for interpreting and enforcing the contract. For example, the contract may provide that, except in case of emergency, no teacher will be required to cover the classes of absent teachers. Administrators frequently react by asking: "Who decides what's an emergency?" Or, the contract may provide that seniority shall prevail in promotions only when the candidates are "substantially equal" in qualifications. A common administrative reaction is: "Who decides when the qualifications are substantially equal?"

In these situations, the administration decides the matter, initially. If the teachers believe that the administration is violating the agreement (by requiring teachers to cover classes of other teachers when there is no emergency, or by failing to promote the most senior of two candidates with substantially equal qualifications), the teachers have recourse to the grievance procedure.

Teachers should not be permitted to impose their interpretation on the administration or get it accepted in any other way. Nevertheless, it is surprising how many administrators fail to recognize their responsibility and authority in these matters. Some administrators are afraid to discipline teachers because the contract did not spell out their right to do so. These administrators did not realize that they retained the initiative in this area, that it was still part of their job to discipline teachers for such actions as reporting late for work. The crucial point is that the administration can take whatever action is not prohibited by the contract. Where the teachers protest that administration interpretation of contract language is incorrect, the administration *still* has the right to take the action based upon its interpretation. If the teachers feel strongly that such action is a violation of the contract, they can and should have recourse to the grievance procedure.

Members of the school board can monitor contracts without becoming embroiled personally in grievance controversies. To illustrate, the board may require a summary report on all grievances filed each month. Such a report might indicate the number of grievances submitted, the number resolved, the resolutions applied, the number of grievances pending, and the nature of those pending complaints. School board members who believe (erroneously) that contract administration can be accomplished only through official board involvement in the grievance process should consider the usefulness of a monthly summary report. It is an important alternative.

Another way to monitor employee contracts is to develop a checklist of pertinent questions about them. Some questions such a checklist should include are:

1. Can the district assign teachers as needed to duties outside their routine workday?

2. Can the district introduce, change or discontinue educational programs without a union veto?

3. Can the district evaluate teachers effectively and take appropriate action on each of those evaluations?

4. Are principals aware of the precise extent of their authority under the teacher contract?

5. Do principals seek approval from grievance representatives before acting on certain provisions of the teacher contract?

6. Are board policies and regulations that affect contract administration explained thoroughly to middle management in the district?

Such questions should be raised during the negotiation process.

When this is impossible, some benefit still may accrue from dissemination of the checklist to management and supervisory personnel; it may elicit information that is not evident from an analysis of grievances.

Administrators who fail to recognize that contract interpretation and administration is, first and foremost, an administrative responsibility are headed for co-management of their school district. And co-management is likely to be a disaster, regardless of the rhetoric about "shared authority" and "professional participation." A good collective contract does not alter the situation whereby teachers teach and administrators administer.

49.   The Role of the School Board in the Grievance Procedure

Should the school board make itself part of the formal grievance procedure teachers use to register their complaints? Except in small districts, it should not. School boards generally are wasting time and inviting trouble when they allow appeals to the board included as a formal step in the contractual grievance procedure.

The reasons for this are not complicated, but they require an understanding of contractual definitions of "grievance." The most common definition is a violation or inequitable or discriminatory application or interpretation of the contract.

Under nearly all such definitions of grievance, an aggrieved employee is allowed to appeal board or administration decisions that allegedly violated the contract. The number and levels of appeal vary from contract to contract, but most include at least one appeal at the building level (to the principal) and at least one at the central office level (to the superintendent or his designee). In some districts, the final step in the grievance procedure is binding arbitration.

Although the argument that an appeal to the school board ought *not* be included as a step in the grievance procedure does not depend upon the presence or absence of binding arbitration, let's assume that in your district the question is this: Should the grievance procedure include an appeal to the board before the grievance is submitted to binding arbitration?

As a concept, at least, most board members probably would agree that school boards ought to concentrate on policy *formulation,* not on policy administration. Policy *formulation* however, was accomplished when the board agreed to the bargained contract. The process of deciding grievance cases is policy *administration.* Handling an employee's claim that the contract has been violated is a matter of determining if established board policy has been violated. This is an administrative function, at least if the board's approach to employment relations is no different from its approach to other policy areas. For example, if the board has established a policy governing student suspensions, it is the administration's responsibility to implement the policy and to determine if the policy has been violated.

The recommendation to observe the distinction between setting policy and administering it is not made out of excessive concern over the jurisdictional rights of administrators. The fact is, however, that when boards involve themselves too heavily in administration, they no longer have sufficient time to perform their vital function of formulating policy.

Even a single grievance can preempt a board's agenda. Witnesses on both sides must be heard, documents read, arguments analyzed, and so on. If just one grievance a month goes to a seven-member board and if each board member devotes no more than two hours to all aspects of the grievance, the board still would be devoting 140 hours of its school year to repeating a procedure that had involved the same grievant, the same witnesses, the same documents, the same arguments, and — virtually always — the same decision that prevailed at the superintendent's level. And, of course, grievances don't always come along in neat packages of one. When 10 or 20 teachers allege a violation, *each* one may claim the right to a hearing before the board.

Contract language aimed at reducing the number of grievances and the time devoted to them will not necessarily protect a board from becoming bogged down in grievance hearings. As if the lost time were not bad enough, a board may also discover that legal restrictions governing board hearings will inhibit prompt action and provide teachers with generous opportunities for converting a grievance hearing into a propaganda show.

The argument against including a board hearing in the grievance procedure grows stronger when one considers that grievance appeals to the board should be superfluous to *both the school board and the employee*. If the grievance is a minor or routine one, there is no reason for the board's getting involved. And if the grievance does have policy or political implications, the superintendent will consult with the board before making a decision. If the superintendent doesn't check with the board in these cases, both he and the board have problems that go far beyond employee grievance procedures. For even greater protection, a board can set policies and guidelines to ensure that its legitimate needs in grievance resolution are taken into account. And this can be accomplished without establishing appeals to the board as a separate and formal step in the grievance procedure.

From an employee's point of view, the advantages in appealing a grievance directly to the board generally are illusionary. A teacher may *believe* that a board will be more sympathetic if it could hear the teacher's story directly, or a teacher may *hope* that a grievance will serve as a wedge driven between a board and its administration. In practice, however, boards seldom overrule their administrators on grievance decisions. If employees want grievances resolved as promptly as possible, they have little reason for insisting upon an appeal to the school board.

Despite these arguments, why are appeals to the board still included in the grievance procedure? One reason relates to the introduction of binding arbitration. When first confronted by union proposals for binding arbitration, boards objected strenuously on the grounds that board prerogatives would be jeopardized. Union negotiators found it easier to "sell" binding arbitration when appeals to the board were included in the grievance procedure. Once in, such appeals are difficult to remove.

Another reason is administrative reluctance to press the issue. Not every superintendent feels secure enough to urge his board to remove itself from the grievance procedure. Additionally, such a recommendation can be construed as a self-serving attempt to hide administrative mistakes.

Also, board members often feel a loss of authority and prestige when they relinquish the authority to decide employee grievances. This need not be the case, of course, because board involvement in the grievance procedure should be governed by board-superintendent relationships, not by board-union ones. Indeed, collective bargaining has helped clarify the distinction between policymaking and administration by making clear who is responsible for approving the collective agreement and who is responsible for applying it.

One of the few good arguments for the inclusion of grievance appeals to the board goes something like this: Board involvement in grievance procedures can yield solid, firsthand knowledge about administrative performance and about the actual impact of board policies on school operations. Insights in either of these areas may well lead to needed changes in district policy. Grievance decisions, the argument goes, can even involve the formulation of board policy. If, for example, a contract is not clear on a certain issue, a grievance may force the board and administration to be more specific, hence to clarify existing policy. Although there is some merit to these arguments, a board's legitimate concerns about the resolution of grievances can be easily handled without making appeals to the board a *separate* and *formal* step in the grievance procedure.

The collective bargaining process offers a good opportunity for eliminating grievance appeals to the board. Union bargainers usually will try very hard to reduce the levels of appeal in grievance procedures, arguing that the prompt disposition of grievances is of prime importance and that several, usually repetitive, levels of appeal are futile. Board negotiators, then, have plenty of union-made reasons for getting rid of grievance appeals to the board or for rejecting a proposal for them, if one is made by the union.

Needless to say, however, some union bargainers *do* want the board to be a separate step in the grievance procedure. Occasionally, a union may think it can use publicity and public relations campaigns to pressure a board into a pro-teacher grievance decision. And sometimes teachers who are board members (outside of districts where they teach) will attempt to use their membership on boards in questionable ways during grievance procedures. On the whole, however, union leaders who have outgrown these games and ploys will accept and even welcome the exclusion of grievance appeals to the board. These union leaders recognize, as should board members and superintendents, that grievance arbitration involves the application of policy (not its formulation or adoption) and, further, that no one gains by adding costly, time-consuming levels to the grievance procedure.

The comments thus far have been directed at districts that have a collective binding arbitration for grievance resolution. What happens in those districts that have neither? The most obvious thing that happens is that board members become more directly involved in grievances. (And this is likely to remain the case.) They become more involved because bargaining, as was mentioned before, helps *clarify* the distinction between formulating policy and implementing it. In the absence of bargaining, the distinction is less clear and board members are more likely to become involved in administration. Also, when the board, rather than an arbitrator, is the last word on deciding if district policy has been violated, administrators are more likely to buck difficult cases to the board.

The foregoing arguments against board adjudication of grievances apply even in the absence of arbitration and bargaining. The arguments can also apply to parent or student grievances, for which a board should establish a broad policy that is implemented by the administrative staff. In any case, the benefits of a board's formally ruling on grievances usually are outweighed by the duplication of administrative procedures, the investment of board time, and the unlikely prospects of a board reaching a "different" decision. And those benefits can, in any case, be achieved without making appeals to the board a *separate, formal* step in the grievance procedure.

50.   Rules of Contract Interpretation

The language of the collective agreement derives from several sources: the proposals and counterproposals; the exchanges and tentative understandings reached in the crucible of negotiations; and the memorandum of agreement drafted (and possibly redrafted) in the clamor and clutter of the negotiating room after settlement has been reached. Ideally, since the precise language of the collective agreement is so important, it should be drafted afresh with an eye toward style, lucidity, and clarity.[1] However, this is not what typically happens.

Usually the job of drafting the exact contract language will be turned over to one of the parties, subject, of course, to approval by the other party prior to execution. In the private sector, management usually assumes this responsibility. In the public sector, at least in the experience of the authors, the reverse is true.

There are obvious advantages in having one of your representatives serve as the initial draftsman. He may (and should) be able to make stylistic changes, primarily in the interests of clarity (except in those areas where the parties prefer ambiguity). He may be able to make substantive changes of a minor nature if the parties agree, after consultation, that the language they used in negotiations or in the memorandum of agreement will create unworkable situations or does not fairly express their intentions. However, the initial draftsman, regardless of which side he represents, is a captive of the negotiating history. This does not mean that the draftsman should not try to improve the language of agreement; it means only that such efforts will probably have limited success.

The teaching of all this is that the representatives of both sides should, at all stages of the negotiations, be mindful of the language

The material in this chapter was extracted from Wollett and Chanin, "The Law and Practice of Teacher Negotiations," Bureau of National Affairs, 1974. Mr. Wollett is a professor of law at the McGeorge School of Law, University of the Pacific, Sacramento, CA; Mr. Chanin is deputy executive director and general counsel, National Education Association, Washington, D.C.

they use and its probable meaning. One of the best indicators of what language means and how collective agreements will be interpreted is found in the decisions of arbitrators in the private sector, who sit as authoritative judges of the meaning and application of over 95 percent of all collective bargaining agreements.[2] While the use of arbitrators to interpret collective agreements in public education has not yet reached this percentage, this is clearly the trend. It is useful, therefore, to examine the rules of contract interpretation and their application by labor arbitrators.

1. Parol evidence

It is generally held that parol evidence is admissible to explain the meaning of an ambiguous agreement. However, an unambiguous written agreement may not be changed or modified by any oral agreement made prior to its execution. An agreement is not ambiguous simply because the parties disagree as to its meaning.

An exception to the parol-evidence rule is the doctrine that a collateral agreement or distinct contemporaneous agreement, even though oral, will be allowed. It has also been recognized that parol evidence may be introduced to show fraud or mutual mistake in the negotiations which led to the execution of the collective bargaining agreement.

Illustration[3]: In accord with the unambiguous terms of a recently negotiated provision, the company downgraded 66 out of 86 employees in a particular group. In agreeing to the provision, the union was assured by the company that its effect would be to downgrade only a "few" of the employees involved. This estimate was given to the union during negotiations at its request and was relied upon by it. The company contended that it had made the estimate in good faith and pointed out that it had indicated it was only an estimate. The arbitrator concluded that since the parties had entered into the contract on the basis of an erroneously assumed state of facts, it was a case of mutual mistake. He ruled, therefore, that the terms of the agreement should be modified to reflect the substantive understanding of the parties — to wit, that the company could only downgrade a "few" employees. He left open the question of what constituted a "few," but ruled that 66 out of 86 was too many.

2. Meeting of the minds

If the contract is ambiguous because there was no meeting of the minds, arbitrators generally will not substitute their own judgment for that of the parties, but will suggest that there be further negotiations.

Illustration4: This case involved the meaning of the vacation requirement of "one year's continuous service." The union contended that this meant that the employee had to work 1,000 hours. The company claimed that it meant "uninterrupted work with permissive absences." The company and the union each took the position that the adoption of the other party's interpretation by the arbitrator would be a change in the terms of the contract. The arbitrator found the language ambiguous, and there was no relevant extrinsic evidence. Stating that he could not substitute his judgment for what should be the product of negotiations, he remanded the matter to the parties for further negotiation.

Although the parties may authorize the arbitrator to decide issues of this type, either in the contract itself or in the arbitration submission, this is unusual. Most arbitrators are prohibited from adding to, subtracting from, or modifying any of the terms of the agreement.

3. Interpretation in light of the law

When there are alternative interpretations, the arbitrator will generally choose the one which makes the contract valid and lawful. The underlying assumption is that the parties intended to create a valid contract.

Illustration5: Two provisions were involved in this case. The first provided that: "Twelve and one-half cents (12^1/$_2$ cents) per hour night-turn premium shall be paid to all employees working...between the hours of 3 p.m. and 7 p.m." The other provision provided that: "Overtime at the rate of time and one-half shall be paid for all hours worked in excess of eight (8)...in one (1) day." The company contended that it was obligated to pay an employee one and one-half times his basic rate plus 12^1/$_2$ cents. The union took the position that the company was obligated to pay an employee his basic rate plus 12^1/$_2$ cents plus an additional one-half of that total. Although the language could reasonably be construed either way, the arbitrator accepted the union's argument. He relied, among other things, upon the fact that, if the company's interpretation were accepted, an employee who worked more than 40 hours in a week would not have the $12^1/_2$ cents shift premium included in the hourly wage upon which overtime was based. This would be contrary to rulings of the Wage and Hour Division under the Fair Labor Standards Act. The arbitrator assumed that the parties did not attempt to establish an illegal procedure.

4. Normal and technical usage of words

Aribtrators generally will give words their usual and popularly accepted meaning in the absence of evidence to indicate that the parties intended them to have a special meaning.

Illustration[6]: The following provision was in issue: "All grievances or disputes arising out of the application, interpretation, or claimed violation of this agreement may be taken up in writing within ten (10) working days of the time of arising. . . ." The company argued that the provision was intended to provide an outside limit on the time during which the union could bring a grievance. The word "may," it contended, should be viewed as compulsory, and since the grievance was not taken up within 10 days the union was precluded from bringing it. The arbitrator ruled against the company, holding that "may" is normally understood as a permissive word and not a mandatory word. In the absence of strong evidence to the contrary, he felt he had no alternative but to hold that the grievance was timely even though brought after the ten-day period.

By the same token, arbitrators generally hold that trade or technical terms will be interpreted in a trade or technical sense unless there is clear evidence to suggest a contrary intention.

5. Construction in light of context

Ambiguous words are often interpreted by analyzing those words with which they are associated.

Illustration[7]: This case arose out of the company's refusal to pay an employee for a holiday. The question was whether the company could require an employee to work on a holiday under Article IX of the contract. This Article provided that an employee who does not work would receive holiday pay unless he was "scheduled to work on the holiday and fails to work, except because of death in the immediate family, or a disabling personal injury or proven unavoidable illness."

The specific question was whether the word "scheduled" had a mandatory connotation in this provision. The word was also used in Article VIII (Hours and Overtime): "It is understood that the company may schedule hours below or above the standard for individuals due to production requirements."

The arbitrator held that in Article VIII the word "schedule" was used in a context of work under an expressed reservation of the company's right to diminish or enlarge worktime above or below standard hours, and in this context he felt that it connoted compulsion. In Article IX, however, he held that it was used in a context connoting a day of freedom from work and of pay for a day not worked. In this context he felt it did not connote compulsion or obligation.

6. Agreement to be construed as a whole

When there are alternative interpretations, arbitrators will generally choose the one which gives meaning and effect to other provisions of the collective bargaining agreement, rather than one which renders them meaningless or creates a conflict.

Illustration[8]: The employer discharged a bargaining-unit employee who was temporarily assigned to a supervisory job. The question was whether this discharge gave rise to a grievance which could be processed under the collective bargaining agreement. The company claimed that it did not, basing its position on the following contract language: "Employees who are members of the bargaining unit shall not be covered by the provisions of this agreement when acting in the capacity of supervisors." The arbitrator rejected the company's contention on the ground that if the clause were taken literally it would render other parts of the agreement meaningless. He cited the following examples, among others:

In determining seniority, any time worked by an employee in a supervisory capacity was to be included; the company was obligated to continue to check off dues for bargaining-unit employees temporarily working in supervisory positions; bargaining-unit employees might bid on vacancies even though working temporarily as supervisors.

7. Consistent meaning throughout agreement

A word that is used in one sense in an agreement is generally considered to have the same meaning when used elsewhere, unless there is evidence to the contrary.

Illustration[9]: Article XX-D of the contract provided as follows:

"In the event the employer requires the transfer or reclassification of any employee, such transfer or reclassification shall be first offered to the senior employees, in the job or shift affected, possessing the ability to perform the work involved and in the order of the seniority."

The company desired to transfer certain employees in the parts inspection classification from the second shift to the first shift. The parts inspection classification was composed of Grade A and Grade B inspectors. The union contended that the word "job" meant classification and that seniority should govern regardless of whether Grade A or Grade B inspectors were involved. The company contended that the Grade A and the Grade B inspectors were different "jobs" albeit within one classification. In sustaining the company's position, the arbitrator relied upon Article XX-A, covering the situation in which an employee desires a transfer. This article referred to "Jobs within a classification or sub-group." The arbitrator concluded that since the word "job" referred to a position within a classification in Article XX-A, the parties must have intended it to have the same meaning in the provision in question.

By the same logic, when parties use different language in different parts of an agreement or in different agreements it is presumed that they intended different meanings.

Illustration[10]: The contract contained a clause entitled "Layoff Pay," which provided certain payment for employees laid off through no fault of their own. The issue was whether the clause also applied to employees retired under the retirement program. The union argued that, under earlier contracts, retired employees did receive such pay upon retirement. This argument boomeranged, since the provision in the earlier contracts had been called "Severance Pay" and used the word "terminated." The arbitrator held that if the word "terminated" in the prior contracts had been understood by the parties to include retirees, the fact that the language was changed in the present contract indicated that they intended to change the meaning.

8. Avoidance of harsh or absurd results

When faced with alternative interpretations, an arbitrator will generally choose the one that leads to a fair and reasonable result, rather than to an unfair or unreasonable one.

Illustration11: As the result of a reduction in the work force, two journeymen carpenters were assigned to lower rated work, while two apprentices, with less seniority, continued to do carpentry work. The union objected since the agreement (Section 8) provided that seniority shall govern in regard to demotions and promotions, and also provided that "The principles of seniority shall apply to apprentices the same as they are presently applied in the basic labor agreement between the parties." The company contended that the latter provision meant seniority *among* the apprentices themselves. The arbitrator adopted the company's view on the ground that the union's theory could lead to absurd results, since Section 8 applied to promotions as well as demotions. If a vacancy occurred and an apprentice met the seniority test he would have to be promoted under the union's view. The entire apprenticeship program would be destroyed if an apprentice could lay claim to a higher rated job before completion of his apprenticeship merely because he had seniority over non-apprenticed employees.

9. To express one thing is to exclude another

It is generally held that when the parties expressly dealt with one or more items of a specific class in an agreement, they impliedly intended to exclude all others in the same class that were not mentioned.

Illustration[12]: In this case, the arbitrator held that since a job description enumerated certain duties, the employee could not be required to perform other nonenumerated duties. The job description apparently did not contain a statement that the duties were illustrative or that the employee could be required to perform other duties.

This problem frequently arises when an agreement specifies reasons for discharge. To avoid this, most contracts provide discharge for "just cause" and preface the specifics with the phrase "by way of illustration, without limitation."

10. Ejusdem generis
When general terms follow an enumeration of specific items, the general terms are interpreted to refer only to things of the same general nature as the specific items.

Illustration[13]: The contractual provision in question provided as follows: "In the case of equally qualified employees seniority shall govern on all occasions when a layoff, transfer or other adjustment of personnel is necessary." The union contended that the phrase "other adjustment of personnel" required allocation of overtime on the basis of seniority. The arbitrator rejected this contention, stating that the parties could not have intended to handle the difficult problem of overtime distribution in such a manner. He held that the phrase in question should take its meaning from what preceded it. Thus, it should be construed to include, in addition to layoff and transfer, such things as promotion and recall.

11. Avoidance of forfeiture
If there are alternative constructions, arbitrators will generally choose the one which does not result in a forfeiture or a penalty.

Illustration[14]: The contract provided that if the arbitrator found that an employee had been unjustifiably discharged, he "shall order reinstatement and payment of retroactive pay to the discharged employee to the date of such discharge." The employees who were unjustly discharged in the instant case suffered no loss of pay during the period in which they were off the payroll. The union contended that this was irrelevant: The language of the contract was clear and it should be construed as a penalty against the company regardless of whether the employees suffered a loss. The arbitrator rejected this argument and held that the provision should be viewed as providing for indemnification. A provision will not be viewed as requiring a penalty or forfeiture, he concluded, unless no other construction is reasonably possible.

12. Experience and training of negotiators

Whether an arbitrator interprets a provision strictly or loosely depends somewhat upon who negotiated it. If it was negotiated by laymen, arbitrators will often apply a less literal construction than if it was negotiated by attorneys.

Illustration[15]*:* The contract provided that: "When an employee is temporarily required to fill the place of another employee receiving a higher rate of pay, he shall receive the higher rate, but if required to fill temporarily the place of another employee receiving a lower rate, his rate shall not be changed." The question was whether this provision was applicable to a voluntary as well as to a compulsory transfer. The company argued that the word "required" indicated that it was intended to apply only when the transfer was compulsory. The arbitrator held otherwise. He noted that the provision was drafted by laymen who were not trained negotiators and who were imprecise in their use of language. Another provision in the contract provided that: "Foremen will not be required to take the place of workmen." The arbitrator pointed out that since the union did not represent foremen, the word "required" obviously must have been intended to mean "permitted." The same construction should be placed on the disputed provision, he held. A review of the entire contract convinced him that brevity and simplicity were substituted for precision. He found many other examples of loose use of language in the contract.

13. Precontract negotiations

It is generally assumed that when parties include a term in an agreement, they intend that term to have the same meaning that it had during the negotiations leading to the agreement.

Illustration[16]*:* This involved a provision which tied wage changes to the "BLS (Federal Bureau of Labor Statistics) cost-of-living index." The question was whether this meant the National BLS Index or the local index for the area in which the plant was located. The arbitrator held that the National Index should be used, even though the contract did not cover the point and the matter had not been specifically discussed in negotiations. He reasoned as follows: The clause was taken essentially from the contract of another company in which the National Index was used; at the time of the negotiations one of the parties had no knowledge that there was a local index, so there could have been no meeting of the minds in this regard; but both of the parties were aware of the existence of the National Index. Moreover, the figures which were used for illustrative purposes were drawn from the National Index. The arbitrator concluded, therefore, that when the parties used the term "BLS Index" during the negotiations they were impliedly referring to the National Index, and that that same reference should be inferred in construing the executed agreement.

The minutes of the negotiating sessions may provide very important evidence, as may oral testimony of the negotiators. On occasion, negotiations have been tape-recorded and the arbitrator has used the tapes in reaching his decision.[17]

The unsuccessful attempt of one of the parties to include a specific statement in an agreement has been interpreted to mean that the opposite of the statement prevails.

Illustration[18]: The contract provided that: "Time and one half shall be paid for all hours in excess of 40 hours in one week, provided, however, if the failure of the employee to make 40 hours is due to:...(b) Unavoidable absence of the employee due to sickness, death in the family, or other cause accepted as satisfactory by the superintendent," daily overtime would be payable. The question was whether a paid, but unworked, holiday should be counted as time worked in computing weekly overtime. During the negotiations, the union had proposed that the word "holidays" be inserted after "sickness" in the above-quoted provision. This request was rejected by the company. The arbitrator held that if the union wanted an unworked holiday to be a reason for not making 40 hours, the parties must have known that it did not count in the computation of the 40 hours.

A somewhat different situation exists when there is a qualified withdrawal of a proposal with a reservation of existing rights.

Illustration[19]: During negotiations, the company proposed that the following provision be included in the agreement: "The Company may designate different starting schedules for jobs within classifications covered by this Agreement." The union objected and the company withdrew the proposal, stating that it believed it had the right to adopt different schedules under the management-rights clause and was merely seeking to clarify this right. The arbitrator held that under the general language of the management-rights clause the company had the right to change schedules notwithstanding its withdrawal of the specific proposal during the negotiations.

14. Custom and practice of parties

The manner in which the parties have dealt with a situation in the past will often be used as a guide in interpreting ambiguous language. The past practice must indicate a mutual, rather than a unilateral, interpretation. This mutuality may result from the failure of one party to object to an interpretation given by the other party, but this involves the question of whether the non-objecting party knew or should have known what was going on.

Illustration[20]: When the union objected to the company's bringing in an independent contractor to wash windows, the company countered that it had been doing so for many years. The union denied that it knew this fact. The arbitrator found that the union disclaimer of knowledge was neither incredible nor negligent, since the only means of distinguishing the outside window washers from the company's own window washers was by the different color of their identification badges. They wore the same uniforms and drove the same trucks. He held that the past practice was not binding in the case.

Compare[21]: The agreement obligated the company to pay a bonus for work on the second and third shifts. The question was whether this provision included watchmen. Although watchmen were not specifically excluded, they were not paid and no claim was made for them until after the above provision had been in operation for several years. The union's claim that it did not know that the company was not paying watchmen was rejected. The arbitrator held that it was the union's obligation to enforce the collective bargaining agreement. The watchmen were the subject of considerable attention in the relationship between the parties, and if the union did not in fact know the watchmen were not being paid this was due to negligence on its part. The past practice was held binding.

Another problem involved in applying this rule is the following: How well-established is the practice? A single incident or even a few incidents do not *necessarily* establish a practice, although they may, depending upon how often the situation has arisen. The past practice need not be absolutely uniform, but may permit of scattered exceptions.

When a party renews ambiguous language in a subsequent contract, the language will generally be construed on the basis of the practice that existed under the preceding contract. The party claiming a change has the burden of clearly showing the changed intent when the new contract was executed.

The basic rule is that past practice is irrelevant if a provision is clear and unambiguous. However, some arbitrators have held that a long-continued, mutually accepted past practice which deviates from the clear language of a contract may amount to a modification of the contractual terms. They often seek to make this result consistent with the general rule by "leaning over backwards" to find an ambiguity.

15. Practice of one of the parties
If the same or a similar contractual provision has been entered into by the union with another employer or vice versa, the practice under that contract is often used as a guideline.

Illustration22: The contract provided that no sick leave benefits "will be paid for the first scheduled working day of any period of absence." The employee in this case was injured after working half his scheduled shift and did not resume work until several days later. The company claimed a deduction for four hours on the day of injury and four hours on the next day, a total of eight hours. The union argued that there should be a deduction only for the four hours on the day of injury. The clause was copied essentially from a contract which the union had with a second company. After the instant grievance had been filed, the union resolved a dispute with the second company in interpreting the clause in the manner contended by the company in the present case. The arbitrator thus ruled in favor of the instant company, viewing the union's deal with the second company as an indirect agreement with its interpretation.

16. Industry practice
Arbitrators will often look to the practice in the industry in which the parties operate for guidance in the interpretation of an ambiguous provision.

Illustration²³: The issue in this case was whether the phrase "length of service" meant the period of unbroken employment (the company view) or the period of total employment without regard to breaks in service (the union view). In adopting the company's interpretation, the arbitrator relied heavily upon the general practice in the industry under similarly phrased provisions.

Arbitrators generally give little weight to practices in other industries.

Illustration²⁴: This case involved the application of a contract provision requiring specified advance notice prior to a change in work assignments to yardmen, who worked with freight cars in the factory yards of a manufacturing plant. The union offered in support of its position the practice under a similar clause in the railroading and common-carrier industry. The arbitrator gave this practice no weight. He indicated that although the yardmen in this case worked on trains, the cited practice grew out of the problems and necessities of a wholly different type of situation, involving the need to have work assignments fit in with train schedules, the distance of the employees away from their homes, the expenses incurred in travelling, and the like. These considerations, he pointed out, were meaningless when dealing with employees in a freight yard who did not travel from their central location.

17. Prior settlements as an aid to interpretation

Prior settlements dealing with the same problem are generally considered to be binding precedents, unless the settlement is specifically stated to be without precedential value. A company and a union will often dispose of many grievances without prejudice in an effort to "clear the slate." One company that had a tremendous backlog of grievances was about to commence negotiations for a new collective bargaining agreement. The company and the union intended to deal with many of the issues underlying these grievances in the negotiations and, accordingly, disposed of many of them on a no-precedent basis, reserving the resolution of the basic issues for the negotiations.

Before using any prior settlement as a guideline, including settlements with prejudice, consideration must be given to any possible changes in either the practice or the contractual language subsequent to the settlement.

18. Interpretation against the draftsman
A general rule of contract law is to construe ambiguity against the draftsman. The rationale is that the draftsman has the burden either to use clear language or to explain what he means. This rule is generally applied to insurance policies and other documents requiring the signing of a printed form. Since, in the collective bargaining situation, the parties are of relatively equal bargaining power in negotiating an agreement, many arbitrators feel that any ambiguity in the final draft is a joint responsibility. Accordingly, this rule is not a favored one among arbitrators and is generally used only when no other rule of construction applies.

It will not be applied if there is no ambiguity or where the final clause differs substantially from the one proposed unilaterally.

Illustration[25]: In this case the union submitted a proposal; the company refused to accept it and proposed a modification; the union, after initial resistance, accepted the modification. The arbitrator concluded that in light of the above, there was really no "draftsman."

Even if the finally adopted ambiguous provision is not substantially different from that proposed by one of the parties, it is often not interpreted against the party proposing it unless the other party was misled, or was under a mistaken impression at the time the language was agreed to.

19. No consideration given to offers to settle a grievance prior to arbitration

Offers to settle a grievance prior to arbitration are not considered relevant in interpreting ambiguous language.

Illustration[26]*:* In this case the union claimed that the company's incentive system was unrealistic. In the processing of the grievance, the company offered to loosen the incentive system somewhat to settle the case. The union refused to accept the concession, and the case proceeded to arbitration. At the arbitration hearing, the union claimed that the company's offer was an admission that the incentive system was inequitable. The arbitrator disagreed. He stated that the acceptance of the union's contention would make the grievance procedure totally ineffective. It would eliminate efforts to compromise since the parties would be afraid of prejudicing their positions.[27]

[1] The actual drafting of the language of the collective agreement is a technical job of great importance. Leroy Marceau has underscored the function of the draftsman in the following language:

"He prevents disputes by making sure that the employer, the union, and the men understand the contract, and that all understand it to mean the same thing. This is not easy. Few men write a sentence that is crystal clear even at the time it is written — the English language slips so easily into vagueness. The draftsman must do *more;* he must write sentences that *remain* clear. His language will be applied in future years, by people who didn't write it, to situations that didn't exist when it was written." Marceau, *Drafting a Union Contract,* xxvii, Little, Brown & Co. (1965).

[2] *Basic Patterns in Union Contracts,* 6th Ed., 51:6, BNA Books, Washington D.C., 1966.

[3] *International Harvester Co.,* 17 LA 592 (Ray Forester, 1951).

[4] *Gulf Engineering Co.,* 29 LA 188 (James Sweeney, 1957).

[5] *Union Switch & Signal Co.,* 9 LA 702 (Aaron Horvitz, 1948).

[6] *M. H. Rhodes, Inc.,* 25 LA 243 (John Hogan, 1955).

[7] *Firestone Tire & Rubber Co.,* 20 LA 880 (George Gorder, 1953).

[8] *American Zinc Co.,* 29 LA 334 (Maurice Merrill, 1957).

[9] *Vickers, Inc.,* 15 LA 352 (Harry Platt, 1950).

[10] *Deep Rock Oil Corp.,* 20 LA 865 (Clyde Emery, 1953).

[11] *Wheeling Steel Corp.,* 21 LA 35 (Mitchell Shipman, 1953).

[12] *General Teleradio, Inc.,* 18 LA 418 (Joseph Rosenfarb, 1952).

[13] *Canadian Industries, Ltd.,* 19 LA 170 (J. A. Hanrahan, 1951).

[14] *Mode O'Day Corp.,* 1 LA 490 (George Cheney, 1946).

[15] *U.S. Pipe & Foundry Co.,* 5 LA 492 (Whitley P. McCoy, 1946).

[16] *Kohlenberger Engineering Corp.,* 12 LA 380 (Paul Prasow, 1949).

[17] *California Electric Power Co.,* 21 LA 704 (J. Grant, 1953). See discussion at p. 4:16, supra.

[18] *Consolidated Paper & Box Mfg. Co.,* 27 LA 126 (Samuel Jaffee, 1956).

[19] *Robertshaw-Fulton Controls Co.,* 21 LA 436 (Sidney Wolff, 1953).

[20] *Weber Aircraft Corp.,* 24 LA 821 (Edgar Jones, 1955).

[21] *Baer Bros.,* 16 LA 823 (Joseph Donnelly, 1951).

[22] *Tin Processing Corp.,* 20 LA 458 (Clyde Emery, 1953).

[23] *Highway Transport Assn.,* 11 LA 1081 (James Hill, 1948).

[24] *Certain-Teed Products Corp.,* 1 LA 354 (George Gorder, 1946).

[25] *Crescent City Warehouse, Ltd.,* 10 LA 168 (Benjamin Aaron, 1948).

[26] *U.S. Steel Corp.,* 26 LA 812 (Sylvester Garrett, 1956).

[27] The basic rules of contract interpretation have been described by Updegraff and McCoy as follows:

"A. 'Primary rules of interpretation' may be briefly summarized as follows: [3 Williston on Contracts (Revised Ed.) ¶618.]

1. The common or normal meaning of language will be ascribed to the provisions of a contract unless circumstances show a special meaning is justified.

2. Where technical words have been used, they will normally be given the intended technical meaning unless it clearly appears by local usage or otherwise that a contrary intention was mutually agreed by the parties.

3. The entire agreement should be read as a whole, and every part of it interpreted with reference to all other parts. It should be so interpreted as to give effect to its entire general purpose.

4. Consideration should be given to the circumstances under which the writing was negotiated or made.

"B. Certain rules of interpretation which are commonly designated 'secondary' may be put as follows: [Restatement of the Law of Contracts, ¶236 *et seq.*]

1. An interpretation which gives reasonable, lawful, and effective meaning to all manifestations in the writing is preferred to an interpretation which leaves a part of such a manifestation unreasonable, unlawful, or of no effect.

2. The principal apparent purpose of the parties is given great weight in determining the meaning to be given to each manifestation of intention or to any part thereof.

3. Where an inconsistency is found between general provisions and specific provisions, the latter ordinarily qualify the meaning of the general provisions.

4. Words or other manifestations of intention which bear more than one reasonable meaning shall be interpreted more strongly against the party by whom they were written unless their use by him was required by law.

5. Written provisions inconsistent with printed provisions in the same agreement are preferred over the printed.

6. If public interest is affected, an interpretation favoring the public is preferred.

"In this connection it will be well to remember that the parol evidence rule, which is not only a rule of evidence but also a rule of construction and interpretation, must always be considered and applied in these cases. [3 Williston on Contracts (Revised Ed.) ¶631.]

"As previously stated, usage or custom is permissible to explain and to assist in interpretation of the meaning of words used in a contract. When usage and custom is relied on, the evidence should establish it in the very broad sense and must further establish that the party against whom it is to be operative understood it and contracted in the light of such knowledge. [Corbin on Contracts, ¶557.]

"An arbitrator can frequently get great assistance from the interpreting statements made by the parties themselves or from their conduct in rendering or receiving performance of the provisions of the agreement. It is fundamental that where the parties have both concurred in a clear and undisputed interpretation of a contract over a substantial period, this conduct strongly supports the conclusion that such mutual interpretation was the intended interpretation of the parties as they negotiated and closed their agreement, [*Ibid*, ¶ *558.*]

Updegraff & McCoy, *Arbitration of Labor Disputes,* 225-6, 2nd Ed., The Bureau of National Affairs, Inc. (1961). *See also* Elkouri and Elkouri, *How Arbitration Works,* 199-218, Rev. Ed., The Bureau of National Affairs, Inc. (1960); Fleming, *The Labor Arbitration Process,* University of Illinois Press (1965).

51. Arbitration: To Go or Not To Go?

Over time, many districts have accepted some form of arbitration to resolve claims of contract violation. In fact, many union negotiators regard binding arbitration as the single most important union objective, at least until it is achieved. In their view, a contract without binding arbitration hardly deserves to be called a contract.

Be that as it may, more and more districts are faced with this decision: Either concede a contract violation or have the union allegation that there was a violation submitted to an impartial third party, who may decide that a violation did in fact occur. Such a decision can be very embarrassing after a district has spent considerable time and money to show that a violation did not occur. Furthermore, a decision on whether to go to arbitration can be extremely important, quite apart from the consequences in the case at hand.

What's involved in the decision to go or not to go to arbitration on a grievance?

Obviously, the administration must review the initial statement of the grievance and its history at the lower levels of the grievance procedure. Is the statement of grievance going to arbitration precisely the same as the original statement? Differences, if any, should be examined very closely, since they are likely to provide important clues to the merits of the grievance. The organization may be relying upon a clause in the contract different from the one originally relied upon because the grievance could not be sustained, or is not as likely to be, on the basis of the original submission.

A review of the action taken at each step of the procedure is also important. Were the reasons for rejection of the grievance explained fully and clearly to the grievant at each step? What reasons did the grievant give for not accepting these reasons, and how would they impress an arbitrator? For example, suppose the teacher organization contends that the grievant should not be precluded from her rights merely because other teachers, for good or bad reasons or none whatever, did not elect to pursue a legitimate grievance. Or suppose the organization contends that it was merely being cooperative in not pursuing previous violations, but it would be grossly unfair to allow management to violate the agreement frequently for this reason.

It is also crucial to review the facts of the case. The administration may be convinced that it is taking an airtight case to arbitration. Practically, however, there is always a risk, if for no other reason than the fact that a human process is involved. Certainly, districts should not rely upon the employee organization to overlook any argument in its favor, even if it has done so at previous levels of the grievance procedure. The teacher organization is virtually certain to be much better prepared at arbitration than at lower levels. Needless to say, the district should be also.

The risks involved in arbitration often extend beyond the immediate case. For example, the contract may provide that teachers cannot be required to teach outside their area of certification or to give up their preparation periods "except in emergencies." It may be that the teachers have been permitting the administration to define "emergencies" very loosely in these situations. If so, the district would not want to run the risk of an arbitrator's definition that would stimulate teachers to press for a more restrictive definition of "emergency." Therefore, the administration has to consider whether it can or should settle the case before going to arbitration. Even though its chances of winning are good, it may be better to resolve the grievance without going to arbitration if an adverse decision poses risks that can be avoided by a concession in the particular situation. In certain situations, management is well advised to provide some sort of remedy while clearly pointing out that its actions are not to be construed as a precedent.

For example, management might say, "We are not obligated by the contract to provide any compensation for the grievant in this situation. However, we recognize that there was a breakdown in communication when the issue arose and that the grievant, who has an outstanding employment record, sincerely believes she has a sustainable grievance. Although we are certain this belief is erroneous, and we will not provide compensation in the future under these circumstances, we are going to pay her on a one-time no-precedent basis, to demonstrate our interest in doing whatever we can to continue our constructive relationships."

Some such communication is essential and not merely to avoid setting an undesirable precedent. Management should avoid giving the impression that it will act positively on grievances only if a contract violation is involved or if pressure is brought to bear on it. Of course, some grievances may have serious implications for bargaining and involve pressure from one or both sides. Nevertheless, insofar as practical, management should adopt the position that it will treat grievances on their merits and that a grievance may have merit even though not sustainable under the contract.

If an issue is important, ordinarily the costs should not deter management from going to arbitration. One should, however, know what the costs are. Fees and expenses for the arbitrator may be only a small portion of total costs. If you are going to arbitration, you should make sure your case is as strong as possible. This means having an experienced party, such as a labor lawyer or negotiator, prepare your case. If you have to go outside your system for this person, the costs of preparation may far exceed your half share of the costs of arbitration. (Arbitrators' fees are $150 to $300 a day for two or three days, plus travel and per diem if the arbitrator is from out of town. Also, the costs of a transcript can be quite high if the issue is a complex one.)

Districts should not make the mistake of thinking that preparation costs are not involved merely because they have competent staff personnel to prepare the case for arbitration. Their time is valuable. Furthermore, the district has to consider whether staff personnel will have to be excused from regular duties for preparation and the arbitration hearing itself. Will the grievant be utilizing other teachers and administrators as witnesses? If so, there may be direct costs for substitutes as well as large indirect costs for the time required for the arbitration sessions. The teacher organization has to worry about the costs of preparation too, but the indirect costs to it are not likely to be as large as they are to the administration.

It is highly advisable to study other arbitration awards on the same issue before making a final decision as to whether to go to arbitration. Typically, management decides to go to arbitration and then reviews arbitration awards for support. This is analogous to a lawyer advising his client to fight it out in court before the lawyer has reviewed the pertinent legal decisions on the issue.

The awards of other arbitrators are not legal precedents. Nevertheless, it pays to study them carefully before going to arbitration. First, the district will get a better idea of how both parties have prepared for arbitration in a case like the instant one. The district may encounter unanticipated arguments for or against its position. If it finds an adverse precedent, it will be better prepared to explain why its case should be decided differently; by the same token, if it finds supporting precedents, it can utilize them effectively in presenting its case. The American Arbitration Association, Commerce Clearing House, and the Bureau of National Affairs publish arbitration awards on a systematic basis with indexes and back copies available for purchase. The American Arbitration Association publication, *Arbitration in the Schools,* is devoted exclusively to arbitration awards in the field of education. It should be consulted carefully for relevant cases.

These are only a few of the steps to be taken by school management in deciding whether or not to go to arbitration. The important thing is to be able to assess the situation from the point of view of the grievant, the teacher organization and the arbitrator before making a final decision on whether to settle or go to arbitration. If the district can assess the case from the viewpoint of its adversary or the arbitrator, it will be in a much better position to assess it from its own. Typically, teachers threaten to go to arbitration more often than they actually resort to it. If they do resort to it, the district should make an all-out effort to win the case. An adverse decision by an arbitrator can be very damaging to administrative prestige and authority. Regardless of the outcome, however, teachers will not go to arbitration casually in the future if the district has shown that it meant business in the past.

52.   Group Grievances

Sooner or later, management negotiators are faced with a demand that the teacher organization have the right to initiate and process a grievance that affects two or more (up to all) teachers. Such grievances are called "group grievances." For example, suppose the agreement provides that teachers are required to work 180 days. School is canceled because of bad weather at 8:30 a.m. on a particular day, and management reschedules it, although some teachers had already reported for work. The agreement says nothing about how much time teachers have to work before they can be credited with one of the 180 days required by the agreement. The teachers claim, however, that rescheduling the day will mean they have to work 181 days, a claim which would be valid if the canceled day is also counted.

Conceivably, those who had already reported for work might be treated differently from those who had not, but it would still be cumbersome to force each teacher who had reported for work to initiate a grievance.

As this example shows, grievances might affect all teachers or a group of teachers. The administration might extend the school day in a way that affects all and is disputed by all. Because of these possibilities, employee organizations seek the right to initiate group grievances. In such cases, no individual teachers need initiate the grievance. The management problem is how to meet legitimate employee needs in this area without opening a Pandora's box.

Typically, the employee organization will seek the right to initiate a group grievance merely upon its own allegation that a grievance affects a group of teachers. The following proposal illustrates this approach: "Whenever the union alleges that a grievance affects all the teachers in a given school, or two or more teachers in different schools, it shall have the right to initiate a grievance upon its own initiative at the lowest level of the grievance procedure which can take the corrective action requested."

Management negotiators should be extremely cautious in negotiating group grievance procedures, especially those that give the union carte blanche to initiate them. It is usually inadvisable to give the union the right to initiate a group grievance merely on the union's "opinion" or "belief" that a group of employees are affected by the grievance. The union leadership may come under severe internal pressure to initiate grievances, especially if it does not have to cite specific employees for whom the grievance is filed.

Quite frequently, union negotiators will contend that group grievances are justified because individuals are afraid to utilize the grievance procedure. This argument should have little merit if the grievance procedure includes a clause prohibiting discrimination or retaliation against anyone using or participating in the grievance procedure. On the other hand, if a grievance really involves an organizational rather than an individual right, there is no objection to permitting the organization *as such* to initiate the grievance. Suppose, for example, that the agreement gives the organization the right to conduct meetings in the schools under specified conditions. The organization (as distinguished from individual teachers) should be able to claim a grievance if it was denied this right although it met the conditions.

The important point is that organizational rights to initiate a grievance should not be based upon a "belief" or "opinion" that a group of teachers is affected by the same act or condition giving rise to a grievance. It should be based upon a claim that the requisite number of teachers are in fact aggrieved by the same act or condition. This may seem like hairsplitting, but consider the following two clauses:

"A. Whenever 10 or more members of the negotiating unit have a grievance based upon the same act or condition, the union may initiate and process a group grievance on their behalf."

"B. Whenever the union alleges that 10 or more members of the negotiating unit are aggrieved by the same act or condition, the union may initiate and process a grievance on their behalf."

Under A, the union would have to demonstrate that 10 or more members of the unit were aggrieved by the same act or condition; under B, such a showing would not be necessary. In the latter case, the union need only show its good faith belief that 10 or more members of the unit are aggrieved. Under A, if there is any tendency for the union to manufacture grievances, management can require a showing that a group is affected. In the absence of such a showing, the group grievance would not be sustained.

As is evident from the preceding discussion, there are many different ways to state the conditions under which a group grievance can be initiated. Sometimes there is a simple numerical standard, *e.g.* 10 or more teachers. Of course, the larger the number, the more unlikely it is that any group grievance will be filed. On the other hand, it is self-defeating for management to require a large number of individual grievances on what is essentially the same issue.

The following clause illustrates a different approach to group grievances: "The union agrees that it will not bring or continue, and that it will not represent any employee in, any grievance which is substantially similar to a grievance denied by the decision of an arbitrator; and the board of education agrees that it will apply to all substantially similar situations the decision of an arbitrator sustaining a grievance."

Under this language, an individual teacher would still have to initiate a grievance where two or more members of the unit alleged the same grievance. However, once the grievance is settled for one teacher by the decision of an arbitrator, other parties would be bound thereby. Thus if the arbitrator decided that the board violated the contract by rescheduling a day canceled because of bad weather, the board would have to apply that decision to other grievances arising out of the same cancellation. If the board and the union disagreed over whether the circumstances of a later grievance were "substantially similar" to an earlier one decided by an arbitrator, then the issue of substantial similarity would go to arbitration. Presumably, neither side would refuse to accept an appropriate precedent, since either would be overruled in arbitration if the subsequent situation were in fact substantially similar to the earlier one.

It might also be necessary to modify any time limits on grievances if this approach is followed. To see why, suppose 100 teachers allege what is essentially the same grievance. Suppose also that the contract requires that grievances be initiated within five working days from the time the grievant knew or should have known about the act or condition giving rise to the grievance. In such case, 99 teachers cannot wait for the outcome of the precedent setting case. To do so would jeopardize their right to initiate a grievance within the five days after the act or condition giving rise to the grievance. Thus, unless the time limits take account of this approach to group grievances, they can work unfairly to the teachers concerned.

Whatever the contract language, group grievances should be authorized only under conditions minimizing the possibility of their abuse. This is especially important in negotiating with inexperienced organizational leadership, which may not be aware of the hazards to itself in a loose group grievance procedure. There are situations in which a group grievance makes good sense for both parties; avoid clauses which go beyond this.

53. Additional Issues, Suggestions, and Sources

Code of Professional Responsibility for Arbitrators of Labor-Management Disputes, American Arbitration Association, New York, N.Y., 1974. This document sets forth the standards of conduct expected of arbitrators from the American Arbitration Association, National Academy of Arbitrators, and/or Federal Mediation and Conciliation Service.

Fairweather, Owen: *Practice and Procedure in Labor Arbitration,* Bureau of National Affairs, Inc., Washington, D.C., 1973. This is a comprehensive analysis of issues that may arise in arbitration. Although oriented to private sector arbitration, a great deal of the analysis would be helpful in public sector arbitration.

Fleming, R.H.: *The Labor Arbitration Process,* University of Illinois Press, Urbana, Ill., 1965. This publication provides a useful perspective on arbitration.

Labor-Management Services Administration, U.S. Department of Labor: *Understanding Grievance Arbitration in the Public Sector,* Superintendent of Documents, Washington, D.C., 1974.

Midwest Center for Public Sector Labor Relations: *Questions and Answers on Contract Administration, A Practitioners Guide,* Indiana University, Bloomington, 1978.

Prasow, Paul, and Edward Peters: *Arbitration and Collective Bargaining,* McGraw-Hill Book Co., New York, N.Y., 1976. This analysis includes a substantial amount of case material presented in an informal way by two highly experienced arbitrators.

Staudohar, Paul D.: *Grievance Arbitration in Public Employment,* Institute of Industrial Relations, University of California, Berkeley, 1977.

Weisberger, June: *Examples of Language and Interpretation in Public Sector Collective Bargaining Agreements,* School of Industrial and Labor Relations, Cornell University, Ithaca, N.Y., 1974.

APPENDIX I

A Glossary of Collective Bargaining Terms

AGENCY SHOP
A provision in a collective agreement which requires that all employees in the negotiating unit who do not join the exclusive representative pay a fixed amount monthly, usually the equivalent of organization dues, as a condition of employment. Under some arrangements, the payments are allocated to the organization's welfare fund or to a recognized charity. An agency shop may operate in conjunction with a modified union shop. (*See also* Union Shop.)

AGREEMENT
A written agreement between an employer (or an association of employers) and an employee organization (or organizations), usually for a definite term, defining conditions of employment, rights of employees and the employee organization, and procedures to be followed in settling disputes or handling issues that arise during the life of the agreement. (*See also* Collective Bargaining.)

AMERICAN ARBITRATION ASSOCIATION (AAA)
A private non-profit organization established to aid professional arbitrators in their work through legal and technical services, and to promote arbitration as a method of settling commercial and labor disputes. The AAA provides lists of qualified arbitrators to employee organizations and employers on request.

AMERICAN FEDERATION OF LABOR — CONGRESS OF INDUSTRIAL ORGANIZATIONS (AFL-CIO)
A federation of approximately 130 autonomous national/international unions created by the merger of the American Federation of Labor (AFL) and the Congress of Industrial Organizations (CIO) in December 1955. More than 80 percent of union members in the United States are members of unions affiliated with the AFL-CIO. The initials AFL-CIO after the name of a union indicate that the union is an affiliate.

This material was prepared by Labor Relations Training Center, (U.S. Civil Service Commission, Bureau of Training), Washington, D.C. 20415

ANNUAL IMPROVEMENT FACTOR
Wage increases granted automatically each contract year, which are based upon increased employee productivity.

ARBITRATION (VOLUNTARY, COMPULSORY, ADVISORY)
Method of settling employment disputes through recourse to an impartial third party, whose decision is usually final and binding. Arbitration is voluntary when both parties agree to submit disputed issues to arbitration and compulsory if required by law. A court order to carry through a voluntary arbitration agreement is not generally considered as compulsory arbitration. Advisory arbitration is arbitration without a final and binding award.

ARBITRATOR (IMPARTIAL CHAIRMAN)
An impartial third party to whom disputing parties submit their differences for decision (award). An ad hoc arbitrator is one selected to act in a specific case or a limited group of cases. A permanent arbitrator is one selected to serve for the life of the agreement or a stipulated term, hearing all disputes that arise during this period.

AUTHORIZATION CARD
A statement signed by an employee authorizing an organization to act as his representative in dealings with the employer, or authorizing the employer to deduct organization dues from his pay (check-off). (*See also* Card Check.)

BARGAINING RIGHT
Legally recognized right to represent employees in negotiations with employers.

BARGAINING UNIT
Group of positions recognized by the employer or group of employers, or designated by an authorized agency as appropriate for representation by an organization for purposes of collective negotiations.

BOYCOTT
Effort by an employee organization, usually in collaboration with other organizations, to discourage the purchase, handling, or use of products of an employer with whom the organization is in dispute.

When such action is extended to another employer doing business with the employer involved in the dispute, it is termed a secondary boycott.

BUMPING (ROLLING)

Practice that allows a senior employee (in seniority ranking or length of service) to displace a junior employee in another job or department during a layoff or reduction in force. (*See also* Seniority.)

BUSINESS AGENT (UNION REPRESENTATIVE)

Generally a full-time paid employee or official of a local union whose duties include day-to-day dealing with employers and workers, adjustment of grievances, enforcement of agreements, and similar activities. (*See also* International Representative.)

BUSINESS UNIONISM ("BREAD-AND-BUTTER" UNIONISM)

Union emphasis on higher wages and better working conditions through collective bargaining rather than political action or radical reform of society. The term has been widely used to characterize the objectives of the trade union movement in the United States.

CALL-IN PAY (CALLBACK PAY)

Amount of pay guaranteed to a worker recalled to work after completing his regular work shift. Call-in pay is often used as a synonym for reporting pay. (*See also* Reporting Pay.)

CARD CHECK

Procedure whereby signed authorization cards are checked against a list of employees in a prospective negotiating unit to determine if the organization has majority status. *The employer may recognize the organization on the basis of this check without a formal election.* Card checks are often conducted by an outside party, *e.g.* a respected member of the community. (*See also* Authorization Card.)

CERTIFICATION

Formal designation by a government agency of the organization selected by the majority of the employees in a supervised election to act as exclusive representative for all employees in the bargaining unit.

CHECK-OFF (PAYROLL DEDUCTION OF DUES)

Practice whereby the employer, by agreement with the employee organization (upon written authorization from each employee where required by law or agreement), regularly withholds organizational dues from employees' salary payments and transmits these funds to the organization. The check-off is a common practice and is not dependent upon the existence of a formal organizational security clause. The check-off arrangement may also provide for deductions of initiation fees and assessments. (*See also* Union Security.)

CLOSED SHOP

A form of organizational security provided in an agreement which binds the employer to hire and retain only organization members in good standing. The closed shop is prohibited by the Labor Management Relations Act of '1947 which applies, however, only to employers and employees in industries affecting interstate commerce.

COLLECTIVE BARGAINING

A process whereby employees as a group and their employers make offers and counter-offers in good faith on the conditions of their employment relationship for the purpose of reaching a mutually acceptable agreement, and the execution of a written document incorporating any such agreement if requested by either party. Also, a process whereby a representative of the employees and their employer jointly determine their conditions of employment.

COMPANY UNION

An employee organization that is organized, financed, or dominated by the employer and is thus suspected of being an agent of the employer rather than of the employees. Company unions are prohibited under the Labor Management Relations Act of 1947. The term also survives as a derogatory charge leveled against an employee organization accused of being ineffectual.

COMPULSORY ARBITRATION. *See* ARBITRATION.

CONCILIATION. *See* MEDIATION.

CONSULTATION

An obligation on the part of employers to consult the employee organization on particular issues before taking action on them. In general, the process of consultation lies between notification to the employee organization, which may amount simply to providing information, and negotiation, which implies agreement on the part of the organization before the action can be taken.

CONTINUOUS NEGOTIATING COMMITTEES (INTERIM COMMITTEES)

Committees established by employers and employee organizations in a collective negotiating relationship to keep an agreement under constant review, and to discuss possible changes in it long in advance of its expiration date. The continuous committee may provide for third-party participation.

CONTRACT BAR

A denial of a request for a representation election, based on the existence of a collective agreement. Such an election will not be conducted by the National Labor Relations Board if there is in effect a written agreement which is binding upon the parties, has not been in effect for more than a "reasonable" time, and its terms are consistent with the National Labor Relations Act. "Contract bars" in state government are established by state laws and state agencies.

COOLING-OFF PERIOD

A period of time which must elapse before a strike or lockout can begin or be resumed by agreement or by law. The term derives from the hope that the tensions of unsuccessful negotiation will subside in time so that a work stoppage can be averted.

CRAFT UNION

A labor organization which limits membership to workers having a particular craft or skill or working at closely related trades. In practice, many so-called craft unions also enroll members outside the craft field, and some come to resemble industrial unions in all major respects. The traditional distinction between craft and industrial unions has been substantially blurred. (*See also* Industrial Union.)

CRAFT UNIT
A bargaining unit composed solely of workers having a recognized skill; for example, electricians, machinists, or plumbers.

CREDITED SERVICE
Years of employment counted for retirement, severance pay, seniority. (*See also* Seniority.)

CRISIS BARGAINING
Collective bargaining taking place under the shadow of an imminent strike deadline, as distinguished from extended negotiations in which both parties enjoy ample time to present and discuss their positions. (*See also* Continuous Negotiating Committees.)

DECERTIFICATION
Withdrawal by a government agency of an organization's official recognition as exclusive negotiating representative.

DISPUTE
Any disagreement between employers and the employee organization which requires resolution in one way or another; *e.g.* inability to agree on contract terms or unsettled grievances.

DOWNGRADING (DEMOTION)
Reassignment of workers to tasks or jobs requiring lower skills and with lower rates of pay.

DUAL UNIONISM
A charge (usually a punishable offense) leveled at a union member or officer who seeks or accepts membership or position in a rival union, or otherwise attempts to undermine a union by helping its rival.

DUES DEDUCTION. *See* CHECK-OFF.

ELECTION. *See* REPRESENTATION ELECTION.

ESCALATOR CLAUSE
Provision in an agreement stipulating that wages are to be automatically increased or reduced periodically according to a schedule related to changes in the cost of living, as measured by a designated index, or, occasionally, to another standard, *e.g.* an average earnings figure. Term may also apply to any tie between an em-

ployee benefit and the cost of living, as in a pension plan.

ESCAPE CLAUSE

General term signifying release from an obligation. One example is found in maintenance-of-membership arrangements which give union members an "escape period" during which they may resign from membership in the union without forfeiting their jobs.

EXCLUSIVE BARGAINING RIGHTS

The right and obligation of an employee organization designated as majority representative to negotiate collectively for all employees, including nonmembers, in the negotiating unit.

FACT-FINDING BOARD

A group of individuals appointed to investigate, assemble, and report the facts in an employment dispute, sometimes with authority to make recommendations for settlement.

"FAVORED NATIONS" CLAUSE

An agreement provision indicating that one party to the agreement (employer or union) shall have the opportunity to share in more favorable terms negotiated by the other party with another employer or union.

FEDERAL MEDIATION AND CONCILIATION SERVICE (FMCS)

An independent federal agency which provides mediators to assist the parties involved in negotiations, or in a labor dispute, in reaching a settlement; provides lists of suitable arbitrators on request; and engages in various types of "preventive mediation." Mediation services are also provided by several state agencies.

FREE RIDERS

A derogatory term applied to persons who share in the benefits resulting from the activities of an employee organization but who are not members of, and pay no dues to, the organization.

FRINGE BENEFITS

Generally, supplements to wages or salaries received by employees at a cost to employers. The term encompasses a host of practices (paid vacations, pensions, health and insurance plans, etc.) that usually add to something more than a "fringe," and is sometimes applied to a practice that may constitute a dubious "benefit" to workers. No agreement prevails as to the list of practices that should be called "fringe benefits." Other terms often substituted for "fringe benefits" include "wage extras," "hidden payroll," "nonwage labor costs," and "supplementary wage practices." The Bureau of Labor Statistics uses the phrase, "selected supplementary compensation or remuneration practices," which is then defined for survey purposes.

GRIEVANCE
Any complaint or expressed dissatisfaction by an employee in connection with his job, pay, or other aspects of his employment. Whether such complaint or expressed dissatisfaction is formally recognized and handled as a "grievance" depends on the scope of the grievance procedure.

GRIEVANCE PROCEDURE
Typically a formal plan, specified in a collective agreement, which provides for the adjustment of grievances through discussions at progressively higher levels of authority in management and the employee organization, usually culminating in arbitration if necessary. Formal plans may also be found in companies and public agencies in which there is no organization to represent employees.

IMPARTIAL CHAIRMAN (UMPIRE)
An arbitrator employed jointly by an employee organization and an employer, usually on a long-term basis, to serve as the impartial party on a tripartite arbitration board and to decide all disputes or specific kinds of disputes arising during the life of the contract. The functions of an impartial chairman often expand with experience and the growing confidence of the parties, and he alone may constitute the arbitration board in practice.

INDUSTRIAL UNION (VERTICAL UNION)
A union that represents all or most of the production, maintenance, and related workers, both skilled and unskilled, in an industry or company. Industrial unions may also include office, sales, and technical employees of the same companies. (*See also* Craft Union.)

INJUNCTION (LABOR INJUNCTION)
Court order restraining one or more persons, corporations, or unions from performing some act which the court believes would result in irreparable injury to property or other rights.

INTERNATIONAL REPRESENTATIVE (NATIONAL REPRESENTATIVE, FIELD REPRESENTATIVE)
Generally, a full-time employee of a national or international union whose duties include assisting in the formation of local unions, dealing with affiliated local unions on union business, assisting in negotiations and grievance settlements, settling disputes within and between locals, etc. (*See also* Business Agent.)

INTERNATIONAL UNION
A union claiming jurisdiction both within and outside the United States (usually in Canada). Sometimes the term is loosely applied to all national unions; that is, "international" and "national" are used interchangeably.

JOB POSTING
Listing of available jobs, usually on a bulletin board, so that employees may bid for promotion or transfer.

JOINT BARGAINING
Process in which two or more unions join forces in negotiating an agreement with a single employer.

JURISDICTIONAL DISPUTE
Conflict between two or more employee organizations over the organization of a particular establishment or whether a certain type of work should be performed by members of one organization or another. A jurisdictional strike is a work stoppage resulting from a jurisdictional dispute.

LABOR GRADES
One of a series of rate steps (single rate or a range of rates) in the wage structure of an establishment. Labor grades are typically the outcome of some form of job evaluation, or of wage-rate negotiations, by which different occupations are grouped, so that occupations of approximately equal "value" or "worth" fall into the same grade and, thus, command the same rate of pay.

LABOR MANAGEMENT RELATIONS ACT OF 1947 (TAFT-HARTLEY ACT)

Federal law, amending the National Labor Relations Act (Wagner Act), 1935, which, among other changes, defined and made illegal a number of unfair labor practices by unions. It preserved the guarantee of the right of workers to organize and bargain collectively with their employers, or to refrain from such activities, and retained the definition of unfair labor practices as applied to employers. The act does not apply to employees in a business or industry where a labor dispute would not affect interstate commerce. Other major exclusions are: Employees subject to the Railway Labor Act, agricultural workers, government employees, nonprofit hospitals, domestic servants, and supervisors. Amended by Labor-Management Reporting and Disclosure Act of 1959. (*See also* National Labor Relations Act; National Labor Relations Board; Unfair Labor Practices; Section 14 (b), Labor Management Relations Act of 1947.)

LABOR-MANAGEMENT REPORTING AND DISCLOSURE ACT OF 1959 (LANDRUM-GRIFFIN ACT)

A federal law designed "to eliminate or prevent improper practices on the part of labor organizations, employers," etc. Its seven titles include a bill of rights to protect members in their relations with unions; regulations of trusteeships; standards for elections; and fiduciary responsibility of union officers. The Labor Management Relations Act of 1947 was amended in certain respects by this act.

MAINTENANCE-OF-MEMBERSHIP CLAUSE

A clause in a collective agreement providing that employees who are members of the employee organization at the time the agreement is negotiated, or who voluntarily join the organization subsequently, must maintain their membership for the duration of the agreement, or possibly a shorter period, as a condition of continued employment. (*See also* Union Security.)

MANAGEMENT PREROGATIVES

Rights reserved to management, which may be expressly noted as such in a collective agreement. Management prerogatives usually include the right to schedule work, to maintain order and efficiency, to hire, etc.

MASTER AGREEMENT

A single or uniform collective agreement covering a number of installations of a single employer or the members of an employers' association. (*See also* Multi-Employer Bargaining.)

MEDIATION (CONCILIATION)

An attempt by a third party to help in negotiations or in the settlement of an employment dispute through suggestion, advice, or other ways of stimulating agreement, short of dictating its provisions (a characteristic of arbitration). Most of the mediation in the United States is undertaken through federal and state mediation agencies. A mediator is a person who undertakes mediation of a dispute. Conciliation is synonymous with mediation.

MERIT INCREASE

An increase in employee compensation given on the basis of individual efficiency and performance.

MOONLIGHTING

The simultaneous holding of more than one paid employment by an employee, *e.g.* a full-time job and a supplementary job with another employer, or self-employment.

MULTI-EMPLOYER BARGAINING

Collective bargaining between a union or unions and a group of employers, usually represented by an employer association, resulting in a uniform or master agreement.

NATIONAL LABOR RELATIONS ACT OF 1935 (WAGNER ACT)

Basic federal act guaranteeing employees the right to organize and bargain collectively through representatives of their own choosing. The Act also defined "unfair labor practices" as regards employers. It was amended by the Labor Management Relations Act of 1947 and the Labor-Management Reporting and Disclosure Act of 1959.

NATIONAL LABOR RELATIONS BOARD (NLRB)

Agency created by the National Labor Relations Act (1935) and continued through subsequent amendments. The functions of the NLRB are to define appropriate bargaining units, to hold elections to determine whether a majority of workers want to be represented by a specific union or no union, to certify unions to represent employees, to interpret and apply the Act's provisions prohibiting certain employer and union unfair practices, and otherwise to administer the provisions of the Act. (*See also* Labor Management Relations Act of 1947.)

NATIONAL UNION
Ordinarily, a union composed of a number of affiliated local unions. The Bureau of Labor Statistics, in its union directory, defines a national union as one with agreements with different employers in more than one state, or an affiliate of the AFL-CIO, or a national organization of government employees. (*See also* International Union.)

NO-STRIKE AND NO-LOCKOUT CLAUSE
Provision in a collective agreement in which the employee organization agrees not to strike and the employer agrees not to lockout for the duration of the contract. These pledges may be hedged by certain qualifications, *e.g.* the organization may strike if the employer violates the agreement.

OPEN-END AGREEMENT
Collective bargaining agreement with no definite termination date, usually subject to reopening for negotiations or to termination at any time upon proper notice by either party.

OPEN SHOP
A policy of not recognizing or dealing with a labor union, or a place of employment where union membership is not a condition of employment. (*See also* Union Security.)

PACKAGE SETTLEMENT
The total money value (usually quoted in cents per hour) of a change in wages or salaries and supplementary benefits negotiated by an employee organization in a contract renewal or reopening.

PAST PRACTICE CLAUSE
Existing practices in the town, sanctioned by use and acceptance, that are not specifically included in the collective bargaining agreement, except, perhaps, by reference to their continuance.

PATTERN BARGAINING
The practice whereby employers and employee organizations reach collective agreements similar to those reached by the leading employers and employee organizations in the field.

PAYROLL DEDUCTIONS
Amounts withheld from employees' earnings by the employer for social security, federal income taxes, and other governmental levies; also may include organization dues, group insurance premiums, and other authorized assignments. (*See also* Check-Off.)

PICKETING
Patrolling, usually near the place of employment, by members of the employee organization to publicize the existence of a dispute, persuade employees and the public to support the strike, etc. Organizational picketing is carried on by an employee organization for the purpose of persuading employees to join the organization or authorize it to represent them. Recognitional picketing is carried on to compel the employer to recognize the organization as the exclusive negotiating agent for his employees. Informational picketing is directed toward advising the public that an employer does not employ members of, or have an agreement with, an employee organization.

PREVENTIVE MEDIATION
Procedures designed to anticipate and to study potential problems of employment relations. These procedures may involve early entry into employment disputes before a strike threatens.

PROBATIONARY PERIOD
Usually a stipulated period of time, *e.g.* 30 days during which a newly hired employee is on trial prior to establishing seniority or otherwise becoming a regular employee. Sometimes used in relation to discipline, *e.g.* a period during which a regular employee, guilty of misbehavior, is on trial. Probationary employee: a worker in a probationary period. Where informal probation is the practice, a worker who has not yet attained the status of regular employee may be called a temporary employee.

RAIDING (NO-RAIDING AGREEMENT)
Term applied to an organization's attempt to enroll members be-

longing to another organization or employees already covered by a collective agreement negotiated by another organization, with the intent to usurp the latter's bargaining relationship. A no-raiding agreement is a written pledge signed by two or more employee organizations to abstain from raiding and is applicable only to signatory organizations.

RATIFICATION
Formal approval of a newly negotiated agreement by vote of the organization members affected.

REAL WAGES
Purchasing power of money wages, or the amount of goods and services that can be acquired with money wages. An index of real wages takes into account changes over time in earnings levels and in price levels as measured by an appropriate index, *e.g.* the Consumer Price Index.

RECOGNITION
Employer acceptance of an organization as authorized to negotiate, usually for all members of a negotiating unit.

REOPENING CLAUSE
Clause in a collective agreement stating the time or the circumstances under which negotiations can be reopened, prior to the expiration of the contract. Reopenings are usually restricted to salaries and other specified economic issues, not to the agreement as a whole.

REPORTING PAY
Minimum pay guaranteed to a worker who is scheduled to work, reports for work, and finds no work available, or less work than can be done in the guaranteed period (usually 3 or 4 hours). (*See also* Call-In Pay.)

REPRESENTATION ELECTION (ELECTION)
Election conducted to determine whether the employees in an appropriate unit desire an organization to act as their exclusive representative. (*See also* Bargaining Unit.)

RIGHT-TO-WORK LAW
Legislation which prohibits any contractual requirement that an

employee join an organization in order to get or keep a job.

RUNOFF ELECTION
A second election conducted after the first produces no winner according to the rules. If more than two options were present in the first election, the runoff may be limited to the two options receiving the most votes in the first election. (*See also* Representation Election.)

SENIORITY
Term used to designate an employee's status relative to other employees, as in determining order of promotion, layoff, vacation, etc. Straight seniority: seniority acquired solely through length of service. Qualified seniority: other factors such as ability considered with length of service. Departmental or unit seniority: seniority applicable in a particular department or agency, rather than in the entire establishment. Seniority list: individual workers ranked in order of seniority. (*See also* Superseniority.)

SHOP STEWARD (UNION STEWARD, BUILDING REPRESENTATIVE)
A local union's representative in a plant or department elected by union members (or sometimes appointed by the union) to carry out union duties, adjust grievances, collect dues, and solicit new members. Shop stewards are usually fellow employees, and perform duties similar to those of building representatives in public schools.

STANDARD AGREEMENT (FORM AGREEMENT)
Collective bargaining agreement prepared by a national or international union for use by, or guidance of, its local unions, designed to produce standardization of practices within the union's bargaining relationships.

STRIKE (WILDCAT, OUTLAW, QUICKIE, SLOWDOWN, SYMPATHY, SITDOWN, GENERAL)
Temporary stoppage of work by a group of employees (not necessarily members of a union) to express a grievance, enforce a demand for changes in the conditions of employment, obtain recognition, or resolve a dispute with management. Wildcat or outlaw strike: a strike not sanctioned by union and one which violates a collective agreement. Quickie strike: a spontaneous or unannounc-

ed strike. Slowdown: a deliberate reduction of output without an actual strike in order to force concessions from an employer. Sympathy strike: strike of employees not directly involved in a dispute, but who wish to demonstrate employee solidarity or bring additional pressure upon employer involved. Sitdown strike: strike during which employees remain in the workplace, but refuse to work or allow others to do so. General strike: strike involving all organized employees in a community or country (rare in the United States). Walkout: same as strike.

STRIKE VOTE
Vote conducted among members of an employee organization to determine whether or not a strike should be called.

SUPERSENIORITY
A position on the seniority list ahead of what the employee would acquire solely on the basis on length of service or other general seniority factors. Usually such favored treatment is reserved to union stewards, or other workers entitled to special consideration in connection with layoff and recall to work.

SWEETHEART AGREEMENT
A collective agreement exceptionally favorable to a particular employer, in comparison with other contracts, implying less favorable conditions of employment than could be obtained under a legitimate collective bargaining relationship.

TAFT-HARTLEY ACT. *See* LABOR MANAGEMENT RELATIONS ACT OF 1947.

UNFAIR LABOR PRACTICE
Action by either an employer or employee organization which violates certain provisions of national or state employment relations acts, such as a refusal to bargain in good faith. Unfair labor practices strike: a strike caused, at least in part, by an employer's unfair labor practice.

UNION SECURITY
Protection of a union's status by a provision in the collective agreement establishing a closed shop, union shop, agency shop, or maintenance-of-membership arrangement. In the absence of such provi-

sions, employees in the bargaining unit are free to join or support the union at will, and, thus, in union reasoning, are susceptible to pressures to refrain from supporting the union or to the inducement of a "free ride."

UNION SHOP

Provision in a collective agreement that requires all employees to become members of the union within a specified time after hiring (typically 30 days), or after a new provision is negotiated, and to remain members of the union as a condition of continued employment. Modified union shop: variation on the union shop. Certain employees may be exempted, *e.g.* those already employed at the time the provision was negotiated and who had not yet joined the union.

WAGNER ACT. *See* NATIONAL LABOR RELATIONS ACT OF 1935.

WELFARE PLAN (EMPLOYEE-BENEFIT PLAN)

Health and insurance plans and other types of employee-benefit plans. The Welfare and Pension Plans Disclosure Act (1958) specifically defines welfare plans for purposes of compliance, but the term is often used loosely in employee relations.

WHIPSÀWING

The tactic of negotiating with one employer at a time, using each negotiated gain as a lever against the next employer.

WORK STOPPAGE

A temporary halt to work, initiated by workers or employer, in the form of a strike or lockout. This term was adopted by the Bureau of Labor Statistics to replace "strikes and lockouts." In aggregate figures, "work stoppages" usually mean "strikes and lockouts, if any"; as applied to a single stoppage, it usually means strike or lockout unless it is clear that it can only be one. The difficulties in terminology arise largely from the inability of the Bureau of Labor Statistics (and, often, the parties) to distinguish between strikes and lockouts since the initiating party is not always evident.

ZIPPER CLAUSE

An agreement provision specifically barring any attempt to reopen negotiations during the term of the agreement. (*See also* Reopening Clause.)

APPENDIX II

American Arbitration Association
Voluntary Labor Arbitration Rules

(as amended and in effect January 1, 1979)

1. **Agreement of Parties** — The parties shall be deemed to have made these Rules a part of their arbitration agreement whenever, in a collective bargaining agreement or Submission, they have provided for arbitration by the American Arbitration Association (hereinafter AAA) or under its Rules. These Rules shall apply in the form obtaining at the time the arbitration is initiated.

2. **Name of Tribunal** — Any Tribunal constituted by the parties under these Rules shall be called the Voluntary Labor Arbitration Tribunal.

3. **Administrator** — When parties agree to arbitrate under these Rules and an arbitration is instituted thereunder, they thereby authorize the AAA to administer the arbitration. The authority and obligations of the Administrator are as provided in the agreement of the parties and in these Rules.

4. **Delegation of Duties** — The duties of the AAA may be carried out through such representatives or committees as the AAA may direct.

5. **National Panel of Labor Arbitrators** — The AAA shall establish and maintain a National Panel of Labor Arbitrators and shall appoint arbitrators therefrom, as hereinafter provided.

6. **Office of Tribunal** — The general office of the Labor Arbitration Tribunal is the headquarters of the AAA, which may, however, assign the administration of an arbitration to any of its Regional Offices.

More information is available from the American Arbitration Association, 140 West 51st Street, New York, NY 10020.

7. Initiation Under an Arbitration Clause in a Collective Bargaining Agreement — Arbitration under an arbitration clause in a collective bargaining agreement may, under these Rules, be initiated by either party in the following manner:

(a) By giving written notice to the other party of intention to arbitrate (Demand), which notice shall contain a statement setting forth the nature of the dispute and the remedy sought, and

(b) By filing at any Regional Office of the AAA three copies of said notice, together with a copy of the collective bargaining agreement, or such parts thereof as relate to the dispute, including the arbitration provisions. After the Arbitrator is appointed, no new or different claim may be submitted, except with the consent of the Arbitrator and all other parties.

8. Answer — The party upon whom the Demand for Arbitration is made may file an answering statement with the AAA within seven days after notice from the AAA, in which event said party shall simultaneously send a copy of its answer to the other party. If no answer is filed within the stated time, it will be assumed that the claim is denied. Failure to file an answer shall not operate to delay the arbitration.

9. Initiation Under a Submission — Parties to any collective bargaining agreement may initiate an arbitration under these Rules by filing at any Regional Office of the AAA two copies of a written agreement to arbitrate under these Rules (Submission), signed by the parties and setting forth the nature of the dispute and the remedy sought.

10. Fixing of Locale — The parties may mutually agree upon the locale where the arbitration is to be held. If the locale is not designated in the collective bargaining agreement or Submission, and if there is a dispute as to the appropriate locale, the AAA shall have the power to determine the locale and its decision shall be binding.

11. Qualifications of Arbitrator — No person shall serve as a neutral Arbitrator in any arbitration in which that person has any financial or personal interest in the result of the arbitration, unless the parties, in writing, waive such disqualification.

12. **Appointment from Panel** — If the parties have not appointed an Arbitrator and have not provided any other method of appointment, the Arbitrator shall be appointed in the following manner: Immediately after the filing of the Demand or Submission, the AAA shall submit simultaneously to each party an identical list of names of persons chosen from the Labor Panel. Each party shall have seven days from the mailing date in which to cross off any names objected to, number the remaining names indicating the order of preference, and return the list to the AAA. If a party does not return the list within the time specified, all persons named therein shall be deemed acceptable. From among the persons who have been approved on both lists, and in accordance with the designated order of mutual preference, the AAA shall invite the acceptance of an Arbitrator to serve. If the parties fail to agree upon any of the persons named or if those named decline or are unable to act, or if for any other reason, the appointment cannot be made from the submitted lists, the Administrator shall have the power to make the appointment from other members of the Panel without the submission of any additional lists.

13. **Direct Appointment by Parties** — If the agreement of the parties names an Arbitrator or specifies a method of appointing an Arbitrator, that designation or method shall be followed. The notice of appointment, with the name and address of such Arbitrator, shall be filed with the AAA by the appointing party.

If the agreement specifies a period of time within which an Arbitrator shall be appointed, and any party fails to make such appointment within that period, the AAA may make the appointment.

If no period of time is specified in the agreement, the AAA shall notify the parties to make the appointment and if within seven days thereafter such Arbitrator has not been so appointed, the AAA shall make the appointment.

14. **Appointment of Neutral Arbitrator by Party-Appointed Arbi-**

trators — If the parties have appointed their Arbitrators, or if either or both of them have been appointed as provided in Section 13, and have authorized such Arbitrators to appoint a neutral Arbitrator within a specified time and no appointment is made within such time or any agreed extension thereof, the AAA may appoint a neutral Arbitrator, who shall act as Chairman.

If no period of time is specified for appointment of the neutral Arbitrator and the parties do not make the appointment within seven days from the date of the appointment of the last party-appointed Arbitrator, the AAA shall appoint such neutral Arbitrator, who shall act as Chairman.

If the parties have agreed that the Arbitrators shall appoint the neutral Arbitrator from the Panel, the AAA shall furnish to the party-appointed Arbitrators, in the manner prescribed in Section 12, a list selected from the Panel, and the appointment of the neutral Arbitrator shall be made as prescribed in such Section.

15. **Number of Arbitrators** — If the arbitration agreement does not specify the number of Arbitrators, the dispute shall be heard and determined by one Arbitrator, unless the parties otherwise agree.

16. **Notice to Arbitrator of Appointment** — Notice of the appointment of the neutral Arbitrator shall be mailed to the Arbitrator by the AAA and the signed acceptance of the Arbitrator shall be filed with the AAA prior to the opening of the first hearing.

17. **Disclosure by Arbitrator of Disqualification** — Prior to accepting appointment, the prospective neutral Arbitrator shall disclose any circumstances likely to create a presumption of bias or which he believes might disqualify him as an impartial Arbitrator. Upon receipt of such information, the AAA shall immediately disclose it to the parties. If either party declines to waive the presumptive disqualification, the vacancy thus created shall be filled in accordance with the applicable provisions of these Rules.

18. **Vacancies** — If any Arbitrator should resign, die, withdraw,

refuse or be unable or disqualified to perform the duties of the office, the AAA shall, on proof satisfactory to it, declare the office vacant. Vacancies shall be filled in the same manner as that governing the making of the original appointment, and the matter shall be reheard by the new Arbitrator.

19. **Time and Place of Hearing** — The Arbitrator shall fix the time and place for each hearing. At least five days prior thereto the AAA shall mail notice of the time and place of hearing to each party, unless the parties otherwise agree.

20. **Representation by Counsel** — Any party may be represented at the hearing by counsel or by other authorized representative.

21. **Stenographic Record** — Any party may request a stenographic record by making arrangements for same through the AAA. If such transcript is agreed by the parties to be, or in appropriate cases determined by the Arbitrator to be, the official record of the proceeding, it must be made available to the Arbitrator, and to the other party for inspection, at a time and place determined by the Arbitrator. The total cost of such a record shall be shared equally by those parties that order copies.

22. **Attendance at Hearings** — Persons having a direct interest in the arbitration are entitled to attend hearings. The Arbitrator shall have the power to require the retirement of any witness or witnesses during the testimony of other witnesses. It shall be discretionary with the Arbitrator to determine the propriety of the attendance of any other persons.

23. **Adjournments** — The Arbitrator for good cause shown may adjourn the hearing upon the request of a party or upon his own initiative, and shall adjourn when all the parties agree thereto.

24. **Oaths** — Before proceeding with the first hearing, each Arbitrator may take an Oath of Office, and if required by law, shall do so. The Arbitrator has discretion to require witnesses to testify under oath administered by any duly qualified person, and if re-

quired by law or requested by either party, shall do so.

25. **Majority Decision** — Whenever there is more than one Arbitrator, all decisions of the Arbitrators shall be by majority vote. The award shall also be made by majority vote unless the concurrence of all is expressly required.

26. **Order of Proceedings** — A hearing shall be opened by the filing of the Oath of the Arbitrator, where required, and by the recording of the place, time and date of hearing, the presence of the Arbitrator and parties, and counsel if any, and the receipt by the Arbitrator of the Demand and answer, if any, or the Submission.

Exhibits, when offered by either party, may be received in evidence by the Arbitrator. The names and addresses of all witnesses and exhibits in order received shall be made a part of the record.

The Arbitrator has discretion to vary the normal procedure under which the initiating party first presents its claim, but in any case shall afford full and equal opportunity to all parties for presentation of relevant proofs.

27. **Arbitration in the Absence of a Party** — Unless the law provides to the contrary, the arbitration may proceed in the absence of any party who, after due notice, fails to be present or fails to obtain an adjournment. An award shall not be made solely on the default of a party. The Arbitrator shall require the other party to submit such evidence as he may require for the making of an award.

28. **Evidence** — The parties may offer such evidence as they desire and shall produce such additional evidence as the Arbitrator may deem necessary to an understanding and determination of the dispute. When the Arbitrator is authorized by law to subpoena witnesses and documents, he may do so upon his own initiative or upon the request of any party. The Arbitrator shall be the judge of the relevancy and materiality of the evidence offered and conformity to legal rules of evidence shall not be necessary. All evidence shall be taken in the presence of all of the Arbitrators and all of the parties except where any of the parties is absent in default or has waived the right to be present.

29. Evidence by Affidavit and Filing of Documents — The Arbitrator may receive and consider the evidence of witnesses by affidavit, but shall give it only such weight as the Arbitrator deems proper after consideration of any objections made to its admission.

All documents not filed with the Arbitrator at the hearing but which are arranged at the hearing or subsequently by agreement of the parties to be submitted, shall be filed with the AAA for transmission to the Arbitrator. All parties shall be afforded opportunity to examine such documents.

30. Inspection — Whenever the Arbitrator deems it necessary, he may make an inspection in connection with the subject matter of the dispute after written notice to the parties who may, if they so desire, be present at such inspection.

31. Closing of Hearings — The Arbitrator shall inquire of all parties whether they have any further proofs to offer or witnesses to be heard. Upon receiving negative replies, the Arbitrator shall declare the hearings closed and a minute thereof shall be recorded. If briefs or other documents are to be filed, the hearings shall be declared closed as of the final date set by the Arbitrator for filing with the AAA. The time limit within which the Arbitrator is required to make the award shall commence to run, in the absence of other agreement by the parties, upon the closing of the hearings.

32. Reopening of Hearings — The hearings may be reopened by the Arbitrator on his own motion, or on the motion of either party, for good cause shown, at any time before the award is made, but if the reopening of the hearings would prevent the making of the award within the specific time agreed upon by the parties in the contract out of which the controversy has arisen, the matter may not be reopened, unless both parties agree upon the extension of such time limit. When no specific date is fixed in the contract, the Arbitrator may reopen the hearings, and the Arbitrator shall have 30 days from the closing of the reopened hearings within which to make an award.

33. Waiver of Rules — Any party who proceeds with the arbitration after knowledge that any provision or requirement of these Rules has not been complied with and who fails to state objection thereto in writing, shall be deemed to have waived the right to object.

34. Waiver of Oral Hearings — The parties may provide, by written agreement, for the waiver of oral hearings. If the parties are unable to agree as to the procedure, the AAA shall specify a fair and equitable procedure.

35. Extensions of Time — The parties may modify any period of time by mutual agreement. The AAA for good cause may extend any period of time established by these Rules, except the time for making the award. The AAA shall notify the parties of any such extension of time ānd its reason therefor.

36. Serving of Notices — Each party to a Submission or other agreement which provides for arbitration under these Rules shall be deemed to have consented and shall consent that any papers, notices or process necessary or proper for the initiation or continuation of an arbitration under these Rules and for any court action in connection therewith or the entry of judgment on an award made thereunder, may be served upon such party (a) by mail addressed to such party or his attorney at his last known address, or (b) by personal service, within or without the state wherein the arbitration is to be held.

37. Time of Award — The award shall be rendered promptly by the Arbitrator and, unless otherwise agreed by the parties, or specified by the law, not later than 30 days from the date of closing the hearings, or if oral hearings have been waived, then from the date of transmitting the final statements and proofs to the Arbitrator.

38. Form of Award — The award shall be in writing and shall be signed either by the neutral Arbitrator or by a concurring majority if there be more than one Arbitrator. The parties shall advise the

AAA whenever they do not require the Arbitrator to accompany the award with an opinion.

39. **Award Upon Settlement** — If the parties settle their dispute during the course of the arbitration, the Arbitrator, upon their request, may set forth the terms of the agreed settlement in an award.

40. **Delivery of Award to Parties** — Parties shall accept as legal delivery of the award the placing of the award or a true copy thereof in the mail by the AAA, addressed to such party at its last known address or to its attorney, or personal service of the award, or the filing of the award in any manner which may be prescribed by law.

41. **Release of Documents for Judicial Proceedings** — The AAA shall, upon the written request of a party, furnish to such party at its expense certified facsimiles of any papers in the AAA's possession that may be required in judicial proceedings relating to the arbitration.

42. **Judicial Proceedings** — The AAA is not a necessary party in judicial proceedings relating to the arbitration.

43. **Administrative Fee** — As a nonprofit organization, the AAA shall prescribe an administrative fee schedule to compensate it for the cost of providing administrative services. The schedule in effect at the time of filing shall be applicable.

44. **Expenses** — The expense of witnesses for either side shall be paid by the party producing such witnesses.

Expenses of the arbitration, other than the cost of the stenographic record, including required traveling and other expenses of the Arbitrator and of AAA representatives, and the expenses of any witnesses or the cost of any proofs produced at the direct request of the Arbitrator, shall be borne equally by the parties unless they agree otherwise, or unless the Arbitrator in the award assesses such expenses or any part thereof against any specified party or parties.

45. **Communication with Arbitrator** — There shall be no communication between the parties and a neutral Arbitrator other than at oral hearings. Any other oral or written communications from the parties to the Arbitrator shall be directed to the AAA for transmittal to the Arbitrator.

46. **Interpretation and Application of Rules** — The Arbitrator shall interpret and apply these Rules insofar as they relate to the Arbitrator's powers and duties. When there is more than one Arbitrator and a difference arises among them concerning the meaning or application of any such Rules, it shall be decided by majority vote. If that is unobtainable, either Arbitrator or party may refer the question to the AAA for final decision. All other Rules shall be interpreted and applied by the AAA.

ADMINISTRATIVE FEE SCHEDULE

Initial Administrative Fee: The initial administrative fee is $75.00 for each party, due and payable at the time of filing. No refund of the initial fee is made when a matter is withdrawn or settled after the filing of the Demand for Arbitration.

Additional Hearings: A fee of $50.00 is payable by each party for each second and subsequent hearing which is either clerked by the AAA or held in a hearing room provided by the AAA.

Postponement Fee: A fee of $40.00 is payable by a party causing a postponement of any scheduled hearing.

APPENDIX III

Sources of Information about Labor Relations in Education

Directory: Midwest Center for Public Sector Labor Relations: *Sources of Information in Public Sector Labor Relations, A Practitioner's Guide,* Indiana University, Bloomington, 1977.

Daily Newsletters: *Daily Labor Report,* Bureau of National Affairs, Washington, D.C.

Weekly Newsletters: *Government Employment Relations Report* (GERR), Bureau of National Affairs, Washington, D.C.; *Educational Labor Relations,* Capitol Publications, Inc., Washington, D.C.

Monthly Publications: *The Arbitration Journal, Arbitration in Schools, Labor Arbitration in Government,* all published by the American Arbitration Association; *Monthly Labor Review,* Bureau of Labor Statistics, U.S. Department of Labor; *Labor Law Journal,* Commerce Clearing House, Inc., Chicago, Ill.

Quarterly Publications: *Industrial and Labor Relations Review,* Cornell University, Ithaca, N.Y.; *Journal of Collective Negotiations in the Public Sector,* Baywood Publishing Company, Inc., Farmingdale, N.Y.

Miscellaneous Sources:

American Federation of Teachers (AFL-CIO), 1012 14th St., N.W., Washington, D.C., 20005, and other labor organizations that include school district employees.

American Association of School Administrators, 1801 N. Moore St., Arlington, Va., 22209.
National School Boards Association, 1055 Thomas Jefferson St., N.W., Washington, D.C. 20007, and other national organizations of school management.

Industrial Relations Research Association, University of Wisconsin, Madison, is the national organization of labor relations specialists. Its programs and publications have devoted increasing attention to public sector labor relations.

Labor Relations Press, P.O. Box 579, Fort Washington, Pa., 19034, publishes the decisions by state labor relations agencies. Subscriptions can be purchased on an individual, state or national basis.

National Education Association, 1201 Sixteenth Street, Washington, D.C. 20036.

National Labor Relations Board, 1717 Pennsylvania Ave., N.W., Washingtón, D.C. 20570.
Publications on collective bargaining under the National Labor Relations Act are available from NLRB or its regional offices.

U.S. Department of Labor, Fourteenth St. and Constitution Ave., N.W., Washington, D.C. 20210.
DOL's Bureau of Labor Statistics publishes the Cost of Living figures generally used in labor contracts. In addition, the DOL publishes the *Monthly Labor Review* and a wide variety of reports on public sector bargaining.

Most of the state labor relations agencies provide an information service, in some cases by contract with private corporations.

A number of universities provide extensive publication programs in public employment relations. Leading ones include the New York State School of Industrial Labor Relations, Cornell University; Institute of Labor and Industrial Relations, UCLA; Midwest Center for Public Sector Labor Relations, Indiana University, and the Institute for Public Employment, Institute of Industrial Relations, University of California at Berkeley.

Index

C

D

W

Waiver, see Zipper clause
Waiver, of right to sue, 177
Waiver, of statutory rights, 170
Weisberger, June, 23, 293
Wellington, Harry, 46, 228
Winter, Jr., Ralph, 46, 228
Wollett, Donald H., 158, 213, 268

Wisconsin Employment
  Relations Commission, 102,
  230
Whipsawing, 311
Work stoppage, 311. See also
  Strikes, Teacher strikes

Z

Zipper clause, 311